Wingshooter's Guide to™

OREGON

Upland Birds and Waterfowl

TITLES AVAILABLE IN THIS SERIES

Wingshooter's Guide to Arizona

Wingshooter's Guide to Idaho

Wingshooter's Guide to Iowa

Wingshooter's Guide to Kansas

Wingshooter's Guide to Minnesota

Wingshooter's Guide to Montana

Wingshooter's Guide to North Dakota

Wingshooter's Guide to South Dakota

Wingshooter's Guide to™
OREGON
Upland Birds and Waterfowl

John Shewey

Wilderness
Adventures
Press™

Belgrade, Montana

This book was made with an easy opening, lay flat binding.

Published by Wilderness Adventures Press
45 Buckskin Road
Belgrade, MT 59714
800-925-3339
Website: www.wildadv.com
email: books@wildadv.com

10 9 8 7 6 5 4 3 2 1

Printed in the United States of America

Library of Congress Cataloging-in-Publication Data:

Shewey, John.
    Wingshooter's guide to Oregon : upland birds and waterfowl / John Shewey.
        p.   cm.
    Includes index.
    ISBN 1-885016-46-7
    1. Upland game bird hunting--Oregon Guidebooks.   2. Waterfowl
shooting--Oregon Guidebooks.   3. Oregon Guidebooks.   I. Title.
SK323.S48   1999
799.2'4'09795--dc21   99-30135
                                                                CIP

Table of Contents

Introduction

Oregon's claim to wingshooting greatness is derived from its remarkable diversity. Across its broad east-west expanse, Oregon assumes countless personalities. Its Pacific Ocean shores rank among the scenic wonders of the continent, complete with precipitous headlands, vast tidal estuaries, and expansive white-sand beaches. The Oregon coast yields immediately to the heavily forested slopes of the Coast Range and Siskiyou Mountains. To the east of these ranges lie the temperate interior valleys of the Willamette, Umpqua, and Rogue Rivers. The Willamette Valley hosted some of the West's earliest settlers, brave pioneers whose 2,000-mile journey across the continent was fraught with danger and hardship.

Then rise the Cascade Mountains, whose elegant snowcapped volcanoes cast scenic grandeur across many Oregon cities. The Cascade Range creates a rain shadow—its western slopes can receive 80 to 120 inches of precipitation per year while the dry eastern descent gathers only a fraction of that total. This rain shadow effect defines the ecosystems that stretch across central and eastern Oregon. Included in this expanse—fully two-thirds of the state's total area—are massive fault-block mountains, dry desert playas, ponderosa / juniper forest, thousands of square miles of sagebrush steppe, sprawling desert sump lakes, breathtaking canyonlands, rugged granite peaks, many acres dedicated to grain agriculture, and many more dedicated to grazing.

Such a vast array of habitat types, ranging from ocean shores to high Cascades to arid deserts, assures equally diverse opportunities for bird hunters. Perhaps Oregon's most remarkable offerings are found in the state's extensive public lands. Introduced chukar partridge thrive on millions of acres of BLM property in eastern Oregon, and grouse and mountain quail abound on huge tracts of national forest. Oregon's agricultural community provides ample habitat for pheasant, valley quail, mourning dove, and Hungarian partridge. Meanwhile, waterfowl enthusiasts find excellent hunting for a wide variety of species on virtually every imaginable kind of watercourse, from wide tidal flats to large rivers to extensive freshwater marshes.

Despite its myriad opportunities for bird hunters, Oregon remains little appreciated by outsiders. The state's pheasant harvest can hardly compare to the prairie states, and it doesn't have sharp-tailed grouse or bobwhite quail or a rich tradition of ruffed grouse hunting. Oregon does, however, rival Nevada for the most extensive opportunity for chukar. Our blue grouse, ruffed grouse, and mountain quail hunting is second to none, but few people realize this save the serious upland hunters themselves. Even game bird biologists are quick to point out that 90 percent of the forest grouse and mountain quail killed each season are taken during opening weekend.

So as you explore Oregon with shotgun in hand and dog at foot, sample the state's many offerings—its long seasons, myriad species, and varied geography. Work the wheat stubble for pheasants and Huns; walk the desert rims for chukar;

seek valley quail in rural tracts; chase the elusive mountain quail across forested inclines; hike the high timber for blue grouse and the riparian bottoms for ruffed grouse, or try your hand at waterfowling on Oregon's diverse watery expanses. Through it all, stop often to appreciate the many scenic treasures, from the roaring Pacific surf to the glistening Cascade glaciers to the precipitous desert canyons.

I would like to acknowledge the contribution of the Oregon Department of Fish and Wildlife. Special thanks to Forrest Maxwell and his German shorthaired pointer, Nash, for our many days afield together.

John Shewey

Oregon Facts

10th largest state in the union
36 counties
97,060 square miles
Highest Point: Mt. Hood, 11,240 feet

296 miles of coastline
21 major estuaries
133,000 acres of tidelands
889 square miles of inland water area
    112,000 miles of rivers / streams
    6,000 lakes and reservoirs

1 National Park (Crater Lake)
3 National Monuments
2 National Recreation Areas (Hells Canyon and Oregon Sand Dunes)
17 National Wildlife Refuges
6 Indian Reservations (9 tribes)
224 State Parks
27.4 million forested acres
    13 National Forests
    789,000 acres of state forest
15.7 million acres administered by the Bureau of Land Management
    58 BLM Recreation Areas

Towns & Cities: 240
Population (1994): 3,082,000
Largest Employer: State Government, 13,000 full-time

Statehood: 1859 (33rd state)
Capital: Salem
Bird: Western meadowlark
Tree: Douglas fir
Animal: Beaver
Flower: Oregon grape
Gemstone: Oregon sunstone
Rock: Thunder egg
Seashell: Oregon hairy triton
Nut: Hazelnut
National Champion Largest Trees: Coast Douglas Fir, Rocky Mt. Douglas Fir, Bigleaf Maple, Black Cottonwood, Black Walnut, California White Fir, Port Orford Cedar, Sitka Spruce (national co-champ), Ponderosa Pine (national co-champ)

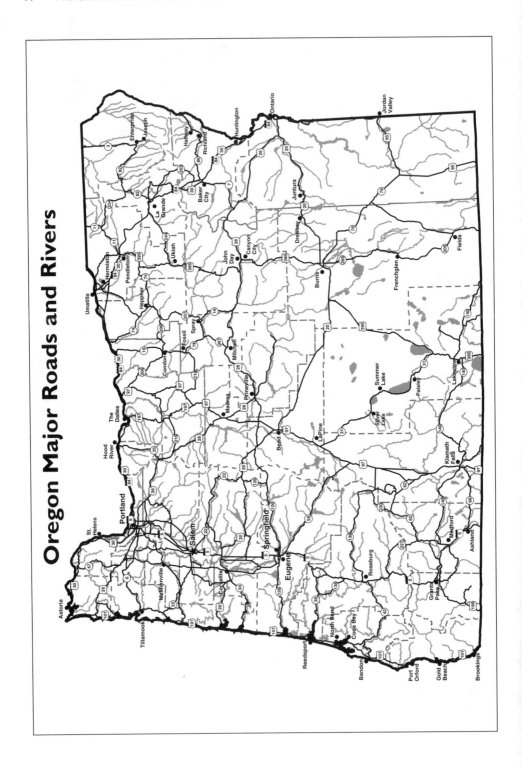

Oregon Major Roads and Rivers

Tips on Using This Book

- Although we have tried to be as accurate as possible, please note that this information is current only for 1998. Ownership of hotels, restaurants, etc., may change, and we cannot guarantee the quality of the services they provide.

- Oregon has two area codes: 503 covers the northwest portion of the state, including Portland and Salem, while 541 covers the remaining portion of the state. These area codes are listed with all phone numbers herein.

- The bird distribution maps are based on information provided by Oregon Department of Fish and Wildlife and are modified by the author to reflect his observations.

- Oregon has almost 3.2 million citizens and therefore many different communities. This guide attempts to pick out the significant towns and cities in each region as related to wingshooting opportunities. Many other towns are located near good bird hunting areas and provide necessary services.

- Always check with ODFW for current hunting regulations, license requirements, license prices, and season dates.

- Remember that access to private lands, posted or unposted, requires landowner permission.

- Oregon's public hunting areas (e.g., wildlife areas and federal refuges) comprise a significant public resource and are therefore covered rather thoroughly herein.

- Always check with motels ahead of time as to whether they allow dogs, even if so listed in this guide. These policies seem to change often, and restrictions as to size of the dog may apply as may additional fees.

- Oregon's public lands and highways are often referred to by their acronyms. The following key should help you navigate:

    FR — Forest Road

    SR — State Route (highway)

    US — United States (federal) highway

    ODFW — Oregon Department of Fish and Wildlife

    UCAP — Upland Cooperative Access Program

    RHAs — Regulated Hunt Areas

    HIP — Harvest Information Program

    CRP — Conservation Reserve Program

    BLM — Bureau of Land Management

NWR — National Wildlife Reguge

NRA — National Recreation Area

NRL — National Recreation Lands

- Motel cost key: $—up to $40
                                $$—$40-60
                                $$$—$60 and up

Highlights of Oregon's Bird Hunting Regulations

License Requirements

- Six months residency in Oregon, immediately prior to application, is required to be eligible to purchase a resident hunting license. Identification is required as follows: An Oregon driver's license, a state nondriver's ID card, or three of the following, one of which must show name and current address indicating six months residence in Oregon—utility/rent receipt, birth certificate, voter registration card, marriage license, passport, Social Security card, or military ID card. Persons not meeting the listed requirements must purchase a nonresident license. A free license is required for landowners hunting most game birds on their own property (see below).
- Hunting licenses are valid through December 31 of each year. Hunts extending into the following year require that year's license. No one may possess more than one valid hunting license.
- Any resident 14 years or older must have a valid hunting license with a waterfowl validation in possession to hunt ducks, mergansers, geese, and coots. In addition, any person 16 years or older must have a signed, valid federal duck stamp in possession to hunt migratory waterfowl.
- Any resident 14 years or older must have a valid hunting license with an upland game bird validation in possession to hunt pheasant, grouse, quail, chukar and Hungarian partridge.
- Any nonresident 14 years or older must have a valid hunting license with a nonresident game bird validation in possession to hunt ducks, mergansers, geese, coots, pheasant, grouse, quail, chukar, and Hungarian partridge. In addition, any person 16 years or older must have a signed, valid federal duck stamp in possession to hunt migratory waterfowl.
- Federal waterfowl stamps and state game bird validations are in effect from July 1 through June 30 of the following year.
- An adult, 21 years or older, must accompany any person under 14 years of age while hunting on other than their own property.

Harvest Information Program (HIP)

- Before hunting, every game bird hunter (except turkey hunters), regardless of age, must obtain a free Harvest Information Program (HIP) validation from a point-of-sale license outlet. Hunters 13 years old and under will receive a free youth license indicating their participation in HIP. Landowners hunting game birds on their own property will receive a free license indicating their participation in HIP. For controlled hunts (i.e., sage grouse and fall turkey) and spring turkey hunts, a regular hunting license is required for landowners hunting on their own property.

Hunter Education Certificate
- All game bird hunters 17 years or younger must have a Hunter Education Certificate in possession to hunt anywhere except on their own property.

Weapons and Shot Restrictions
No one may hunt game birds:
- With a shotgun larger than 10-gauge.
- Other than with shotguns; re-curve, long and compound bows; hawk, or falcon, except that rifles and handguns may be used to take blue and ruffed grouse.
- With a shotgun that can hold more than three shells.
- With lead, bismuth, or tungsten-iron shot larger than BB or steel shot larger than F; or with any tracer shells.
- Toxic shot restrictions are listed where appropriate under federal refuges, state refuges, and wildlife areas. In addition, the possession and use of shot other than federally approved nontoxic shot is always prohibited while hunting migratory waterfowl and coots. Steel shot plated with copper or zinc is allowed.

Shooting Hours
Game birds may be hunted only from one-half hour before sunrise to sunset, except Canada geese may be hunted in September only from sunrise to sunset.

Trespass
No one may hunt on the enclosed or cultivated land of another without permission. Enclosed land may be indicated by fence, ditch, road, hedge, railroad right-of-way, or any distinctive boundary.

Boats and Motor Vehicles
No one may:
- Hunt or shoot game birds from or with the aid of a motor-driven land conveyance or floating sinkbox.
- Drive, rally, or chase any game bird from any motor-driven land, water, or air conveyance or sailboat.
- Shoot game birds from or with the help of any motorboat or sailboat unless the motor has been shut off and/or sail furled, and movement therefrom has stopped. Sail and motor-propelled craft may be used only to pick up dead or injured birds.
- Operate a snowmobile or all-terrain vehicle while carrying a loaded firearm or bow unless all arrows are in a quiver.

Baiting
No one may:
- Hunt game birds by aid of baiting or hunt at or near a baited area.
  "Baiting" means to expose, deposit, distribute or scatter corn, wheat, salt or other feed to lure game birds near a hunting area. "Baited area" is any area that has been baited.

A ring-necked pheasant explodes from ideal cover in eastern Oregon.

Decoys and Calls

No one may:

- Hunt game birds by the use or aid of any live birds for decoys.
- Hunt game birds by the use of records or tapes of bird calls or sounds, or electrically amplified imitations of bird calls or sounds.

Disguising Sex

No one may disguise the sex or kind of any game bird. The feathered head must be left attached to all upland game birds in the field or while in transit. The head or one fully feathered wing must be left attached to all migratory waterfowl, doves, and pigeons.

Waste

All game birds must be retrieved, if possible, and kept by the hunter in the field.

Possession and Transport

Game birds shipped or given to another person for transport during the season or within 48 hours after the season closes must be accompanied by a written note listing the number and kinds, date killed, name and address of possessor, and signature, address and hunting license number of the hunter. Birds transported more than 48 hours after the season closes must bear a shipping permit or metal seal of the department of fish and wildlife.

Other Restrictions
No one may:
- Hunt in areas closed by the state or federal government, within city limits (unless otherwise authorized), or on school grounds, public parks, cemeteries, public road or road right-of-way, or railroad right-of-way.
- Shoot from or across any public highway or railroad right-of-way.
- Take fur animals, except in compliance with furbearing mammal regulations.
- Disturb or remove the traps of any licensed trapper from public lands.
- Hunt game birds with a light, use a net or snare, or sell or waste any part of a game bird. Note: temporary rules are in effect regarding the sale and purchase of some game bird feathers. Contact the department for details.
- Hunt in Safety Zones created and posted by the department of fish and wildlife.
- Disturb, damage, remove, alter or possess any official department of fish and wildlife sign.
- Hold any wild bird in captivity without a permit or destroy the nests or eggs of birds.
- Release any species of bird in the state without a permit from the department of fish and wildlife.
- Permit dogs to run at-large or train dogs in game bird nesting habitat during the months of April through July, except as authorized by the fish and wildlife commission.

1998-99 Oregon Game Bird License and Permit Fees

Resident Hunter . . . .$ 15.00
Sports Pac . . . .$ 101.00
Nonresident Hunter License (age 14 and older) . . . .$ 53.00
Resident Combination Angler and Hunter License . . . .$ 32.50
Resident Juvenile Hunter License (age 14-17 years inclusive) . . . .$ 4.00
Resident Landowner/Youths Under age 14 . . . . Free
Disabled War Veteran's Hunting License* (residents only) . . . . Free
Permanent Pioneer Hunter License*
     (residents only, age 65 with 50 years in Oregon) $2.00–12.00
Senior Citizen Hunting License*
     (residents only, age 70 with five years in Oregon) . . . . Free
Resident Waterfowl Validation (required of all resident
     waterfowl hunters age 14 and older) . . . .$ 6.00
Resident Upland Game Bird Validation (required of all persons
     age 14 and older hunting pheasant, quail, partridge and grouse) . . . . . .$ 6.00
Nonresident Game Bird Validation (required of all nonresidents age 14
     and older hunting waterfowl, pheasant, quail, partridge and grouse) . . .$ 26.00
Harvest Information Program Validation
     (required of most game bird hunters) . . . . Free
Resident Controlled Fall Turkey Permit . . . .$ 11.00

Nonresident Controlled Fall Turkey Permit . . . .$ 41.00
Sage Grouse Permit . . . .$ 1.00
Sauvie Island Annual Parking Permit . . . .$ 10.50
Sauvie Island Daily Parking Permit . . . .$ 3.00

*Applications are available at ODFW Portland headquarters and regional offices, and these licenses may be obtained by mail only through the Portland office.

1998/99 Season Dates/Bag Limits
Upland Birds

Blue and Ruffed Grouse
Western Oregon and Hood River and Wasco Counties . . . . .Sept. 1–Jan. 10
Eastern Oregon . . . . .Sept. 1–Nov. 29
Bag Limits . . . . .3 each species daily; 6 each species in possession

Sage Grouse (Permit Season Only)
Permit season details published in Early Game Bird Synopsis; application deadline was August 22.
Season Dates . . . . .Sept. 12–16
Bag Limit . . . . .two grouse per season

Mountain Quail
Western Oregon and Hood River & Wasco Counties . . . . .Sept. 1–Jan. 10
Bag Limit . . . . .10 daily, 20 in possession
Klamath and Wallowa Counties . . . . .Oct. 17–Dec. 31
Bag Limit . . . . .2 daily, 2 in possession
Remaining Eastern Oregon . . . . .No open season

Valley Quail
Western Oregon . . . . .Oct. 17–Nov. 15
Eastern Oregon . . . . .Oct. 17–Dec. 31
Bag Limit . . . . .10 daily, 20 in possession

Cock Pheasant
Western Oregon . . . . .Oct. 17–Nov. 15
Bag Limit . . . . .2 roosters daily, 6 in possession
Eastern Oregon . . . . .Oct. 17–Dec. 13
Bag Limit . . . . .2 roosters daily, 8 in possession

Chukar and Hungarian Partridge
Wallowa, Union, Umatilla, Morrow & Grant Counties . . . . .Oct. 10–Dec. 31
Remaining Eastern Oregon . . . . .Oct. 10–Jan. 31
Bag Limit . . . . .8 daily, 24 in possession

Wild Turkey (Spring Season)
Entire state excluding Snake River Islands . . . . .April 15, 1999–May 31, 1999
Bag Limit . . . . .One male turkey
Season Limit . . . . .2 male turkeys (and a third with a bonus turkey tag)

Wild Turkey (Controlled Fall Season)
Douglas and Jackson Counties, by permit only . . . . .Oct. 15–Nov. 15
Daily and Season Bag Limit . . . . .1 turkey, either sex

Mourning Dove
Entire State . . . . .Sept. 1–Sept. 30
Bag Limit . . . . .10 daily, 20 in possession

Band-tailed Pigeon
Entire State . . . . .Sept. 15–23
Bag Limit . . . . .2 daily, 2 in possession

Common Snipe
Entire State . . . . .Concurrent with duck season
Bag Limit . . . . .8 daily, 16 in possession

Waterfowl

September Canada Goose
Clatsop, Columbia, Multnomah, Clackamas, Washington,
    Tillamook, Yamhill, Marion, Polk, Benton, Lincoln, Linn,
    and Lane Counties . . . . .Sept. 5– Sept. 18
Bag Limit . . . . .5 daily, 10 in possession
Douglas, Coos, Curry, Jackson, Josephine, Klamath, Lake,
    Sherman, Wasco, Gilliam, Morrow, Umatilla, Union, Baker,
    and Malheur Counties . . . . .Sept. 5– Sept. 11
Bag Limit . . . . .3 daily, 6 in possession
Note: The taking of cackling Canada geese, Aleutian Canada geese, and white-fronted geese is prohibited during the September season.

Duck (Including Merganser)
Entire State . . . . .Oct. 3– Jan. 16
Bag Limit . . . . .7 daily, 14 in possession*
*Within the daily bag limit of 7 ducks you may not have more than: 2 hen mallards,
  1 pintail, 2 redheads and 1 canvasback.

Coot
Entire State . . . . .Oct. 3–Jan. 16
Bag Limit . . . . .25 daily, 25 in possession

Black Brant

Entire State . . . . .Nov. 7–Nov.20

Bag Limit . . . . .2 daily, 4 in possession

Goose

Klamath, Lake, Harney, and Malheur Counties .Oct. 3–Jan. 9

Remaining Eastern Oregon . . . . .Oct. 10–Jan. 16

Bag Limit .4 dark/3 white daily, 8 dark/4 white in possession*

*The daily dark goose limit may not include more than two white-fronted geese or four in possession and one cackling Canada goose or two in possession. White geese are snow and Ross' geese. Dark geese are all other geese except black brant.

Northwest Oregon General Zone . . . . .Oct. 10–Jan.10

Bag Limit . . . . .4 dark/3white geese daily, 8 dark/6 white in possession*

Open Area: Those portions of Multnomah, Clackamas, Marion, Linn and Lane Counties outside the Northwest Oregon Permit Zone (see permit zone description in synopsis), except that portion of Lane County west of US 101 is closed to all Canada goose hunting.

Southwest Oregon General Zone . . . . .Oct. 10–Jan. 16

Bag Limit . . . . .4 dark/3white geese daily, 8 dark/6 white in possession**

Open Area: Coos, Curry, Douglas, Josephine and Jackson Counties except that those portions of Douglas, Coos and Curry Counties west of US 101 are closed to Canada goose hunting.

Northwest Oregon Permit Zone . . . . .See Oregon game bird regulations synopsis for open areas and season dates

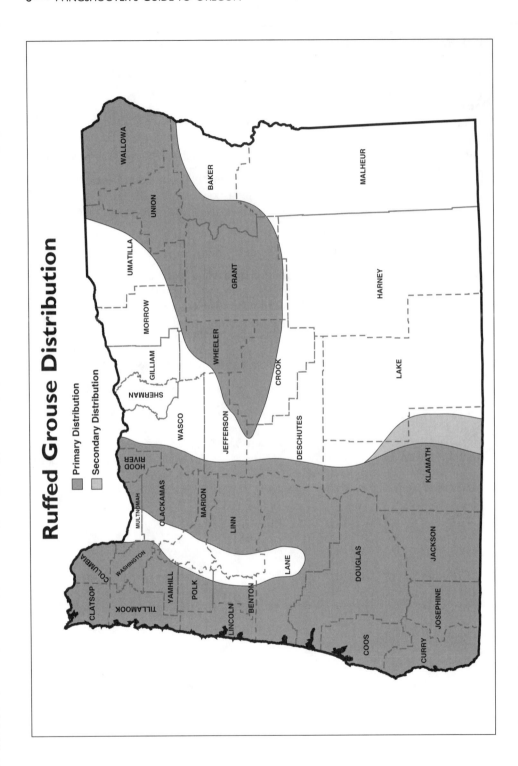

Ruffed Grouse Distribution

- Primary Distribution
- Secondary Distribution

Upland Game Birds

Ruffed Grouse

Bonasa umbellus

QUICK FACTS

Local Names
Ruff or ruffs; forest grouse, ruffled grouse, fool hen

Size
Ruffed grouse range from about 1 to 2 pounds and stretch 15 to 19 inches in length.

Identification in Flight
Ruffed grouse explode suddenly, often from heavy cover, with a thunderous flapping of wings. The black-barred tail is evident in flight. They twist and turn expertly through brush and branches. Birds that have not been hunted sometimes flush to the branches of a nearby tree, where they sit nervously before rocketing out of the foliage. Western Oregon's ruffed grouse tend toward a rich cinnamon-red color; eastern birds are usually ashy-gray or reddish-gray.

- Western Oregon abounds with ruffed grouse habitat, and the birds are not necessarily tied to riparian areas owing to the high moisture content in the forests and to myriad seeps and springs. Birds can range up to about 5,000 feet or more in elevation but are most common up to 3,000 feet.
- Eastern Oregon ruffed grouse are tied closely to riparian areas.
- Western Oregon grouse season runs from September 1 until early January.
- Eastern Oregon forest grouse season runs from September 1 until late November.
- The 1998 bag limit was 6 forest grouse with a maximum of 3 each species (ruffed and blue grouse)
- Grouse hunters are required to purchase an Upland Game Bird Validation.
- In 1996 Oregon hunters harvested 73,820 ruffed grouse.

Appearance

Oregon's western ruffed grouse are strikingly patterned in rich reddish-rust, brown, black, and white. Arthur Cleveland Bent called them "the darkest, most richly colored, and one of the handsomest races of the ruffed grouse" (*Life Histories of North American Gallinaceous Birds*, 1932). Oregon's eastern ruffed grouse range from the red phase to a distinctive ashy-gray with black and white highlights. Along the

Ruffed grouse on maple leaves.

eastern slope of the Cascade Range, reddish or reddish-gray phase birds predominate while the gray-phase grouse occur more commonly in the mountains of northeastern Oregon. The ruffed grouse derives its name from the ruff of black feathers around its neck, which is far more pronounced in adult males. Males and females sport a short crest and a squared-off tail with a black subterminal band. When fully fanned, the tail is a thing of beauty, and the age and sex of the bird can be determined by the tail size and pattern.

Sound and Flight Pattern

Ruffed grouse are mostly silent, but upon close approach to a family covey, the hunter might hear gentle clucks. During the breeding season, males display from a "drumming log" (or stump), fanning their tails and producing with their wings a drum-roll-type sound sometimes likened to the distant starting of a chain saw or motorcycle. Drumming generally occurs during the spring breeding season, especially at dawn and dusk, but often during late afternoon.

The thunderous whir of the ruffed grouse's short, powerful wings has startled many a hunter into missing easy shots. Often the birds hold in heavy cover, exploding from the ground at the last moment and then weaving a fast path through the lower tree limbs. Their flight speeds approach 40 miles per hour. Though ruffed grouse seldom take flight, their high-speed negotiations through thick cover often leave the hunter with nothing to shoot. This is especially true in the dense forests and bottomlands of western Oregon.

Habits and Feeding

During September, brood flocks consist of a hen and two to eight young. Occasionally, abundant food sources will attract two or more broods to the same feeding location. Hunting pressure quickly breaks up the brood coveys. In areas seldom hunted, coveys of two or three birds sometimes remain together through most of the season, although singles are more typical by winter.

Early in the fall, ruffed grouse rely heavily on fruits, berries, greens, and insects; by late autumn, their diet begins to shift to the buds of alder and aspen (red alder in western Oregon; alder and aspen in eastern Oregon). As snow blankets the ground, they climb trees to feed on the buds. The Oregon crabapple appears to be a major food source in areas of western Oregon where this tree abounds. Thick berry patches attract ruffed grouse, along with blue grouse and mountain quail. In western Oregon, ruffed grouse seem fond of young bracken fern shoots, whose dense stands also provide excellent cover for feeding, dusting, or day-roosting coveys.

Ruffed grouse feed most actively from early to midmorning and then again during late afternoon. In between, they rest and dust. During September, when the weather remains warm, the grouse often spend midday in the shelter of heavy bracken fern or berry growth along the edges of mixed wood lots, usually near water.

Seasonal Patterns

Spring for a male ruffed grouse means daily drumming from his chosen log or stump, which will serve in that capacity for generations of grouse if the habitat remains appropriate for their existence at the site. He mates with one or more hens, and then the hens lay 9 to 12 eggs. The chicks hatch in about three weeks and can fly, weakly, at about one week after hatching.

The broods disperse in the fall, with the young males seeking their own drumming sites. Sometimes they advertise these sites with late autumn drumming. In western Oregon, ruffed grouse need not live exclusively along the streams and rivers, for the water-rich Coast and Cascade Ranges offer countless tiny seeps and springs, often far from the nearest creek. At the same time, heavy dew provides additional moisture. Eastern Oregon grouse are closely tied to riparian zones. Unless the habitat changes, ruffed grouse utilize the same coverts for generations, so a hunter who locates birds should hunt that area in successive seasons, as the birds generally don't wander too far away.

Winter mortality is generally high for ruffed grouse, and severe winters can deplete the numbers quite rapidly. In western Oregon, unusually cold, wet weather during the late spring and early summer months can decrease nesting success and increase chick mortality.

Preferred Habitat and Cover

Western Oregon abounds in ideal ruffed grouse habitat. The birds thrive in moist, mixed woodlands and in western Oregon, such habitat is available in extensive stands of mixed hardwoods and conifers. Douglas fir, cedar, true firs, and hemlocks are the dominant low-elevation evergreen trees in western Oregon. Where these are mixed with stands of varied-age alder and maple, ruffed grouse are likely to thrive. Added to this bonanza of grouse habitat are the myriad berry species available as food and cover. These include red and blue huckleberry, salmonberry, thimbleberry, blackberry, and others. Bracken fern and sword fern provide additional cover and food.

Stands of alder and maple, mixed with a few conifers and understoried by berries and ferns, provide perfect cover for ruffed grouse, especially when these areas border openings, including stream channels, logging roads, clearcuts, and natural meadows.

In eastern Oregon, ruffed grouse depend on riparian zones for appropriate habitat, which takes the form of alder and aspen stands of varying ages mixed with young conifers. During the winter, when snow covers the ground, look for grouse feeding early and late in the leafless alders and aspens—often they seek refuge from severe weather under the protective canopy of conifers. Year-round seeps and springs also hold ruffed grouse in eastern Oregon. Look for moist areas in aspen groves and mixed thickets, especially in partially timbered draws and side canyons.

Hunting Methods

Ruffed grouse hold reasonably well for staunch pointing dogs and are also ideal for flushing breeds that work very close, well within average shotgun range. A good retrieving dog is critical to finding birds that fall in heavy cover.

Ruffed grouse are easiest to find during their morning and afternoon feeding times, when they frequent edges and clearings. During midday, hunt mixed timber or stands of aspen or alder. In eastern Oregon, look for springs, seeps and creeks surrounded by mixed hardwood and conifer cover. These areas serve as both feeding and day-roosting areas for ruffed grouse.

In western Oregon, where dense forest often hinders access, try walking old logging road spurs, especially where they cut across low ridges or run alongside streams or seeps. Look for water along these roads and cover these areas thoroughly. Ruffed grouse often dust on logging roads and feed along the road margins, especially if the road hangs above a creek and runs through mixed cover. Watch for dusters on the roads—grouse often leave a few feathers along with tracks.

Oregon offers excellent prospects for ruffed grouse.

Table Preparations

Ruffed grouse ranks among the best of upland fare, especially when young birds have fed heavily on berries. Field-dress the birds soon after harvest during warm days and store in the cooler with ice. Breasts can be prepared with a wide variety of recipes, but take care to keep them moist during the cooking process.

Shot and Choke Suggestions

All Season—No. 7½ or 8 shot
Choke—Improved and modified

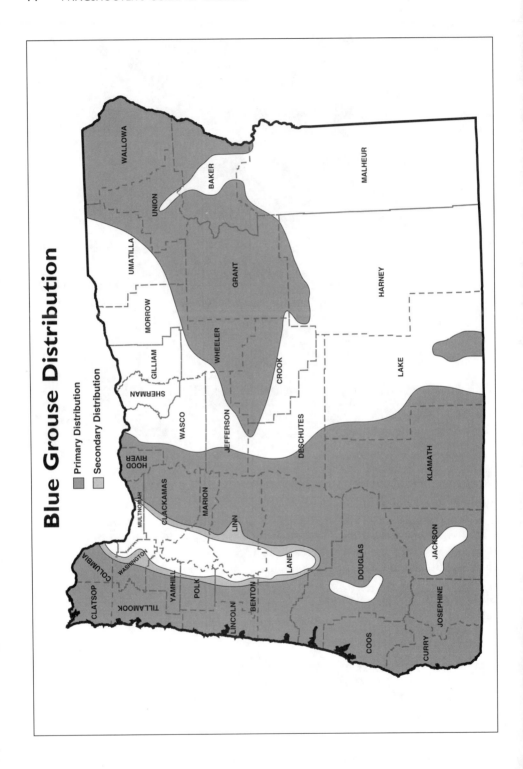

Blue Grouse Distribution

■ Primary Distribution
☐ Secondary Distribution

Blue Grouse

Dendragapus obscurus

QUICK FACTS

Local Names

"Blues," fool hen, pine grouse, pine hen, hooter

Size

Males, 20 to 22 inches in length; females smaller; weight, 2½ to 4 pounds; young and females noticeably larger than most ruffed grouse.

Identification in Flight

Loud, explosive flushes reveal a bird that appears uniformly dark gray. They often flush to the branches of a conifer and then either sit tight or reflush with a very rapid downward launch. Escape flights are often low and darting through trees, typically downhill on a ridge or slope.

- Blue grouse migrate uphill during late fall.
- Blue grouse in Oregon are closely tied to Douglas fir and true firs (e.g., grand fir, silver fir, and subalpine fir)
- As the season progresses, blue grouse become increasingly arboreal; when snow falls, they spend most of their time in trees.
- Western Oregon grouse season runs from September 1 until early January.
- Eastern Oregon forest grouse season runs from September 1 until late November.
- The 1998 bag limit was 6 forest grouse with a maximum of 3 each species (ruffed and blue grouse).
- Grouse hunters are required to purchase an Upland Game Bird Validation.
- In 1996, Oregon hunters harvested 33,120 blue grouse.

Appearance

Male blue grouse are large, robust grayish birds. Females are somewhat lighter and more mottled but otherwise quite similar. On the ground, blue grouse look like large, dark chickens; in flight, the male's long tail is conspicuous. Adult males are generally not found with females and their brood coveys. Oregon's blue grouse have a gray terminal band on the tail.

Sound and Flight Pattern

Blue grouse vocalize very little, although females and brood birds utter faint clucking notes at times. During the late spring mating season, males earn the name hooter by delivering, with their air sacks, a series of low-pitched hoots that might

Eastern Oregon male blue grouse displaying.

easily be mistaken for an owl. These hooting notes carry quite well through the woods, but locating a hooting bird is a difficult proposition.

On the wing, blue grouse often flush to a nearby tree, sometimes perching in plain sight to look over the threat, other times concealing themselves at the base of a densely foliated branch. If the birds then reflush from the tree, they will do so with a rocket-like downhill charge, often dodging through nearby trees and branches and usually heading downslope to the protection of a steep ridge. If caught in the open, blue grouse flush low and away and again usually make haste for a downhill retreat or the top of a distant conifer.

Habits and Feeding

Blue grouse frequent forested ridges, especially those with openings, such as natural meadows, clearcut edges, and exposed outcroppings. Any such areas that include heavy berry growth are likely to harbor blue grouse. The birds feed heavily on huckleberries, currants, gooseberries, serviceberries, thimbleberries, and others, along with a wide variety of greens and other plant matter. Blue grouse often feed

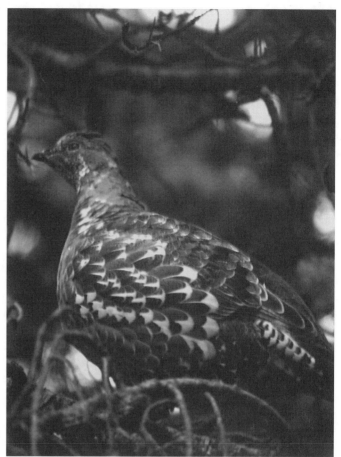

*Blue grouse
in a pine tree.*

along the margins of natural meadows, where they eat a variety of greens. They feed most actively from early to midmorning and again during late afternoon. In between those times, blue grouse dust, preen and roost, sometimes on the ground in protective cover, sometimes in the safety of a conifer. As winter approaches, blue grouse migrate upslope to timbered ridges and saddles where they live almost exclusively on fir needles until the following spring.

During September, expect to find brood coveys of three to eight birds. Prime feeding areas sometimes attract several broods, so large concentrations sometimes occur in forest clearings with dense berry growth. Brood coveys begin to break up as fall progresses. The large, adult males live a solitary existence, often frequenting the top and upper third of steep, timbered ridges, where safety is just a few wingbeats away.

Seasonal Patterns

Blue grouse exhibit a unique seasonal migration pattern in that they move downhill during spring for mating and nesting and then migrate back to the ridgetops and high, timbered slopes to spend the winter. Here, they feed on fir needles and live an arboreal life. During the early part of hunting season, they may occur on the same slopes occupied by ruffed grouse in western Oregon or along the top of the highest timbered ridges. Early or late in the season, ridgelines, saddles, and forested buttes are good bets for hunters.

Preferred Habitat and Cover

Blue grouse are tied closely to coniferous forest and especially to Douglas fir. Forests in the Cascades and Coast Ranges are comprised of a mix of Douglas fir, true firs, mountain and western hemlock, and cedar. Some of the best blue grouse habitat occurs in the zone where Douglas fir is mixed with hemlock and subalpine fir, typically at elevations of 3,000 to 7,000 feet in the Cascades. Grouse are especially drawn to timbered ridges and saddles where natural meadows and forest edges break up the timber stands. These areas often feature seeps and springs where birds take water if needed.

On the east side of the Cascades and in the mountains of eastern Oregon, blue grouse are distributed throughout the Douglas fir forests and are at times found in regions of surprisingly sparse evergreen cover. Such areas include the lower edges of the forest where it reaches down into river canyons. In some parts of northeastern Oregon, blue grouse occupy the same slopes as chukars, with the former being found higher on the ridge. Throughout their range, blue grouse are closely tied to their preferred foods, including berries and various greens.

Hunting Methods

Blue grouse hunters can walk logging roads, spurs, and skid roads where these cut across high ridges. Often, blue grouse can be spotted from a vehicle as they dust or feed along the road edges. In many places, logging spurs lead close to the top of steep ridges. From the end of these roads, hunters can climb and then walk the ridgetops. Given a choice, choose the side where the ridge drops away suddenly and thoroughly work clearings and berry patches. Blue grouse often day-roost and feed around outcroppings of rock on steep ridges, so walk and hunt these areas carefully. Throughout their range in Oregon, blue grouse tend to occupy the same places that are occupied by fire lookouts, so hunt these buttes and ridgetops as well.

Blue grouse hold for staunch pointing dogs, which are especially useful when hunting large clearings and parklands. In open areas, where the birds are subject to light hunting pressure, young blue grouse are well matched to young pointing dogs, often allowing close approach by both man and dog. An effective retriever will aid in finding wounded birds, since they habitually run into dense cover.

Ruffed grouse and blue grouse from the Oregon Cascades.

Table Preparations

During the early part of the season, blue grouse feed heavily on berries, so their white meat offers excellent eating. During warm weather, dress them immediately and store on ice.

Shot and Choke Suggestions

Heavily timbered ridges—No. 6 to 7½ shot, improved-modified choke.
Open areas, especially late season—No. 6 shot, modified choke

Grouse on the Grill

A few years ago, Labor Day weekend began on a September 1st Saturday, which of course also marked the beginning of grouse season in Oregon. Several friends with honest 9-to-5 jobs had planned a weekend climb of the South Sister, Oregon's third highest peak. Since the woman-of-the-time and I lived close to the mountain in the town of Bend, it was arranged that we would host this little weekend adventure. During the weeks leading up to the climb, I grappled with a single perplexing issue, the magnitude of which can only be appreciated by fellow bird hunting enthusiasts: How do I persuade the whole gang that Sunday would be the better climb day without informing a bunch of nonwingshooters that my hidden agenda was to avoid missing the grouse opener at all costs?

My solution, of course, preyed upon the good tastes of my friends, for all of them did and still do profess a distinct appreciation for exceptional food and fine wine. I began two weeks ahead of time, casually mentioning that if the timing was right, I might very well be able to harvest a few grouse prior to the climb and thus prepare fodder for a post-climb barbecue. Having long since gained a somewhat suspect reputation as the best barbecuer in the bunch, I knew I was slowly burying the hook. A few days later, I was again working the grouse-on-the-grill-would-be-such-a-pleasant-way-to-end-the-weekend angle. The wife finally took the bait, asking, "When does grouse season open?"

"Well," I replied, "it actually starts Saturday morning, and if I'm going to feed six or eight people, I'm going to need a limit of birds, and if I'm to have any hope of killing a limit I'll need to be the first hunter on the ridge on Saturday morning. I was thinking that if we moved the climb to Sunday, I could spend Saturday getting the birds and then preparing the marinade."

Two weeks of sowing seeds had produced the desired results: The wife was persuaded and the friends were likewise persuaded in order. We would climb Sunday; I would hunt Saturday. Perfect.

At least, I thought it was perfect. Killing a limit of six grouse never comes as an easy task. And I had talked it up way too much. I had no choice but to put out, so to speak. Saturday morning found me walking a favorite ridge at sunrise. The first three birds came easy when I stumbled onto about 15 blue grouse feeding in an expansive patch of gooseberry. By the time I'd busted the third of those big blues, the remaining birds had disappeared over the steep slope that fell precipitously away to the west. No pursuing them down there. The next three birds took most of the day, and by evening I'd covered 10 or 12 miles, most of it in 90-degree heat. I was pretty well spent and had a 10,000-foot mountain to climb the next morning.

What's more, I still had lots of work ahead, breasting and sectioning grouse into skewer-sized strips and then preparing the marinade along with all the other

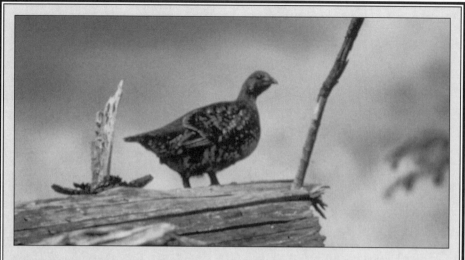

ingredients for the skewers. All these tasks were completed by 10PM, the grouse meat soaking in my favorite marinade, where it would remain for the next 16 hours. In preparation for our 4AM departure, all the friends had wandered off to bed before I finished with the birds. I probably need not mention that 4AM came far too soon. As is our custom, the climbing began at 5AM, before sunup.

Not until we'd covered the first three miles did I begin to feel the effects of my previous day's many miles afoot. Then came the steep stuff in the form of 3,000 feet of rock, scrim, and cinder that, if any more vertical, would defy hiking. We veterans of Oregon chukar and grouse hunts learn early the value of bearing down and mindlessly putting one foot in front of the other. We made the summit by 9AM, and I hobbled back to the vehicles about three hours later with my knees pretty well wiped out.

All the way down the mountain, the rest of the gang waxed poetic about the forthcoming grouse dinner, now mere hours away. Picking up the rear, I simply trudged along on spent legs, wondering what I'd gotten myself into with this master plan of mine.

The barbecued grouse skewers received rave reviews from all quarters, although eight hungry climbers stretched the meat pretty thin. Soon everyone drifted into cozy chairs and sleepy conversation, save the chef, who busily, even though exhausted, cleaned the kitchen and grill. That latter task finally accomplished, I commandeered a corner of the couch. It occurred to me shortly thereafter that despite my efforts to engineer the whole weekend around opening day of grouse season, it was in fact the friends who had determined my destiny all along. That reality derived from one friend's comment: "Ya know, John, those grouse were terrific, but next year maybe we should climb on Monday, then you'll have time to get two limits and really feed us like kings."

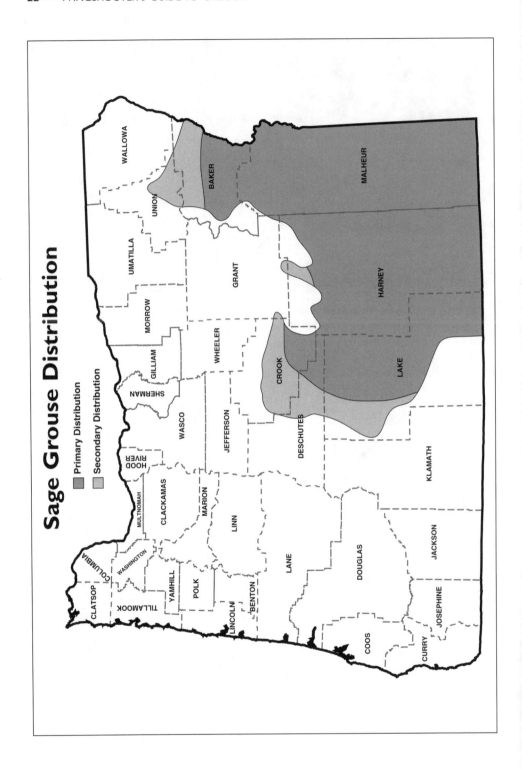

Sage Grouse Distribution

■ Primary Distribution

▨ Secondary Distribution

Sage Grouse

Centrocercus urophasianus

QUICK FACTS

Local Names

Sage hen, sage cock, sage chicken, bomber

Size

North America's largest native grouse, cocks range from 25 to 35 inches with a wingspan of 36 to 38 inches. They weigh 3 to 7 pounds; adult hens are substantially smaller, averaging 3 to 4 pounds.

Identification in Flight

The dark upper half and black belly contrast rather strikingly with the bird's white underwings. Its flush is loud and explosive, and they often fly for considerable distances on their long wings.

Throughout its huntable range in Oregon, the sage grouse does not share habitat with sharp-tailed grouse, thus the only possible confusion could come from hen pheasants in those areas where both species inhabit fringe agricultural regions.

- Oregon's sage grouse season is limited to a permit-only, short-duration season during which a hunter may harvest only two birds, the wings from which must be turned in to ODFW. The season permit is issued through a drawing with application deadlines (always during August) being listed in the Oregon Early Game Bird Synopsis.
- Oregon's 1998 sage grouse season extended from September 12 to 16. The highest tag allotments, as usual, went to the Beatty's Butte and Whitehorse Units (200 permits) along with the Steens and Warner Units (150 permits). In all, 12 units in southeastern Oregon are open to sage grouse hunting.
- Oregon's permit-only sage grouse season is designed primarily as a method of collecting wings for analysis by biologists, and these wings must be turned in to ODFW.
- Sage grouse thrive in some of Oregon's most remote areas.
- Sage grouse are known to travel substantial distances during seasonal migrations.
- In Oregon's southeast deserts, where sage grouse are most numerous, they often prefer high plateaus (occurring at over 9,000 feet in the Steens Mountains).
- Sage grouse rely on sagebrush as a staple winter food but switch to a more varied diet during spring, summer, and fall.
- Sage grouse once lived throughout eastern Oregon, but widespread removal of sagebrush steppe for agricultural purposes caused their extirpation from the Columbia Basin and most of northeastern Oregon.
- Since 1991, an average of 755 hunters harvested an average of 796 sage grouse each year.

Sage grouse from southeastern Oregon.

Appearance

The male sage grouse is a remarkable and striking bird with its black belly, richly mottled plumage, and long, sharp tail plumes. During their February-April mating season, males strut in full regalia on the traditional "leks." This mating ritual, both a visual and audible wonderment, ranks among the most unique wildlife chronicles in western North America. Female sage grouse share the male's rich mottling of brown, tan, and gray, but lack the face pattern and large tail, though they, too, have long pointed tail plumes.

Sound and Flight Pattern

Cock sage grouse often utter a soft, deep kuk-kuk-kuk when flushed; hens cackle quietly. Both sounds are often overpowered by the explosive, rapid beat of stiff wings. Sage grouse sometimes flush and then, to the hunter's consternation, fly great distances, sometimes disappearing from sight. Birds that have seen no hunting pressure are less prone to such long flights, as are hens and their broods.

Habits and Feeding

Male sage grouse take no part in the rearing of chicks. Broods typically range from six to eight young. Brood flocks tend to mix, forming larger flocks during late summer and fall. Winter flocking begins in earnest by late autumn, and these winter flocks may include upward of 100 birds, although flocks of 15 to 40 are more typical most years. Sage grouse, while nonmigratory, do seek new ranges during the different seasons. When snow falls, they move to higher, windlashed plateaus or to lower elevations. Their winter food consists largely of sage, while during the remainder of the year they feed on a wide variety of plant foods. Sage grouse get moisture from their foods and from dew but are nonetheless drawn to water sources when these are available. Because sage grouse are active early in the morning, some of the best hunting areas feature a waterhole atop a high plateau that is tilted slightly to the east or southeast (to absorb the first sunlight).

Seasonal Patterns

In Oregon, mating season for sage grouse begins in the bitter chill of February, with peak activity on the leks occurring during March and early April. Large leks can feature dozens of cocks competing mightily for dozens of hens. Leks are located in areas more open than the surrounding sage steppe, often on sparsely vegetated playas, dry meadows, or windblown barrens. These open areas are significant because they allow female sage grouse to evaluate the various strutting males. Also, mating activity on the leks makes these normally secretive birds more at risk from predators, so open areas allow them a better chance of seeing and fleeing from harm. Strutting always occurs early in the morning with peak activity around sunrise. On the lek, the most dominant males occupy the most central locations and do most of the mating. Less dominant males dance at the edges and often continue strutting after the other birds have left for the day or for the season. After mating, males disperse and hens are left to nest and raise the chicks, often not far from the leks. Flock formation begins in the summer and fall, mostly with the hens and their broods; during summer, males often stray great distances.

Preferred Habitat and Cover

Sagebrush, specifically *Artemesia tridentata*, forms the critical element in determining sage grouse range. In Oregon, undisturbed and unaltered sagebrush desert is most abundant in the southeast corner of the state, which also offers countless acres of the high sage plateau country favored by the birds. Here the birds also find the mix of greens and grasses that comprise their diet from spring through autumn. During September, when Oregon's short sage grouse season occurs, the birds frequent areas featuring watering holes, dense sage stands for loafing and preening, and prime feeding areas in low-growth sage stands. They also occur on the fringes of alfalfa and other crop fields where these places meet good grouse range in southeastern Oregon. During wet years, sage grouse populations may be high but with birds and flocks widely scattered—wet years produce an abundance of good grouse habitat, so birds

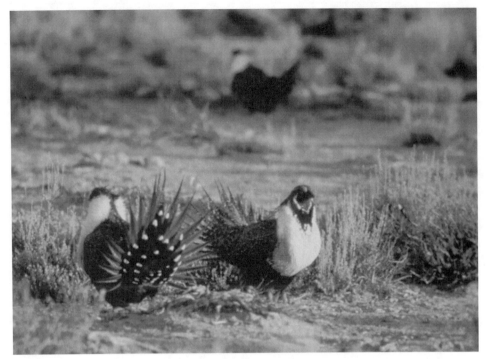

Male sage grouse displaying.

disperse. Conversely, drought years limit good habitat to greenbelts and watering areas, where sage grouse congregate.

Hunting Methods

Hunting sage grouse in Oregon begins at home with good USGS topo maps and BLM maps. Look for water sources, especially in the form of waterholes located atop large plateaus at elevations ranging from 4,000 to 7,000 feet. After choosing likely locations, begin the hunt very early—as soon as legal shooting hours begin. The hunt may require lots of walking, but concentrate your efforts within a mile or so of the water sources. Look for sign in the form of chicken-like droppings that are usually green-white in color. Such droppings, along with feathers, accumulate in favorite roosting, dusting, and loafing areas. Also look for tracks, especially around watering holes. A good pointing dog (or two or three) can save lots of walking. Bear in mind that Oregon's September season is often accompanied by warm or even hot weather that can be hard on dogs in this arid climate. Hunting early in the morning allows the dog ample cool weather and good scenting conditions. Beware of rattlesnakes, especially when the sun begins to warm the rocks, and make sure the dog's feet are well conditioned.

Table Preparations

Opinions vary on the palatability of sage grouse, but I suspect much of the bitter taste often associated with the birds results from hunters not gutting the birds immediately, especially when warm weather prevails. Young birds offer the best flavor and will, of course, comprise most of the kill.

Shot and Choke Suggestions

No. 5 to 6 shot, modified and full chokes.

Sage Grouse Hunters, Harvest and Birds/Hunter by Hunt Unit in 1997

Hunt Unit	Hunters	Harvest	Birds/Hunter
Sumpter	5	3	0.6
Lookout Mt.	10	8	0.8
Beulah	100	102	1.0
Malheur River	44	32	0.7
Owyhee	45	45	1.0
Whitehorse	141	199	1.4
Steens Mt.	77	84	1.1
Beatty's Butte	162	158	1.0
Juniper	66	64	1.0
Silvies	9	9	1.0
Wagontire	62	43	0.7
Warner	83	92	1.1

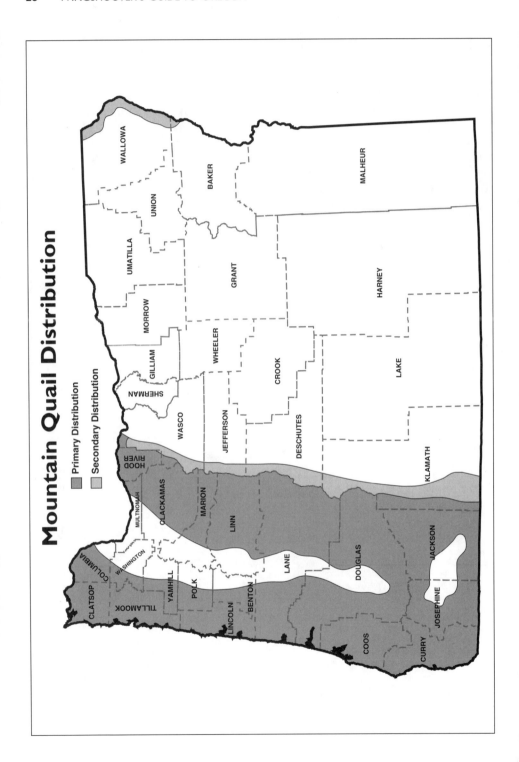

Mountain Quail Distribution

■ Primary Distribution

▨ Secondary Distribution

Mountain Quail

Oreortyx pictus

QUICK FACTS

Local Names
  None known

Size
  10 to 12 inches in length (largest of the quail)

Identification in Flight
  Mountain quail explode from the brush with a rapid whir of wings and usually with lots of excited chirping. Looping or direct flights are typical, and these birds are adept at dodging through the branches.

- Mountain quail prefer steep, brushy, rocky areas in the mountains of western Oregon.
- Mountain quail exist in low densities in central Oregon and northeastern Oregon, but no hunting season is currently in place owing to sparse populations, except in Wallowa and Klamath Counties.
- Mountain quail season runs concurrent with grouse season in western Oregon.
- The 1998 bag limit on mountain quail was 10 birds (2 birds in Wallowa and Klamath Counties).
- Quail hunters are required to purchase an Upland Game Bird Validation.
- In 1996 Oregon hunters harvested 54,633 mountain quail.

Appearance

The adult mountain quail is an unusually handsome bird with its steel-blue/gray breast and bronze-olive-colored back. The flanks are strikingly marked with broad white and dark bands, while the chestnut-colored face is outlined in white. The mountain quail's plume is long and straight, sometimes tilting to the rear. The female is similar in overall appearance, although her plume is shorter.

Sound and Flight Pattern

Mountain quail vocalize often and readily, especially when a hunter and dog work the covey. Members of a broken covey call to each other with sharp chirps and soft clucks. The call is loud and resonant and often accompanied by a series of sharp whistles. Mountain quail fly only when necessary, but their short, powerful wings allow them to steer a rapid course through dense vegetation. Coveys tend to break up in all directions, with some birds running and others taking flight. Often, a hunter hears the bird fly away but is never afforded a shot owing to the thick brush preferred by mountain quail.

Mountain quail.

Habits and Feeding

Mountain quail feed most actively during the morning and late afternoon hours, when they frequent berry patches, road edges, clearcut edges, and other such open areas. Their diet consists of myriad berries, seeds, greens, and some insects. Family coveys are most common, but good feeding areas may attract several such coveys, at which time all the individuals feed together in the same area. Mountain quail dust frequently, so hunters should study roads and logging landings for dusting areas and then hunt these places regularly.

In southwestern Oregon, where mountain quail populations are strongest, brood coveys of 6 to 15 birds occupy the same general area throughout the season and will at times group with other coveys during winter. The result is a covey of 50 or more birds, reminiscent of a winter covey of valley quail. In the central and north Oregon Cascades and Coast Ranges, mountain quail densities are not quite as high, so large winter coveys are rarely seen. Instead, individual brood coveys tend to occupy the same general area, so once hunters learn the location of several coveys, they can hunt these areas regularly,

Seasonal Patterns

During the fall, brood coveys of mountain quail tend to center their activities on a particular location, often near their night roosting site. These sites have been deemed "headquarters." A covey of mountain quail will use its headquarters for roosting, preening, dusting, and foraging. The birds venture out for feeding during morning and again during late afternoon or evening.

Around midautumn, mountain quail coveys may migrate to different elevations, and many individuals leave to mix with associated coveys nearby. At this time, hunters may find coveys missing from the areas they occupied during the early part of the season. During winter, coveys again settle into a routine.

Preferred Habitat and Cover

Mountain quail occupy some of the most difficult terrain in the forests of western Oregon, due to their preference for areas of dense shrubbery located on steep hillsides at elevations up to about 6,000 feet. They are birds of the edges, so clearcuts from 5 to 15 years old often provide ideal habitat, especially if water and mixed older conifers occur nearby. Brushy, rocky slopes and outcroppings provide good cover as well. Good mountain quail habitat includes dense growth of berries, seedbearing grasses, and flowers, legumes, bracken fern, and various other greens. Dusting areas include just about any disturbed area, from clearcuts to logging roads to gopher mounds.

Hunting Methods

Consistently shooting mountain quail requires that the hunter locate several coveys and then hunt the coveys regularly. To find coveys, many hunters spend mornings and evenings driving and walking logging roads in appropriate habitat, looking for quail or quail sign (dusters and tracks) on the roads. Once birds are located, hunters can pursue the covey on foot. In future visits, hunters can park the vehicle at a distance and walk up on the covey's headquarters area unannounced.

When walking the logging roads and spurs, watch closely for dusting areas, which often contain feathers. It's likely the birds are nearby as they tend not to wander too far from their favorite haunts. These birds often vocalize with subtle chirps and sometimes scamper nervously about in the understory. The hunter who keeps ears and eyes open will find more quail.

A good retriever is essentially mandatory for mountain quail hunting because downed birds often land in cover too dense for humans. A close-working flusher can be a big asset, and a pointing dog with good lungs and a strong uphill gait can pressure running birds into holding. In either case—flushers or pointers—the dog that hunts mountain quail on a regular basis has the opportunity to learn the peculiar habits of these running, wild-flying quail.

Table Preparations

The hunter fortunate to pull off a few good shots will be rewarded with exceptional white meat from mountain quail. Breasts are smaller than those of ruffed grouse but larger than valley quail. During the typically warm weather of September, dress or breast the birds soon after the kill and store on ice.

Shot and Choke Suggestions

All Seasons/locations—No. 7½ or 8 shot; improved or open bore.

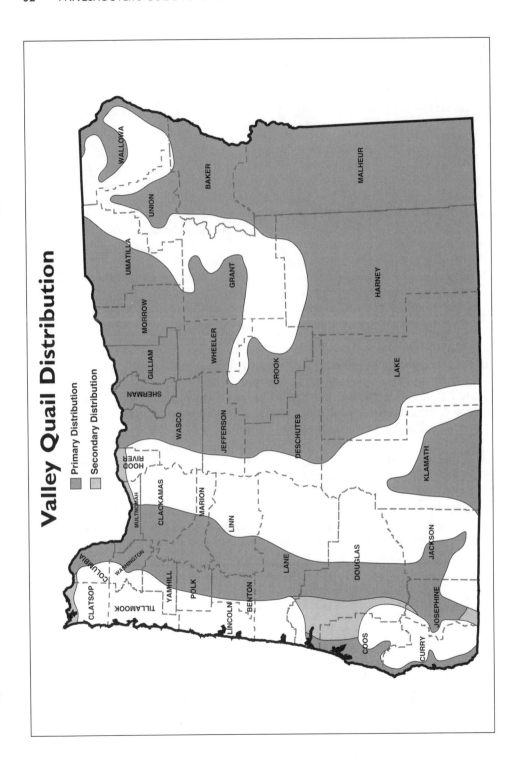

Valley Quail Distribution

■ Primary Distribution
■ Secondary Distribution

Valley Quail

Callipepla californica

QUICK FACTS

Local Names
California quail, quail, topknot quail

Size
Approximately 8 inches in length; Oregon's smallest upland game bird

Identification in Flight
Valley quail explode from cover with rapid, buzzing wingbeats, often chirping as they go. Only rarely does an entire covey flush in unison; instead, individuals or pairs flush one after another until all the birds have relocated.

- Valley quail are native only to the counties bordering California but were widely introduced around Oregon beginning in the late 1800s and now thrive throughout most of the state. They are Oregon's most widely distributed upland game bird.

- Valley quail are closely tied to brushy edge habitat in agricultural and suburban areas.

- In central and eastern Oregon, valley quail are closely tied to water sources, including riparian areas, farms, ranches and towns.

- In western Oregon, valley quail season runs concurrent with pheasant season. In eastern Oregon, valley quail season extends to December. 31.

- The 1998 bag limit on valley quail was 10 birds.

- Quail hunters are required to purchase an Upland Game Bird Validation.

- In 1996, Oregon hunters harvested 87,468 valley quail.

Appearance

The handsome male valley quail features a characteristic, drooping black topknot, shaped something like a question mark. His face is boldly patterned in black and white, while its head is chestnut-colored and borders a yellowish forehead. Both male and female have striped flanks and a scalloped belly. The back is deep blue-gray to olive-gray. The hen valley quail lacks the boldly patterned face and the topknot is noticeably shorter. With practice, wingshooters can usually pick males out of the flushing coveys.

Valley quail feeding.

Sounds and Flight Pattern

Valley quail prefer to run, which they do remarkably well, but will flush with little provocation as they are capable fliers. The flush depends on the cover—in western Oregon, good flushing dogs can work quail out of large blackberry stands, in which case, the birds often explode out the top of the berry bushes or run through and flush out the opposite side. The combination of high, arcing flights and straightaway ground-level flushes makes for interesting shooting. In sparse cover, valley quail typically flush low and somewhat straightaway, wrapping around any object that distances them from the threat. Their flushing speed is not particularly great, so shooters can pick distant birds first and work back in, creating an opportunity for easy doubles and an occasional triple.

Most characteristic of the valley quail's many vocalizations is the male's distinctive breeding call, a series of three (typically) slurred musical notes, the middle one loudest and highest. The call is sometimes described as a question for the female quail: "where ARE you." This breeding call is typically delivered over and over from a low perch during the mid- to late spring courtship season. This same call, along with a shortened two-note version of it, is heard regularly during the summer and fall. In addition, valley quail utter a variety of chirps and chips.

Habits and Feeding

Valley quail begin feeding early in the morning, then dust, preen, and rest during midday. They forage again in the late afternoon or evening. The valley quail's diet consists of a wide variety of plant materials, including myriad seeds, buds, and greens. In agricultural areas they are drawn to waste grain. Valley quail frequent watering areas; in the arid regions of central and eastern Oregon, in fact, the coveys rarely wander far from water.

Coveys of valley quail sometimes walk surprising distances to feed, picking their way through cover to a favorite foraging area and then often employing a sentinel to keep an eye out for danger. With a sentinel bird at guard, the rest of the quail pick away at their chosen food, often dusting and preening while foraging. Their distinctive bobbing walk and antics while feeding make for enjoyable observation.

Seasonal Patterns

During spring, male valley quail establish a territory for calling. They announce their presence each morning and evening with their distinctive "where-ARE-you" calls. The calling perch is usually elevated. After breeding, the female and male raise the young together. A typical spring scenario finds the male valley quail perched silently atop a lookout post while the female leads the young in search of food, generally in heavy cover where the broods of as many as 15 chicks remain protected from numerous predators. During good years, some valley quail will double clutch.

Family coveys remain together through the summer and most of the fall. In areas of prime habitat, two or more family coveys may occupy the same area. As winter approaches, family coveys converge, forming large winter coveys. In eastern Oregon, during high-productivity years, winter coveys might include more than 100 individuals. Large winter coveys in western Oregon typically number 20 to 50 individuals.

Throughout their range in Oregon, valley quail are closely tied to water. In water-rich western Oregon, however, the birds have lots of cover from which to choose. In central and eastern Oregon, valley quail are closely tied to riparian areas, farms, ranches, and towns. They may share habitat with chukars and pheasants in sagebrush environments and agricultural environments, respectively. In some habitats, they are the most abundant game bird.

Preferred Habitat and Cover

Valley quail can be found along river and creek bottoms where there is good, brushy cover and adjacent open areas, especially in parts of the Willamette Valley, where blackberry and other extensive shrubbery provides ideal cover, and around rural, suburban and urban areas in eastern Oregon where suitable water sources are easily found.

Valley quail need edges for feeding, heavy brush stands for cover, and elevated, heavy brush cover for roosting. In many areas of Oregon, they are a common urban

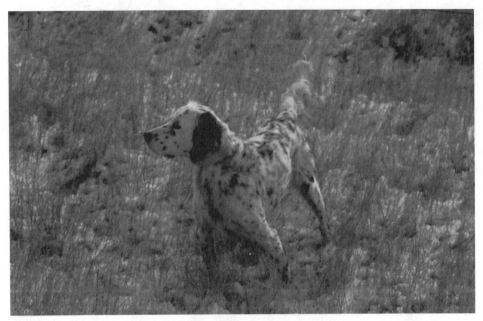

This setter has a lock on birds.

bird and are easily attracted to backyard bird-feeding stations where appropriate escape and roosting cover are found.

Hunting Methods

Because of the brushy habitat in which valley quail thrive, a good dog should be considered mandatory. This is especially true in western Oregon, where extensive blackberry growth sometimes makes downed birds impossible to find and retrieve without a dog. Valley quail are perfectly suited to pointing dogs because, after a covey is broken up, pointing breeds can locate and hold the singles and doubles. These birds do have a propensity for running, but a fleet-footed pointer can stop them, especially after the covey is scattered. Flushing breeds must work close and cover the ground thoroughly.

In agricultural areas, hunters should work fencelines, brushy edges, watering areas, and drainages. In central and eastern Oregon, look for quail along brushy creeks, draws with springs or seeps, irrigation canals, and riparian margins along rivers. In prime habitat, keep an eye peeled for tracks on dusty roads. Valley quail feed actively during the early morning and late afternoon/evening, when they sometimes wander away from heavy cover. Once a covey is located, the initial flush sends birds in all directions. Then hunters and dogs can effectively work the singles and doubles.

Valley quail.

Table Preparations

Though quite small, the plump breasts provide superb eating and can be prepared in a variety of ways. Be sure to draw the birds immediately during warm weather.

Shot and Choke Suggestions

Improved, No. 7½ or 8 shot.

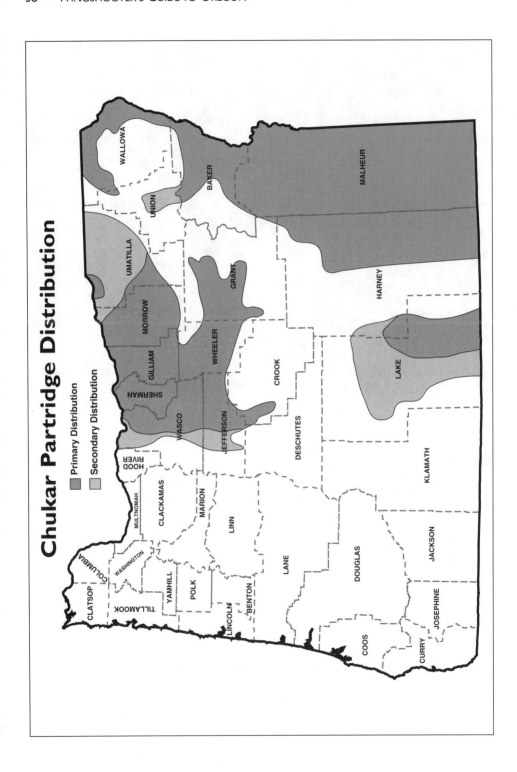

Chukar Partridge Distribution

■ Primary Distribution
▨ Secondary Distribution

Chukar Partridge

Alectoris chukar

QUICK FACTS

Local Names

Chukar

Size

Both sexes range from 13 to 15 inches in length; adult males average 19.6 ounces in weight, while adult females average 15.7 ounces.

Appearance in Flight

Chukar are quick flyers that prefer to flush and fly downhill. On the wing, they exhibit fast wingbeats like that of a quail, and their handsome face pattern and striped flanks are often clearly discernible. Being covey birds, chukars often flush in unison. They are superb athletes on the ground, able to run uphill and climb rimrocks and talus slides like mountain goats.

- Chukar are nonindigenous partridge native to central Europe but widely introduced in western North America, especially in Oregon, Idaho, and Nevada.

- Chukar populations fluctuate rather widely from year to year and are largely determined by spring nesting and rearing conditions as well as by winter weather.

- Chukar are closely tied to water in their arid habitat and will make daily or twice daily trips to water sources until autumn weather brings moisture to the high rims and slopes.

- Southeastern Oregon offers an abundance of public land that allows wing-shooters expansive opportunity to hunt on many thousands of acres of prime chukar habitat.

- Chukar hunters and their dogs must be in good physical condition to hunt the steep, arid country these birds inhabit.

- Pointing dogs are especially well suited to hunting chukars; flushing dogs need to work fairly close.

- The 1998 daily bag limit on chukar was 8 birds.

- Partridge hunters are required to purchase an Upland Game Bird Validation.

- In 1996, Oregon hunters harvested 61,782 chukars.

Appearance

The chukar partridge, a most handsome game bird, is elegantly adorned with black and white bars on its taupe flanks, a soft gray mantle and a striking black-and-white face pattern. This beautiful plumage is then further enhanced by the chukar's bright red legs and bill.

Sound and Flight Pattern

Chukar are readily identified by their call, from which derives their name: "chuka, chuka, chuka." The call often rings from high above, near the rimrocks, and is especially pronounced early in the season before the birds have learned the virtues of silence. Often, the call of the chukar simultaneously tells the hunter that birds are present and the he or she has a lot of climbing to do before reaching said birds. Once a covey is broken, members call to announce their location. Chukar flush with a whir of short, powerful wings and fly low and away downslope, often wrapping around a ridge or spine before landing again. Chukar flush in coveys, although often a few stragglers are late in exiting.

Habits and Feeding

Cheatgrass forms an important ingredient in the chukar's diet. When available, chukars feed readily and heavily on waste grain, namely in areas where wheat fields sit atop canyon slopes occupied by chukar populations. Prior to the arrival of autumn or winter moisture, chukars generally make their way to water in the morning and then feed their way upslope. In the late afternoon, after feeding, preening, and loafing on the slopes, the birds again move down to water prior to roosting in the rimrocks, talus, or other cover. Clutch birds feed heavily on insects.

After the first rain or snow, chukar need no longer make regular trips to open water. Instead, they disperse to higher slopes and obtain water from pools in the rocks or moisture on the vegetation. Cool winter weather further reduces their need for water.

Seasonal Patterns

Family clutches remain separated until fall, when they begin joining to form larger winter coveys. During good years, areas of ideal habitat may produce winter coveys of more than 100 birds. Coveys remain closely associated with available water sources until rains arrive in mid- to late autumn. Substantial moisture during the late fall allows chukar coveys to disperse to higher and more remote slopes. During winter, the birds prefer south-exposure slopes, which offer warmer temperatures owing to direct sunlight.

Preferred Habitat and Cover

Chukars are most at home in arid, steep, rugged canyons where streams or rivers provide a water supply. They roost in rimrocks, talus slides, brushy draws, and other such covers. Perfect habitat combines steep slopes with abundant cheatgrass,

Chukar with brood at guzzler.

myriad talus slides, and cover in the form of rabbit brush, sage, and bunchgrass. If the same slope has wheat fields on flatlands above and a year-round stream below, all the elements for ideal habitat are in place for these hardy partridge. During winter, chukar seek areas devoid of snow and are most comfortable on south exposures where they gather what little warmth is offered by the sun.

Hunting Methods

Success in chukar hunting requires that hunters always seek ground at or above the level at which the birds will be found. Such position can be accomplished in one of three ways: Early in the season, you can ambush the birds as they seek water at the canyon bottoms, typically at midmorning and again during late afternoon. Otherwise, you have to get to their level by either walking up or hunting an area where you can drive to the top. Topo maps produced by the Bureau of Land Management and United States Geological Survey show roads that provide access to the top of many canyons. Otherwise, you're stuck with the option of hiking up the steep slopes inhabited by chukar, which is one reason for the old adage that the first time you hunt chukars you do so for the enjoyment of it, and every time thereafter you are motivated solely by revenge. That adage also derives from the chukar's maddening

An eastern Oregon triple: pheasant, chukar, and Hungarian partridge.

tendency to run rapidly uphill, never flushing unless approached from above or pinned down by a dog.

Once you reach appropriate altitude, start walking the contour and give up elevation only begrudgingly. Even walking a contour can be exhausting, especially on steep, rocky, unstable ground where one leg remains forever higher than the other.

A good dog or dogs help immensely in finding chukars, especially later in the season when the birds appreciate the value of stealth and silence. Pointing breeds are especially well-suited to chukar hunting: the birds usually hold well for a dog, and pointers can cover lots of ground while the hunter continues along on the same contour, only walking up or downhill to flush birds in front of the dog. Also, speedy pointing breeds have the ability to catch up with birds running uphill, thus pinning them down until the gunner can get there.

Often chukars reside atop the canyons, where flat or rolling country makes for much easier walking. These birds always remain but a short flight or run from the safety of the canyon edge, where they can disappear with a burst of speed. Thus in many areas, a viable tactic involves getting to the top and then hunting along at the edge of the slope or just down from the edge. In some places—the breaks of the John Day River for example—wheat stubble attracts birds to the top of the slopes.

Table Preparations

The white-meat chukar ranks amongst the best of wildfowl with a mild, tender flavor. Birds should be drawn soon after the kill, especially in warm weather. They lend themselves to numerous preparations.

Shot and Choke Suggestions.

Early season with pointing dogs—No. 5, 6, or 7½ shot, modified chokes.

Late Season with pointing dogs—No. 5 to 6 shot, modified and full chokes.

Any season with flushing dogs—No. 5 to 6 shot, modified and full chokes.

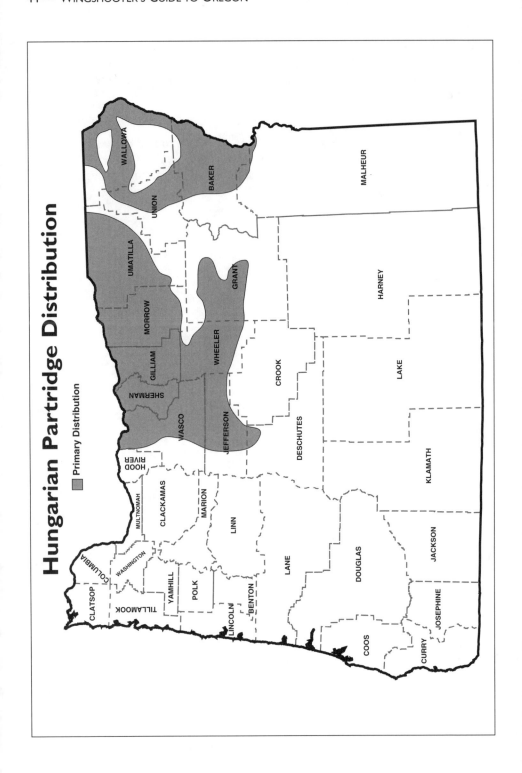

Hungarian Partridge Distribution

Primary Distribution

Hungarian Partridge

Perdix perdix

QUICK FACTS

Local Names

Hun, gray partridge

Size

12 to 13 inches in length with a wingspan of 15 to 17 inches and weighing up to a pound.

Appearance in Flight

Hungarian partridge are strong, quick flyers with rapid wingbeats not unlike a quail. They are capable of quick twists and turns and often wrap around a ridge or hill before landing again. They typically flush as a covey, sometimes with a few stragglers.

- The Hungarian partridge is a non-native game bird introduced widely in North America. They are indigenous to central Europe. The first stocks in Oregon occurred in 1900 and 1912.
- The Columbia Basin, especially its southern half, offers Oregon's best Hun populations with fairly strong populations in the Snake River basin counties.
- Huns were initially planted in western Oregon but failed to survive there.
- Huns are typically hunted incidentally to pheasant and chukar.
- The 1998 daily bag limit on Hungarian partridge was 8 birds.
- Partridge hunters are required to purchase an Upland Game Bird Validation.
- In 1996, Oregon hunters harvested 11,380 Huns.

Appearance

The Hungarian partridge is a handsome bird characterized by a grayish plumage throughout, a chestnut-colored belly, cinnamon-colored head and a rust-colored tail, this latter feature usually visible in flight. Generally Huns are easily told from chukar and valley quail, the only other upland birds with which they might be confused. They sometimes occupy wheat stubble alongside chukar and pheasant, and their habitat overlaps that of the valley quail near ranch and farm buildings and around brushy draws on grasslands and grain fields.

Sound and Flight Pattern

Upon flushing, Huns usually utter a series of fairly loud squealing calls. Their initial burst of rapid, explosive wingbeats soon gives way to an alternating series of flaps and glides. The covey tends to depart in tight formation. If a covey is broken, individuals will call to one another and reassemble.

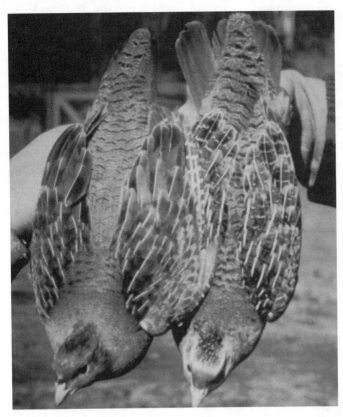

Hungarian partridge.

Habits and Feeding

Generally, Huns are early risers and begin their quest for food by daybreak or before. After a morning feeding, the coveys water, loaf, dust and preen before an afternoon feeding. Huns feed on a wide variety of seeds and grains, specially waste grains in wheat fields. They also consume some insects and green vegetative matter. Much of their water intake comes from morning dew and from irrigation, but when available, they drink from streams, seeps, and ditches. During winter, snow provides a source for water. Like other game birds, Huns gather grit from the edges of roads, especially those running alongside good feeding areas, such as wheat fields and prairies.

Seasonal Patterns

Huns are strictly covey birds, and as such, their entire life history is defined by these social flocks. During late spring, the hen lays 12 to 17 eggs, so ideal nesting and rearing conditions can produce large family coveys. Hens and cocks rear the young together. The hot summer months are spent in the coolest, most comfortable part of their range, especially if water becomes a commodity not easily gathered. By fall, family broods assemble into larger coveys where they remain throughout the winter and early spring. Severe winter weather drives the coveys to areas offering the best combination of cover and available feed. In the absence of large accumulations of snow, the birds often reside in sheltered, brushy draws. If snow fills such places, they may feed on windswept knolls and windward slopes where grain and seed is most easily gathered.

Preferred Habitat and Cover

Hungarian partridge are most abundant in the grain country of eastern Oregon, especially where wheat and other grain tracts are bordered by grasslands. The best Hun country features geography characterized by rolling hills, draws, grassy slopes, and high, shortgrass knolls. Large tracts featuring a mix of native grasses and brushes offer ideal cover for Huns, especially when bordered by large grain fields. Early in the season, when eastern Oregon is hot and dry, coveys often occupy irrigated lands or moist draws, especially those with water.

Hunting Methods

Consistent success hunting Hungarian partridge generally means covering lots of ground with the aid of good pointing dogs. Huns can range widely across expansive tracts of good habitat, but productive areas tend to remain that way over time. Birds are most active during morning and late afternoon when they forage for food; otherwise they tend to collect grit, loaf, preen, and dust on exposed rises, slopes or, in cold or hot weather, under heavier cover. Once a covey is found and flushed, hunters can follow along for subsequent flushes until the covey is broken. Then, with the aid of dogs, hunters can work the singles as they call to regroup. Unless the covey is pursued rather ardently, it will rarely break. Huns begin moving about very early in the day and are quite wary. Nonetheless, hunters who begin the pursuit at daybreak are rewarded by perfect scenting conditions for the dogs and it is the bird dog that really defines a successful hunt for gray partridge. Without dogs, consistent success on Huns is highly improbable.

Table Preparations

The Hungarian partridge offers darker meat than that of the chukar partridge. In fact, Hungarian partridge compares favorably to valley or mountain quail. During hot weather, birds should be drawn immediately and cooled as soon as possible. When so treated, the breasts offer fine eating and lend themselves to a variety of preparations.

Shot and Choke Suggestions

Chokes—Modified chokes for singles barrels; for doubles, improved/modified early in the season with pointing dogs; improved/full late season or with flushing dogs.

Shot—No. 7½ or 6 (with single guns, try two 7½s followed by a load of 5s or 6s).

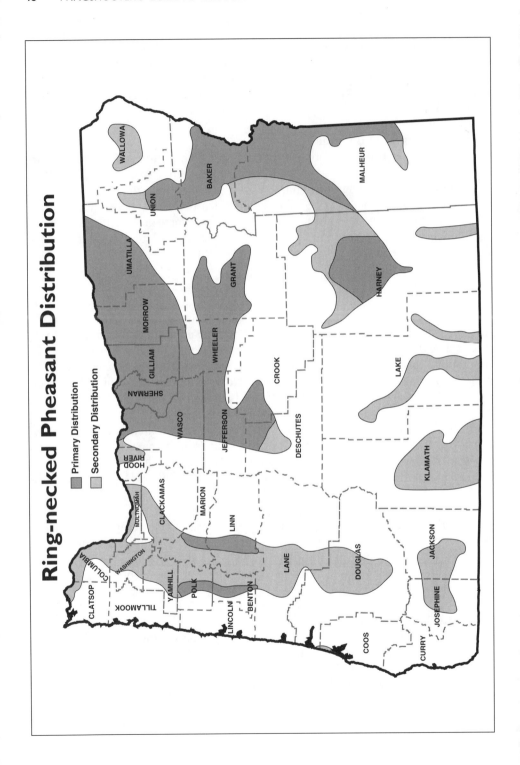

Ring-necked Pheasant Distribution

■ Primary Distribution
▨ Secondary Distribution

Ring-necked Pheasant

Phasianus colchicus

QUICK FACTS

Local Names

Pheasant, ringneck, rooster, cockbird

Size

Roosters up to 3 feet long, including tail; weight from 2 to 3½ pounds with a wingspan of 32 to 34 inches. Hens, which are fully protected, range from 20 to 25 inches.

Appearance in Flight

Male pheasants appear much darker in flight than the brownish hens. In good light, the rooster's resplendent plumage is quite obvious and it frequently cackles loudly upon being flushed.

- Ring-necked pheasants are the most sought-after upland game bird in Oregon.
- Oregon hosted the nation's first-ever introduction of ring-necked pheasants in 1882. The first birds were transported by sea directly from China by Judge Owen Denny.
- The 1998 daily bag limit on pheasants was two roosters.
- Hen pheasants are fully protected in Oregon and may not be harvested.
- Pheasant hunters are required to purchase an Upland Game Bird Validation.
- In 1996, Oregon hunters harvested 80,850 pheasants.

Appearance

The rooster ring-necked pheasant ranks as the most stunning and colorful of North America's upland game birds. Their glossy, deep green head terminates at a gleaming white neckband and is highlighted further by a bright red cheek and ear patches. The body plumage is a mix of orange, brown, gray, black, iridescent purple, and bronze. The long, brownish tail is heavily banded with black. The hen is mottled brown and tan throughout.

In a few places, hunters may encounter a darker pheasant known as the Sichuan pheasant. This bird, darker overall and lacking the white neck ring, is a subspecies of the better-known version and was planted experimentally between 1992 and 1997 in hopes of finding a pheasant better suited to the sparsely vegetated habitat found throughout much of the Willamette Valley. Funding shortfalls killed the program after some 24,878 Sichuans were released in 14 township-sized areas. Success of the introduction remains to be determined.

Sound and Flight Pattern

The loud, raspy display call of the male pheasant is a familiar and pleasing sound throughout much of Oregon's agricultural area. Otherwise, the hunter is most likely to hear the excited cackling of a flushed and rapidly departing rooster. Pheasants flush explosively and unpredictably. Their flight is strong and rapid for short distances. Once on the wing and headed hard away, they flap and glide alternately, then hit the ground at a full run, especially when cover is sparse. Their escape flight may cover half a mile or more.

Habits and Feeding

Pheasants rise early to begin feeding around daybreak, especially early in the season when warm weather dominates the afternoon. As the season progresses, shorter, colder days prompt pheasants to remain active longer and later in the day. In western Oregon, the birds must cope with extensive rainy spells, during which pheasants seek deep, protective cover from which they emerge only long enough to feed. Any sun break brings birds out to sun themselves and preen lazily, especially during midmorning.

Seasonal Patterns

The springtime rooster courting behavior begins early each day and consists of strutting about and calling from a favorite ground perch. His red wattle becomes bright and swollen, the ear tufts erect, and tail fanned. Each raspy call is delivered with plenty of body English. The hens seek protective cover for their ground nests and lay 8 to 12 eggs. Like most upland game birds, chicks are capable of short flights at about one week of age. While pheasants don't really form coveys, good years sometimes lead to flocks of 20 or more birds concentrated around ideal food sources. Otherwise, they spend fall and winter as singles, doubles, or small flocks. Winterkill can take a heavy toll on pheasants, especially when heavy snow occurs with or prior to bitter cold.

Preferred Habitat and Cover

Pheasants are closely tied to agriculture and fare best when grain production is inefficient, meaning that lots of native cover remains in the form of rows and coverts and that lots of waste grain remains after harvest. In western Oregon, such habitat is increasingly scarce as clean farming—most noticeably by the grass-seed industry—leaves little in the way of cover and food for pheasants.

The best pheasant cover in the Willamette Valley now exists along the valley fringes, where more varied terrain includes smaller agricultural plots planted with a greater variety of crops and interrupted more frequently by rows and islands of wild vegetation, including native and introduced grasses and shrubs. When seeking pheasant cover in western Oregon, look for tracts of fallow land featuring a mix of tallgrass cover, blackberry patches, vegetated fence- and ditchrows, scotchbroom groves, and scattered mixed stands of cottonwood, ash, Douglas fir, and oak. This kind of habitat is most abundant on small plots of land where hunters might be well served to gain permission from several landowners with abutting properties. With

A rooster pheasant holding in thick cover.

permission to cross fences and hunt several side-by-side parcels of land, pheasant hunters increase their odds of covering enough suitable habitat.

In eastern Oregon, pheasants have fared better owing to more extensive habitat. They occupy agricultural lands along with riparian areas, always using the most diverse cover available to them. Throughout most of eastern Oregon, pheasants are closely tied to available water. They thrive in agricultural areas where grain fields mix with large plots of fallow or native grass and shrub cover; add a permanent stream, river, canal, or ditch system, and you have ideal habitat. Hunting pressure exerts a profound effect on pheasants, which explains why roosters surviving on public hunting areas soon head for the heaviest, most impenetrable cover. Where it exists, roosters are especially fond of heavy cattail cover.

Hunting Methods

Throughout Oregon, a pheasant hunter's success is largely determined by his or her dog and by his or her choice of locations. Long before the season begins, pheasant hunters should seek permission to hunt private lands as these areas habitually

Pheasant in the Willamette Valley.

offer the best prospects on a season-long basis. Hunters should also familiarize themselves with the daily routine of the birds on the land they intend to hunt.

The hunt itself can take many forms. Working in pairs or groups, hunters can force running roosters into the edges of cover, where the birds often stop and hold for pointing dogs. The solo hunter—and I often fit this category—should hunt the cover thoroughly behind a good dog. Try walking a ditch, row, or draw through good cover, forcing birds to run ahead or to run into side-coverts where they can then be pursued systematically.

A flushing dog, trained to work well within gun range, makes an excellent pheasant breed because he or she can follow and often outmaneuver a running, zigzagging rooster. In many cases, of course, it is left to the hunter to keep up with both dog and pheasant. Flushing dogs also shine when hunting heavy cover, such as cattail stands, where the staunch point of a pointing breed goes completely unseen by the hunter.

With a flusher fighting through heavy cover, hunters can walk the edges and wait for birds to fly out.

Pointing dogs make fine pheasant hunters assuming they learn how to cope with running birds, which for many dogs is simply a matter of experience. Nash, a German shorthair belonging to a good friend, exemplifies a pheasant-wise pointer: He follows along behind running roosters, figuring out their escape route, while rarely pushing them hard enough to flush. It's a game of point-creep-trot, point-creep-trot some more until the rooster sits tight. On occasion, Nash even outguesses a rooster, circling ahead of the bird and cutting it off before the pheasant runs clear out of the county.

Table Preparations

Among the best of wild game, pheasants lend themselves well to roasting, baking, and many other preparations. The birds should be drawn immediately, especially in hot weather. A good marinade helps prevent overdrying of the white-meat breasts and dark thighs. Because of their tendency to dry during cooking, pheasants are ideally suited to recipes that take advantage of baking bags or crockpots.

Shot and Choke Suggestions

Choke—Modified for singles; improved/modified for doubles or modified/full for late season in sparse cover

Shot—Strong field loads of No. 6 or No. 5; even magnum No. 4 for long shots late in the season or on sparse cover.

Pheasants in the Fog

December's chill arrival cast away the last remnants of a mild autumn above the breaks of the John Day River, where countless acres of wheat stubble carpeted every semblance of tillable ground. The wheat traced the contours of the canyon rims, in places stretching for straight miles, otherwise reaching out on fingers of land that hung above the deep gorges where the river's many tributaries flow.

My hunting companion, Forrest, ground the big pickup to a halt inside one of the few fencelines just off the highway. A scant dressing of snow highlighted the fields, and a thick fog hung precariously above, not yet committing itself to the inevitable blanketing of the landscape in a ghostly cloak. Seasoned by many hunts on these plateaus, Forrest expressed foreboding at the fog, warning that it could very easily get a man all twisted around and confused. "Like some of the women I've known," I quipped. Luckily, Forrest knew the lay of the land.

Nash, Forrest's veteran German shorthair, eagerly awaited the chase, for he too had spent many a day searching these rims and fields for the lustrous scent of chukar, pheasant, and Huns. My own pup, a year-old Weimaraner named Jake, would spend most of his day attached to a long lead, an exercise that would prove far more tiring for me than for him.

We struck out toward the edge of the canyon, where we dropped down just below the wheat stubble and into the low-growth sage and cheatgrass, the latter being a critical ingredient in the diet of chukar. The dogs picked up bird scent almost immediately, but before Nash could work out the puzzle, a large covey of chukars flushed wild from the slope below, well out of range. These birds had been hunted for the better part of three months and were no doubt operating on threadbare nerves.

The steep, rocky slope below plunged almost 2,000 feet down to a large creek, and while all of this lay below the fog, a glance uphill reminded us that the white cloak was descending ever more rapidly and would soon envelop us. Working our way along a contour, we soon found another covey of chukar; these also flushed wildly, but close enough that we killed two birds. Or rather Forrest killed two birds while I tried desperately to manage a 65-pound dog on a lead in one hand and a shotgun without a chambered shell in the other.

The second covey, which we flushed from flat ground at the edge of the stubble, split in two, one-half going over the edge, the other half appearing to wrap around the contour. The increasingly dense fog made the task of watching the covey flight impossible, so we simply guessed at their general direction. Forrest continued down along the sagebrush below the stubble, while I walked up into the field. Moments later I heard two quick shots and then the whir of wings so close that I held the gun at ready. I realized then that unless a chukar flew by within 15 or 20 yards, I would have no chance of seeing a target in the fog.

I called out to Forrest so that he would be forewarned of my approach. I found him with yet another dead bird. That would be our last chukar of the day, however, because we could no longer see Nash. The dog would disappear for 10 minutes at a time, a sure sign with Nash that he had found and pointed birds for us. Yet in the dense fog we had no hope of locating the dog. Forrest resigned himself then and there to a beeper collar, which he purchased before the end of that season.

In any event, our primary concern now lay in finding our way back to the truck. The enveloping fog obscured everything, and only Forrest's general sense of direction on familiar territory brought us eventually to the faint outline of the pickup parked adjacent to the quiet old highway.

Midafternoon arrived with a whisper of cold air that served mostly to the gel the fog into a thick blanket, simultaneously white and opaque. Far-off sounds seemed near; close sounds seemed distant. We steeled ourselves for one last hunt, this time through a huge expanse of wheat stubble likely inhabited by pheasants and maybe by Hungarian partridge. Our only frame of geographic reference was a slight farmer's access road that led straight away through the stubble.

We parked on the road and vowed to follow it both into the field and then back out, knowing full well that any deviance from that plan might leave us hopelessly lost in an endless sea of wheat stubble. After several hundred yards the road dipped slightly onto one of the many fingers of land reaching out over the canyon below. Much to our delight a minor drop in elevation granted us just enough visibility to see the dog working at 50 yards, which proved enough to allow us a chance to fire on a covey of Huns held at bay by Nash.

As we worked deeper into the field, both dogs—Jake still on lead—caught strong bird scent. Well educated in the way of pheasants, Nash began working his magic, deciphering the escape plans of a rooster and his harem. Finally Nash locked up in a solid, classic pose. Upon our approach, the rooster flushed low and fast but not fast enough to escape Forrest's steady gun. Upon the shot, three additional birds flushed, but these were all hens. Nash promptly returned the dead rooster, and we continued our sweep of the field.

The afternoon passed too quickly, with Nash locating several more roosters, some of which wove an intricate escape through the stubble and others that found their way to our game pouches. Soon revoked was our brief respite from the fog, and as the gray veil descended once again, Nash pointed yet again and I will not soon forget that one: At the extreme range of our limited vision, Nash stood rock solid in the day's most elegant point. Waves of drifting fog made Nash's staunch figure seem to appear and disappear in turn, and we stood there for a moment admiring that scarcely describable act that has for generations drawn sportsmen to the pointing breeds.

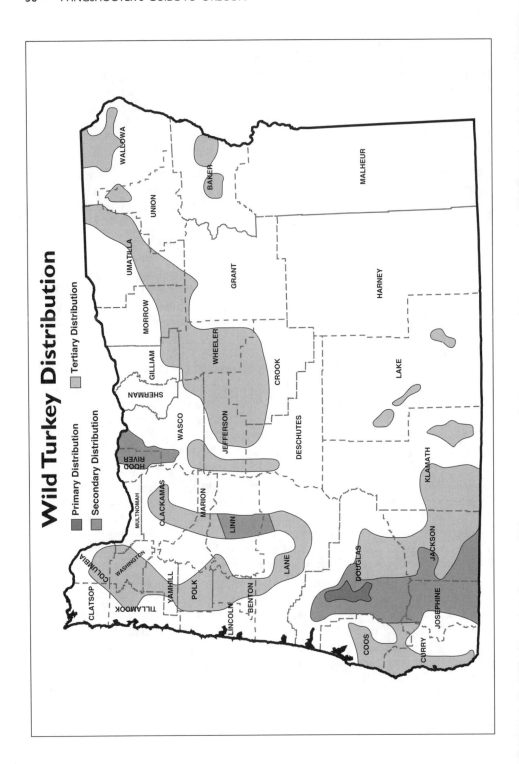

Wild Turkey

Meleagris gallopavo

QUICK FACTS

Local Names

Tom, turkey, gobbler

Size

Males can weigh 25 pounds, but 15- to 20-pound toms are more typical. Females weigh 8 to 12 pounds. The male is 3 to 4 feet long with a wingspan of 4 to 5 feet.

Identification in Flight

Wild turkeys prefer to run and are exceptionally good at doing so, reaching top speeds upward of 20 miles per hour. They are strong flyers as well, though, and can use their long powerful wings to disappear quickly. In flight they can hardly be confused with any other fowl.

- Wild turkeys are not native to Oregon and were first introduced by biologists in 1961.
- Oregon has two subspecies of wild turkey. Merriam's turkeys were introduced first, but Rio Grande turkeys have since proven more successful and more adaptable to a variety of habitat types. The first Rio Grande turkeys were introduced to Oregon in 1975, and management efforts now focus primarily on this subspecies.
- Some 5,000 wild-caught turkeys have been released in Oregon to establish breeding populations throughout much of the state. The Rio Grande turkeys come from Texas, Oklahoma, Kansas, and California.
- Oregon's first statewide turkey season was held in 1987 and since that time, turkey hunting has grown more than tenfold.
- Oregon's most dense turkey populations occur in Douglas, Jackson, and Josephine Counties. Other strong populations thrive in Hood River and Wasco Counties. Turkeys are found in almost every county in Oregon.
- Oregon's spring turkey season (male turkeys only) is held during April and May. An either-sex fall season is held in Douglas and Jackson Counties, during which dogs may be used (consult synopsis).

Appearance

The wild turkey, North America's largest upland game bird, is a striking bird, with the hen being adorned in rich tones of brown, chestnut, tan, and black. A glossy iridescent cast highlights the male's black and dark brown plumage. Long, mottled

Rio Grande turkey.

tailfeathers, each tipped with a black subterminal and a tan or buff-colored terminal band, form a broad fan that the male raises and spreads during the courtship dance. The turkey's head is devoid of feathers, and the tom sports a bright red wattle. Tom turkeys also grow a long beard on their breast, which, on an old bird, might be 10 to 12 inches long. The wing quills are alternately barred with black and white.

Sound and Flight Pattern

Turkeys use myriad sounds in many varieties. The most familiar of the turkey's sounds, of course, is the male's spring gobbling, and sometimes, during the fall and winter. Hunters learn to mimic several of the turkey's calls. A turkey's flight can be both surprisingly agile and humorously labored. When leaving a high night-roost at dawn, turkeys essentially launch themselves and then flap and glide seemingly in an effort to land on the ground with some degree of dignity. Once a turkey gains a head of steam, however, its flight is powerful and direct. Most often, turkeys remain on the ground, where they use their strong legs to distance themselves from predators.

Habits and Feeding

Turkeys consume a wide range of foods, with the extensive list including many fruits, seeds, nuts, and legumes. In western Oregon and in the Columbia Gorge, where oak stands abound, acorns are one of many favorite foods. Turkeys feed actively during the morning, then preen, dust, and loaf during midday, often feeding at the same time. During late afternoon, turkeys again move about in search of food prior to roosting.

Seasonal Patterns

Early spring marks the beginning of turkey courtship activities. Toms disperse from the winter flocks and begin fighting for dominance and then gobbling and strutting for hens. Toms mate with as many hens as possible. Hens build simple ground nests and lay from 6 to 15 eggs. During the 28-day incubation period for the eggs, toms continue to gobble and strut in an attempt to attract unmated hens or hens whose first clutch failed. Research in Oregon shows that about 50 percent of nests are lost to weather, predation, or abandonment. Then, half the successful broods are lost to weather and predation. Hens of the Rio Grande subspecies are prolific renesters, which partly explains the success of this bird in Oregon.

After the chicks hatch, the hen remains with the brood throughout the summer and fall. Sometimes several broods join together forming large droves. During the late fall, young toms ("jakes") may separate from the brood, forming flocks of their own. In regions where snow accumulates, turkeys move downslope to areas where food is more easily gathered.

Preferred Habitat and Cover

In Oregon, wild turkeys utilize a variety of habitats. In southwestern Oregon, turkeys prefer hardwood cover, especially oak, but often range into mixed coniferous forest, brushy edges, and farmlands. Farther north, along the fringes of the Willamette Valley, turkeys occupy similar ranges, but here oak stands are often mixed with a variety of other hardwoods. The Columbia Gorge offers substantial oak and mixed oak/conifer woodlots that are preferred by turkeys. In central and eastern Oregon, turkeys prefer riparian areas, along with open stands of ponderosa pines.

Hunting Methods

Turkey hunting is a game of ambush, wherein a well-concealed hunter, by imitating the sounds made by a hen, calls a gobbler into firing range. Successful hunters almost always scout out locations well ahead of the season, learning as much as possible about the movements and daily patterns of local birds. In scouting for turkeys, look carefully for sign, including tracks and droppings. Turkey tracks are unmistakable, since no other upland bird leaves such a sizeable impression. Male turkeys leave large, elongated j-shaped droppings. Also look for feathers, dusting areas, and large scratches where turkeys tear through leaf cover in search of food. Dusting and preening stations typically include lots of feathers and droppings.

Once you find a turkey population, start searching for a place from which to call. Calling areas should be in fairly open terrain, not only because turkeys avoid dense brush but also to allow you unrestricted visibility. The calling station should also be at least 150 yards from a roosting site if one is known. Select a tree at least as wide as your shoulders and taller than your head, thereby breaking up your profile while also

Rio Grande turkey in Marion County.

protecting you from careless hunters who might stalk your decoys or your calls. (Turkey hunting has rapidly become the most dangerous variety of upland game bird hunting, primarily because people fail to take simple precautions). Wild turkeys can easily detect motion and sound, so hunters must remain motionless and well camouflaged.

Arrive at your calling location before dawn, then begin listening for turkeys. If you have scouted and then set up in the vicinity of a known roost, listen for wing rustling and soft calls. When you begin calling, do so softly and infrequently at first. Aggressive calling can spook experienced toms, but only experience in turkey calling and turkey hunting can help hunters determine how and when to call.

Oregon's fall turkey season, held by permit in Douglas and Jackson Counties, allows hunters a second opportunity to harvest a turkey of either sex, and the use of dogs is permitted. Hunters must apply for a permit by September 15, and the season limit is one turkey. Consult the Early Game Bird Season Synopsis for details. During the statewide spring season, hunters are allowed two male turkeys (only one per day, however) and a third bird if the hunter possesses a bonus turkey tag (available for Douglas, Josephine Coos, Curry, and part of Jackson County). The general spring season requires that hunters simply purchase a turkey tag, these being available throughout the year from ODFW license dealers.

Table Preparations

As one might expect, wild turkey makes exceptional table fare. The birds should be drawn as soon as possible.

Shot and Choke Suggestions

In Oregon, only shotguns and bows may be used to hunt turkeys. Shotguns must be 10, 12, 16 or 20 gauge and shot size can be no larger than BB and no smaller than #6. Recurve, long, and compound bows are legal. Generally, the specific size shot depends on the area being hunted, but loads of No. 2 and 4 assure clean kills assuming hunters lure the turkey into optimum range of 25 yards or less. Full chokes help center the shot charge around the turkey's head.

Top Ten Game Management Units by Total Turkey Hunters, Harvest and Hunter Success, 1993-1997

Hunt Unit	Total Hunters	Total Harvest	% Hunter Success
Melrose	5,375	2,482	46
Rogue	3,881	755	19
McKenzie	2,249	529	24
White River	5,638	478	8
Dixon	1,458	409	28
Evans Creek	1,596	337	21
Willamette	1,209	318	26
Tioga	651	257	39
Alsea	866	212	24
Sled Springs	860	205	24

Migratory Game Birds

Mourning Dove

Mourning doves live throughout most of Oregon where suitable habitat exists. Local populations and migrating flocks generally depart with the first cold weather in September or October, especially in central and eastern Oregon. Some of the state's best dove shooting occurs in the grain-agriculture belt of the Columbia Basin, but western Oregon hunters can find good sport along the Willamette River and in nearby grass and grain fields. The tender breast meat of these small game birds lends itself well to many different preparations.

Habits

Doves flock daily to feeding areas, especially those with an abundance of waste grain. During the afternoon (and often during the morning) they fly to favorite waterholes. They collect grit at favorite gravel sites. Deciphering the daily habits of doves can be as easy as watching for and observing concentrations of birds prior to and during the season.

Hunting Methods

Doves are best ambushed at either the feeding or watering locations, where hunters can set up in good cover and await the daily or twice-daily flights. Mourning doves are notoriously fast flyers and have caused the demise of many a box of shotgun shells. No. 7½ and 8 shot is best combined with a modified choke.

Oregon Harvest

Since 1990, an average of 4,850 Oregon dove hunters harvested an estimated average of 42,570 doves annually.

Band-tailed Pigeon

Though recent decades have witnessed a severe decline in band-tailed pigeon populations, sufficient numbers still exist to allow for a limited hunting season in Oregon, where the birds both nest and migrate. The season occurs during September, and hunters should check the current synopsis for details. The best hunting occurs in the Coast Range and, in places, along the coast itself. Some opportunity also exists in the Cascade Range. Wherever band-tailed pigeon are pursued, successful hunters have one thing in common: They have located a concentration of birds, often by knowing the location of favorite flight paths or of the mineral springs so coveted by the pigeons.

Habits

Band-tailed pigeons occur in flocks ranging from a dozen to a hundred birds, although smaller flocks are the rule these days. During migration, they stop at

Band-tailed pigeons migrate through western Oregon.

favorite mineral springs, often for days on end, and habitually fly between roost, mineral springs, and feeding sights, these latter typically taking the form of berry patches. Elderberries are a favorite food. Traditionally, some locations on the coast offered excellent pigeon shooting. The birds can still be found migrating through these areas: Look for pigeons roosting in large spruce and fir snags or in tall, live trees along the highway and around the estuaries. Grouse hunters should carefully note the location of any pigeon sightings because, being creatures of habit, the birds are likely to remain there until bad weather or food shortage forces them on.

Hunting Methods

Most pigeon hunting takes the form of pass-shooting at birds as they fly between roosting sites, springs and feeding sites. In the mountains, look for tall saddles that lie in line with the flight path used by the birds. Hunters can also flush loafing flocks from tall conifers or flush pigeons from berry patches and springs. Pass shooting at these fast-flying targets requires modified or full chokes and No. 6 or 7½ shot along with a good lead and long follow-through.

Harvest

Band-tailed pigeon harvest surveys indicate about 1,400 hunters take an estimated 3,000 birds annually.

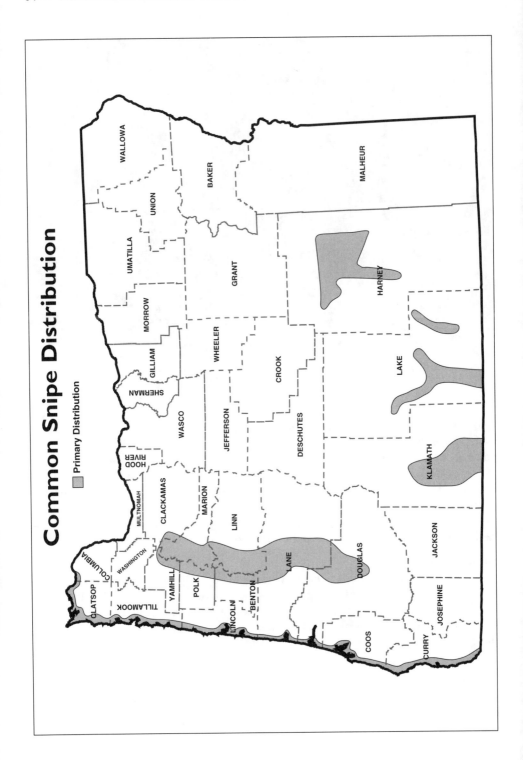

Common Snipe Distribution

■ Primary Distribution

Common Snipe

Oregon offers some of the premier snipe hunting found in the western U.S. The birds migrate along the coast in large numbers, stopping over at numerous estuaries and dairy fields to feed and rest. Common snipe also migrate through the Willamette Valley and through parts of eastern and central Oregon. Snipe hunters who locate the right habitat on the coast might encounter a hundred or more snipe in an outing during late fall or early winter. More modest numbers still provide great wingshooting at a bird that ranks among the most challenging targets.

Habits

Common snipe feed in moist areas where their long, pliable, sensory-tipped bill can penetrate the mud in search of the myriad invertebrates on which they feed. On the coast, look for them on the estuaries, especially where grasses, rushes, and sedges abound on wet ground. Also hunt dairy pastures, with the landowner's permission, of course. In the Willamette Valley and other parts of Oregon, snipe often frequent wet depressions in muddy, fallow fields. They migrate through eastern Oregon as well and are common on fringes of marshes such as Summer Lake and Malheur Lake, where they prefer shortgrass, sedge, and bulrush cover.

Hunters must be able to distinguish common snipe from similar shorebirds, all of which are fully protected. A wildlife manager at one of Oregon's popular waterfowling areas once cautioned me that, in checking the "snipe" harvested by hunters, he sees more dead dowitchers and other shorebirds than actual common snipe. A combination of habit and habitat traits allows for easy identification:

1. Snipe rarely form tightly organized flocks and do not flush in unison as a flock like many other shorebirds.
2. Upon flushing, snipe typically utter one to three (or more) nasal notes announcing their name, "snipe" or "scaip." They will continue these calls as they attain altitude.
3. Upon flushing, snipe rise several feet, then twist and turn while flying away low and hard; then they rise quite suddenly, often flying a big, high circle and landing again somewhere in the same covert.
4. Snipe rarely feed on the same open sand or mud expanses frequented by dowitchers and other shorebirds. Instead, snipe feed in low cover, along stream or ditch margins, in wet dairy pastures and muddy fallow fields, snipe often occur with killdeer, which are readily distinguishable.
5. Both dowitchers and common snipe sometimes buzz decoy spreads. The voices are different, however, and the flight pattern of a dowitcher is softer and less erratic.

Hunting Methods

Serious snipe hunting is mostly a walk-em-up game. Many pointing dogs want little to do with these fowl, and some dogs won't even retrieve them. However, snipe flush readily, typically holding tight and allowing for close approach. When walking

Close-up of a common snipe.

good cover, pause every 20 or 30 yards—sometimes snipe hold so tight that they allow you to walk right by, but stopping for a moment often unnerves them. If a snipe escapes your shot or flushes out of range, stand motionless and watch the bird's flight. Often they fly in a big circle and land in the same covert—their wide, circular path sometimes brings them back in range for a challenging passing shot. After a freeze, look for snipe along the unfrozen shorelines of streams and ditches, where the mud remains soft enough to allow the birds to feed. Improved and modified chokes are ideal when combined with light loads No. 7½ or 8 shot.

Harvest

From 1990 to 1995, an average of 848 hunters harvested 3,241 snipe, annually.

Permission To Hunt WHAT?

Imagine the confusion involved in asking a farmer for permission to hunt snipe on his property. Most regard you with either suspicion or thinly veiled bemusement. Often you get that smirking somebody-just-fell-off-the-turnip-truck look; others whisper back into the house, "Hey Martha, come here, you gotta hear this."

But a snipe addict must persist. After a few years of serious snipe shooting, I arrived at a complex but workable solution, one that I recommend for anyone playing this game. In my freezer I keep a couple of frozen snipe. On hunt day, I put a frozen bird into my vest along with a small bird book and a copy of the game bird regulations. Upon initial greetings with a farmer, I steel myself for the inevitable reaction to my request. If any of the aforementioned responses happens, I then proceed, with the help of my educational aids, to convince the landowner first of the snipe's existence and then of its validity as a game bird.

More often than not, such conversations convince the landowner that these snipe are a far cry from the entirely elusive critters that we, as gullible kids, chased around the woods with a gunny sack and flashlight. Moreover, the property owner generally grants me permission to work his soggy fields in search of these long-billed little fowl.

Those childhood snipe days were indeed elusive but not appreciably more so than the common snipe (alias jacksnipe and Wilson's snipe), whose twisting, turning flight characteristics can reduce shotgunners to lonely conversation with their own egos. Generally the snipe zigs when you zag and zags when you zig. By the time their zigs and your zags arrive at a common point in space, the snipe has rocketed beyond effective range. Then, just for good measure, the occasional snipe that you have dead to rights manages to fly right through the shot pattern, its small, streamlined body escaping a string of No. 8s.

Yet for all its fine qualities as a shotgunner's target, the common snipe remains underhunted almost to the point of absurdity. During migration, common snipe swarm to the Northwest coast, where they sometimes overwinter in surprising densities before returning to their breeding grounds in the far north and in the mountains and high desert of Oregon. They are easy to find once you learn their habitat and a few of their basic habits. Find a heavily used covert along a major migration route and you may well be rewarded by a 50-flush day. Yet virtually nobody pursues snipe.

Larry Pecenka, an assistant manager at Fern Ridge Wildlife Area near Eugene, once told me that hunters on this expansive preserve report killing only about 20 snipe per year, most of which are incidental kills by duck hunters. Yet Fern Ridge fills with snipe during the late fall and winter. Fern Ridge is typical of snipe habitat, offering expansive soggy fields, marshlands

Oregon snipe hunting is often overlooked by many hunters or is incidental to hunting other birds.

and wet grasslands. Even so, only two or three serious snipe hunters work the area each season.

Closely related to the woodcock of the East and Midwest, the common snipe is a handsome and rather minuscule shorebird with an infamous habit of flying quickly and erratically out of gun range. The majority of snipe killed in Oregon are indeed incidental kills by duck hunters, too many of whom assumed that any shorebird with a long bill and long legs is a snipe and is therefore fair game.

In fact, managers at both Fern Ridge and Sauvie Island (a large public hunting area on the Columbia River near Portland) express concern about the frequency of duck hunters killing dowitchers, plovers, yellowlegs, and other shorebirds. Ray Johnson an ODFW manager at Sauvie Island told me once that he sees "10 other shorebirds killed by hunters for every snipe I have seen killed here."

Pecenka agreed, saying, "Unfortunately, other longbills like dowitchers and yellowlegs are killed by hunters who have not learned how to identify snipe; potential snipe hunters should know their birds."

All other shorebirds found in Oregon are fully protected by federal and state law, so hunters must learn to identify snipe before going after them. Those who first learn to identify common snipe and then learn how to find the birds can enjoy a great deal of untapped wingshooting.

Common snipe are about the same size as a robin though different in shape. They sport a long, slender bill and fairly long legs. When flushed, they appear mottled brown above and white below. In hand, the snipe's back proves to be richly patterned with brown, tan, rust, and black. The underside of the wings are lined with black and white barred feathers.

Habits and habitat identify snipe as readily as appearance. Unless they have been shot at repeatedly, snipe almost always utter one or two notes immediately upon flushing. This call is a hoarse, nasal-sounding rendition of their name: "snaaip, snaaip." The calls continue as the snipe gains altitude. In addition, unlike many other shorebirds, snipe almost always flush as individuals rather than in unison as a flock. Most other shorebirds flush and fly away in groups. If a large number of birds is present, they will flush in ones and twos, often coming up like popcorn in a popper, especially after the shooting starts. Even if a dozen or more snipe flush from a small area, several more will likely hold tight, not moving unless almost stepped on by the hunter.

Many similarly-sized shorebirds flush and fly in tight flocks, turning and twisting in unison. Snipe never fly in such a manner. Sometimes, a dozen or more snipe will travel together, but these flocks are loosely organized and their twists and turns are not unified. They often fly quite high and then plunge suddenly to the ground.

Also, snipe almost always flush from cover, the exception being birds that are feeding in wet plowed fields. Most other shorebirds occur in groups or even large flocks on exposed mudflats, beaches, or pond margins. Snipe flush from grasses and rushes but rarely from an exposed area far from cover.

The flush, usually complete with one or two nasal notes, is perhaps the single best identifying characteristic of the common snipe. But the bird's flight pattern identifies it as well: up a few feet off the ground and then hard away with a twisting, turning, zigzagging flight full of more moves than a mourning dove could ever dream up—that is a typical snipe flush. In addition, they often fly high into the air, make one to three wide circles of the area and then plunge back to earth within a few hundred yards of where they flushed.

After learning to identify snipe, hunters should concentrate on finding ideal habitat. In Oregon, snipe habitat varies from region to region but includes grassy estuary margins (including islands), fields with standing water, short-grass margins of freshwater marshes, soggy bulrush coverts, dairy pastures, and creekbeds. When a hard freeze strikes overnight and snipe can no longer stick their bills into the frozen mud of flooded fields and pastures, the birds are quick to move to the edges of free-flowing streams, canals, and ditches.

A limit of common snipe from an Oregon estuary.

Snipe seasons follow a federally mandated framework and in Oregon are held concurrent with duck season. An eight-bird limit is in effect.

A snipe hunter can benefit handsomely from some preseason scouting to find ideal habitat on both public and private lands. Before the season begins, secure permission to hunt private tracts. But keep the bird book and game bird synopsis—and maybe a frozen snipe from last year—close at hand when you knock on a farmer's door.

Waterfowl

DUCKS

Between 1990 and 1996, an average of 22,625 hunters harvested an estimated 245,457 ducks and 2,712 coots annually. Mallards comprised nearly 47 percent of the annual harvest, followed by American wigeon (14 percent) and green-winged teal (12 percent). In 1997, with many birds available and liberal limits, hunters harvested an estimated 423,806 ducks.

Dabbling Ducks

Dabbling ducks, often called puddle ducks, are so named because they frequent shallow water, where they feed by tipping and reaching underwater with their heads and necks. Dabblers jump straight off the water with powerful wings. In Oregon, a variety of dabbling ducks occur on virtually all water types, including slow-moving rivers, small ponds and lakes, marshes, large sump lakes, and estuaries. Dabblers, especially mallards, wigeon, pintail, and gadwall, often feed in grain stubble. With the exception of the rare Eurasian wigeon, all of the dabblers that occur in Oregon also nest within the state, but northern migrants comprise a majority of most species by late autumn. Color, wing pattern, and flight characteristics are major aids in identifying the different species.

Hunting Methods

Because of their widespread distribution and the variety of wetland habitats available to them in Oregon, dabbling ducks present myriad opportunities for all kinds of hunting. Most dabblers respond to decoy spreads and calling, and these classic methods remain the foundation of duck hunting on most water types. In some places (sheltered ponds, creeks, canals), jump shooters can find excellent sport. Even pass shooting can be productive in places such as Summer Lake and coastal estuaries.

Regardless of method, duck hunting peaks at dawn and dusk when dabblers are on the move between feeding and roosting areas. Inclement weather only improves hunting because wind and rain causes ducks to stir and move more frequently. All-day hunting often accompanies storm fronts. Understanding the schedule and flight routes used by ducks in a particular place allows hunters to set up in the right places at the appropriate times.

Many dabbling ducks circle above to survey decoy spreads before pouring in to the landing zone. Mallards, pintail, and wigeon frequently approach in this manner. Teal and shoveler often buzz decoy spreads, flying directly in or over—wood ducks are apt to do this as well. Early in the season, when locally produced birds comprise the bulk of the duck population, hunters often find that most species respond readily to calling and decoying. Later, after birds have been shot at quite a bit and when the northern migrants arrive, they are more wary.

The mix of dabbler species in Oregon varies somewhat from region to region. Mallards, pintail, and wigeon abound everywhere. Northern shovelers are widely dispersed across the state. In eastern Oregon, cinnamon teal and gadwall are quite abundant, whereas locally produced blue-winged teal, though common in eastern Oregon, tend to depart early in the fall. In western Oregon, green-winged teal are prevalent, but there are also tremendous flocks of wigeon, especially along the coast, in the Willamette Valley, and along the lower Columbia. The largest and most spectacular flocks of mallards assemble during late fall in the Columbia Basin of northeastern Oregon, where tens of thousands of birds form massive flocks that descend on large fields of grain stubble.

Gun and Shot Suggestions

Gauge—10 and 12; 16 and 20 for close range decoy shooting or teal hunting.

Choke—Modified or modified/improved for double guns.

Shot—Only federally approved, nontoxic shot may be used for waterfowl hunting. No. 4-2-BB size shot is ideal, and light "scatter" loads of No. 6 are ideal for dispatching cripples.

Species and Identification

Mallard—*Anas platyrhynchos*

Length	20 to 28 inches.
Male	Bright green head and dark, chestnut-colored breast; white belly and white underwing linings; black rump; yellow bill; and bright orange feet.
Female	Mottled brown; orange bill with black spotting.
Wing	Dark gray above with purple speculum bordered on both sides by white bands.
Identification in Flight	Large size; powerful and direct flight; dark head, neck, and breast (male).
Common Range	Found throughout the state.
1997 Harvest	185,702.

Drake pintail and mallard.

Northern Pintail—*Anas acuta*

Length	20 to 30 inches.
Male	Large, streamlined duck with long, pointed tail; gray mantle highlighted with black and white; white throat and breast; brown head with white streak extending up along sides; blue bill with black streak on top.
Female	Mottled brown but paler than female mallard; bill similar to male's.
Wing	Long and sleek with copper-colored speculum bordered on the trailing edge by white.
Identification in Flight	Long neck and streamlined appearance evident; graceful and fast.
Common Range	Found throughout the state.
1997 Harvest	37,152

American wigeon on saltwater.

American Wigeon—*Anas americana*

Length	18 to 23 inches.
Male	Rust-colored breast and flanks; white belly; large, iridescent green eye streak that covers a full third or more of the face and back of the neck; white cap and forehead; black-and-white speckled cheeks and throat; blue bill with black base and tip.
Female	Rust-colored flanks; mottled brown above; bill same as in male; juvenile males similar but often showing some green in the head.
Wing	Entire shoulder covered by white patch that is quite evident in flight; white shoulder most evident in males; green speculum.
Identification in Flight	Combination of white shoulder and characteristic wavering. flight whistle identifies this medium-sized duck; flight is usually rapid and often erratic; compact flocks.
Common Range	Found throughout the state.
1997 Harvest	48,446

Eurasian Wigeon—*Anas penelope*

Length	16 to 20 inches.
Male	More gray overall than American wigeon; rust-colored head with cream-colored crown and forehead; large white wing patch.

Hen and drake gadwall at Summer Lake Wildlife Area.

Female	Similar to female American wigeon.
Wing	Same as American wigeon.
Identification in Flight	This regular visitor along the Pacific Coast is most often seen as a single specimen among a flock of American wigeon or sometimes with flocks of mallards or pintail.
Common Range	Found only occasionally along the coast and in the Willamette Valley.

Gadwall—*Anas strepera*

Length	18 to 23 inches.
Male	Grayish overall with distinctive black rump; white belly; unique head profile (sharply sloping, high forehead); black bill.
Female	Gray brown overall; white belly; orange bill with black spots.
Wing	White patch in speculum bordered above in the male by a rust-colored band.
Identification in Flight	Medium-sized; streamlined; white belly and wing linings sharply bordered by darker feathers; fast, somewhat erratic.
Common Range	Abundant numbers in eastern Oregon; numbers are increasing in western Oregon.
1997 Harvest	23,174

Northern Shoveler—*Anas clypeata*

Length	18 to 20 inches.
Male	Huge bill; green head; white breast; rust-colored flanks and belly.
Female	Huge bill; mottled brown overall.
Wing	Entire shoulder is light blue gray; green speculum.
Identification in Flight	Large bill; blocky appearance; contrast between dark head, white breast, dark belly (male); small flocks.
Common Range	Found throughout Oregon.
1997 Harvest	31,602

Green-winged Teal—*Anas crecca*

Length	12 to 16 inches (smallest dabbler).
Male	Striking coloration includes tan breast spotted with black, silvery gray flanks, yellow undertail coverts, cinnamon-colored head with green eye stripe.
Female	Mottled brown and tan overall.
Wing	Green speculum; long and narrow.
Identification in Flight	Quick, twisting and turning flight; swift wingbeats; tightly formed flocks that dive, twist, and turn in unison; green speculum.
Common Range	Found throughout Oregon; especially abundant in western Oregon.
1997 Harvest	46,002

Cinnamon Teal—*Anas cyanoptera*

Length	14 to 17 inches.
Male	Rich cinnamon red overall with blue gray wing coverts visible in flight.
Female	Mottled brown overall. (essentially indistinguishable from female cinnamon teal).
Wing	Blue gray coverts (shoulders) and green speculum.
Identification in Flight	Small flocks; fast, erratic flight.
Common Range	Most common in eastern Oregon but occurs throughout the state.
1997 Harvest	868 combined with blue-winged teal.

Hen and drake green-winged teal.

Blue-winged teal drake.

Blue-winged teal—*Anas discors*

Length	14 to 16.5 inches.
Male	Striking slate gray head with white crescent in front of eye; tan flanks and breast spotted with black.
Female	Mottled brown and tan overall (essentially indistinguishable from female cinnamon teal).
Wing	Blue gray coverts (shoulders) and green speculum.
Identification in Flight	Fast and erratic; twisting and turning in small, compact flocks.
Common Range	Primarily found in eastern Oregon; migrates south early.
1997 Harvest	868 combined with cinnamon teal.

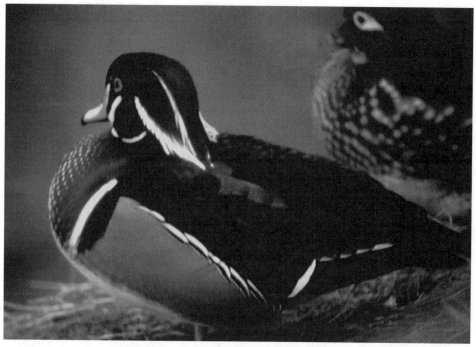

Wood duck drake.

Wood Duck—*Aix sponsa*

Length	15 to 21 inches.
Male	The most colorful of North American waterfowl; unmistakable in its stunning array of color and pattern.
Female	Grayish overall with soft crest and white eye patch and speckled breast.
Wing	Purple speculum.
Identification in Flight	Erratic flight often accompanied by distinctive call; distinctive long tail.
Common Range	Found throughout state but most common in western Oregon.
1997 Harvest	8,314

Waterfowling on Oregon's Estuaries

For duck and goose hunters accustomed to hunting freshwater environs, Oregon's estuaries offer a unique and entirely different set of circumstances. Tides play a critical and defining role in estuarine waterfowling. Tidal changes trigger the movements of ducks and geese that feed, rest, and roost on the estuaries. These same tidal variations and the water levels they create determine the strategies and tactics employed by hunters.

In most instances, mazelike networks of tidal creeks drain the estuaries. At low tide, these creeks may be little more than mere trickles in the bottom of ditchlike streambeds several feet deep. At high tide, however, four or more feet of additional water overwhelm the same creeks. The unwary hunter might plunge shoulder deep into a creek only two feet wide. Moreover, estuaries offer several different grades of mud. In places sandy mud makes for firm footing, while in other places, the worst kind of quick-mud can easily suck a man several feet deep. In many places, the mud proves easy to traverse when covered with water, but impossible to negotiate when exposed by the receding tide.

Likewise, if you launch a boat on the estuaries, be wary of tide changes that can leave a boat high and dry—and probably stuck in the mud. Conversely, an incoming tide can snatch up a beached boat and carry it away. In many instances, a boat provides the best means of navigating the estuaries, but the boat should be matched to the task at hand. Small duck boats—even canoes and prams—can safely traverse many reaches of the estuaries, but sturdier craft are in order if you spend any time near the river mouths. Hunters afoot can find plenty of accessible waterfowling locations on many Oregon estuaries.

As with duck hunting anywhere, the waterfowler who spends some time scouting the territory will have an advantage in figuring out where and when to set up. Early morning and evening hunts are usually the most productive, but tidal fluctuations often cause ducks to move about during the day. Once you figure out the pattern for a particular place, you can form the best possible hunt strategy.

In many instances, estuary hunters set up decoy spreads in one location for the morning hunt and then move to another location to take advantage of changing water levels. One of my favorite places, for example, offers good high-tide decoying in the wide, middle reaches of a tidal creek. Here I wrap the spread around the point of a small island where the creek reaches its widest point of about 20 yards.

However, when the tide ebbs, the creek is divested of most of its water and then I move the decoy spread to a sandbar area on the edge of the main river channel. The bank offers a wash of wood debris, so each season we build a makeshift blind around a huge log that long ago washed down the estuary. In a strong wind, I arrange the decoys in two parallel lines, leaving a landing zone in the middle. I also like to throw a few decoys in the mouth of the creek, where the minute current makes them dance back and forth.

The decoy spread itself can make or break an estuary duck shoot. In some locations, large concentrations of mallards, wigeon or pintails exhibit a distinct pattern of moving from feeding location to roosting location. A dozen decoys and the right location and you're in business. If you are set up outside of that prime feeding or resting area, you may need large decoy spreads and strong calling skills to tempt high-flying flocks to deviate from their plan. Likewise, if divers, such as canvasback and scaup, are your quarry, a large open-water spread achieves the best results.

In other places, birds use many different areas and can be decoyed without expansive spreads. In the places I frequent, two dozen decoys suffice most of the time. Three dozen allows for even better results because you can split the spread into a main unit and a smaller auxiliary setup.

Jump shooters enjoy consistent success on any estuary that is drained by an extensive network of tidal creeks. A midtide stage (or even a low tide) is best for jump shooting because until you are nearly on top of them, ducks can't see you coming. This is an especially efficient method of hunting green-winged teal since these tiny buzz-bombs frequent the tidal creeks and usually prove difficult to frighten from their favorite area. Often you can flush a flock once, hit a bird or two, and then watch them settle down in the next creek. Jump shooters need a good retrieving dog because tidal creeks are quite often too deep or too muddy for safe wading.

Setting out decoys near Coos Bay.

Diving Ducks

Oregon offers extensive habitat for diving ducks. Coastal bays and estuaries provide expansive migrating and winter range for divers of many species. Oregon's large rivers also host good numbers of diving ducks. Huge rafts of scaup, for example, assemble on the Columbia River. Some diving ducks—the ringneck being the most obvious—are closely tied to freshwater while others (at least during the winter) rarely venture away from the saltwater environs. Among the species found predominantly along the coast are the harlequin duck and red-breasted merganser. Among waterfowlers, the most sought-after divers include canvasback, redhead, and scaup. Others—especially mergansers and buffleheads—are of little interest to most duck hunters. Many diving ducks respond to decoy spreads, but hunters who specialize in pursuing canvasback, redhead, and scaup employ special tactics. These ducks often occur in large rafts on big, open waters, where large, species-specific decoy spreads and sinkboats produce the best results.

Hunting Methods

Most diving duck hunting occurs incidentally to hunting for dabblers. Some species of divers—buffleheads, goldeneyes, ring-necked ducks, and hooded mergansers, for example—respond readily to spreads of decoys intended for dabblers. Often, divers swim into the decoy spreads. Less desirable targets, such as buffleheads, make great natural decoys when allowed to swim along and feed among the hunter's decoys.

Purposeful hunting for divers generally centers on the most desirable species: canvasback, scaup, and redheads. On some of Oregon's bays and estuaries, sinkboat hunters can work over large rafts of decoys. Without the benefit of a sinkboat, which are rarely seen these days, set up large species-specific decoy spreads along likely flight paths. Often a point of land jutting well into the bay or estuary provides the best opportunity for decoying divers, which head straight into the decoys without circling like the dabblers.

On estuaries, cover is a premium, especially out on points and exposed shorelines. Use natural materials to construct a blind against an old root-wad or tree trunk or use stakes and camo netting to arrange a ground blind on open shores.

Often a mixed spread of dabbler and diver decoys produces excellent results, especially in areas where both types of ducks abound. Use one type or the other as the main spread, then arrange the others some distance away. A large raft of diver decoys, arranged in lines, can be bolstered with the addition of a dozen mallard decoys set closer in or grouped inside and to one side. Similarly, a dozen or so bluebill or canvasback decoys might be clustered outside a main spread of dabbler decoys.

Gun and Shot Suggestions

Gauge—10 or 12.

Choke—Modified for open water; modified/improved for smaller waters.

Shot—Only federally approved nontoxic shot may be used for waterfowl hunting.
No. 2-BB-BBB for large open-water divers; No. 4-2-BB for ring-necked ducks and other small divers.

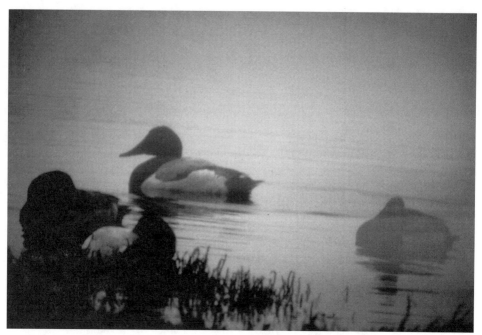

Canvasbacks.

Species and Identification

Canvasback—*Aythya valisineria*

Local Names	"Cans"
Length	19 to 22 inches.
Male	Gleaming white back and flanks contrasting vividly with black breast; chestnut red head; distinctive slope to the forehead and bill.
Female	Grayish back; sandy brown head; distinctive slope to forehead and bill.
Wing	White and light gray.
Identification in Flight	Distinctive black-white-black pattern of male's body; flickering of white in the wings; rapid wingbeat and fast, direct flight; wedge-shaped flocks.
Common Range	Found throughout the state.
1997 Harvest	1,960

Redhead—*Aythya americana*

Length	18 to 22 inches.
Male	Black breast and rump contrasting with white belly and gray back; bright red head; blue bill tipped in black.
Female	Dark rusty brown overall with blue bill tipped in black.
Wing	Pale gray secondaries contrast with darker shoulders.
Identification in Flight	Male's black-white-black body pattern; pale gray secondaries; low, direct flight in compact, wedge-shaped flocks.
Common Range	Found throughout the state, but most common in eastern Oregon.
1997 Harvest	2,345

Ring-necked Duck—*Aythya collaris*

Local Names	Bluebill, ring-billed duck.
Length	14 to 18 inches.
Male	Small, dark duck with gleaming white flanks; white vertical stripe on sides below neck; dark gray bill with a white ring at the base and near the tip and with a black tip; peaked crown.
Female	Dark gray brown overall; faint white eye ring; bill like male's but less striking.
Wing	Black with gray stripe along trailing edge
Identification in Flight	Fast, agile flight; twisting and turning; generally in small flocks but may raft in large concentrations.
Common Range	Found mostly western Oregon, but some found throughout.
1997 Harvest	7,626

Lesser Scaup—*Aythya affinis*

Local Names	Bluebill.
Length	15 to 18 inches.
Male	Glossy purple head, which often appears black; black breast; white belly, flanks and mantle; at close range and in hand, duck's mantle is heavily vermiculated with black; blue bill; head pointed toward the rear.
Female	Head shape same as male; brown head and breast; gray brown flanks and mantle; white patch surrounds base of bill.
Wing	Distinctive, black leading edge contrasts vividly with broad white stripe extending through secondaries, then bordered on the trailing edge by a narrow dark stripe.

Identification in Flight	Wing pattern is distinctive and also aids in separating the lesser scaup from the similar greater scaup. Flight typically low, direct, and fast.
Common Range	Found throughout, but most numerous in eastern Oregon's large marshes and along the Columbia River.
1997 Harvest	7,106

Greater Scaup—*Aythya marila*

Common Names	Bluebill.
Length	15 to 20 inches.
Male	Glossy greenish head that typically appears black; black breast and rump; white belly, flanks and mantle; mantle vermiculated with black but not so heavily as in lesser scaup. Head shape rounded instead of peaked; pale blue bill.
Female	Brown overall; flanks lighter; back gray brown; trace of white at base of pale blue bill.
Wing	Distinctive; white stripe extends through secondaries and well into primaries and is bordered in front by black shoulders and at the rear by a narrow black lining.
Identification in Flight	Distinctive wing pattern; low, fast, direct flight.
Common Range	Mostly found in western Oregon, specifically along the coast and lower Columbia River.
1997 Harvest	5,490

Common Goldeneye—*Bucephala clangula*

Local Names	Whistler.
Length	16 to 20 inches.
Male	Large, plump black-and-white duck; head is rounded and glossy dark green, often appearing black with round white spot in front of yellow eye; neck, breast, belly and flanks bright white; mantle and rump black; black bill.
Female	Gray body and large, rounded brown head.
Wing	Black with broad, square white patch extending most of the way across inner half of wing.
Identification in Flight	Distinctive white wing patch; wings whistle loudly; fast, direct flight, typically in small flocks, often flying high.
Common Range	Found throughout the state.
1997 Harvest	1,919

Common goldeneye.

Barrow's Goldeneye—*Bucephala islandica*

Local Names	Whistler.
Length	16 to 20 inches.
Male	Generally similar to common goldeneye, but head glossy purple with crescent-shaped white patch in front of eye; more extensive black on back.
Female	Brown head and gray brown body; yellowish bill.
Wing	Similar to common goldeneye but with narrow black stripe extending across white patch.
Identification in Flight	Distinctive white wing patch; wings whistle loudly; fast, direct flight, typically in small flocks, often high.
Common Range	Found throughout, but mostly in western Oregon.
1997 Harvest	780

Ruddy Duck—*Oxyura jamaicensis*

Local Names	Stiff-tailed duck.
Length	15 to 16 inches.
Male	During fall and winter, male is grayish overall with lighter checks contrasting with brown cap; long, stiff tail; broad flat bill; (breeding season male is rusty throughout with a black head, large white cheek patch, and bright blue bill).
Female	Similar to winter male but with dark line across light check.

Wing	Gray.
Identification in Flight	Rapid wingbeats, low, direct flight; long tail.
Common Range	Found throughout the state.
1997 Harvest	681

Bufflehead—*Bucephala albeola*

Local Names	Butterball.
Length	13 to 15 inches.
Male	Tiny in size but plump; brilliant pattern of black and white; glossy black head with large white patch extending over back half of crown; large white wing patches with black stripes at base of wings and down center of back; gleaming white flanks and breast.
Female	Also tiny but plump; brownish overall with small white patch behind eye.
Wing	Male's wing black at tip, white through center and black at base; female has gray wings with a small white patch on the inner secondaries.
Identification in Flight	Low to water, fast and direct, sometimes twisting and turning as they follow narrow watercourses.
Common Range	Found throughout the state.
1997 Harvest	10,365

Hooded Merganser—*Lophodytes cucullatus*

Local Names	Hoody.
Length	16 to 19 inches.
Male	Spectacular black head with fanlike white crest outlined in black; black back; white breast with a vertical white stripe dividing two black stripes at the front of rust-colored flanks; long, white-edged tertials; small, thin black bill.
Female	Soft gray overall with cinnamon brown, fanlike crest.
Wing	Both sexes have small white speculum; male's have gray patch along leading edge of shoulder.
Identification in Flight	Fast and streamlined in flight; note male's wing pattern.
Common Range	Found in western Oregon.
1997 Harvest	1,011

Common Merganser—*Mergus merganser*

Common Name	Fish duck.
Length	22 to 27 inches.
Male	Very large with bright white breast, belly, and flanks; black back; green head; long, narrow, bright red bill.
Female	Gray with white belly and breast; brown, crested head; long, thin red bill.
Wing	Male has extensive white speculum and shoulder patch; female has gray shoulders and small white speculum.
Identification in Flight	Low, fast flight; very large size.
Common Range	Found throughout the state.
1997 Harvest	823 (combined with red-breasted)

Red-breasted Merganser—*Mergus serrator*

Length	19 to 26 inches
Male	Very large; green head with shaggy crest; white collar; bright red bill; tan, spotted breast; black mantle with black extending down sides in front of shoulders; gray flanks.
Female	Brownish gray, lighter below but with no distinct border between lighter underparts and darker upper parts as in common merganser; thin red bill; cinnamon-colored head with shaggy crest; red eye.
Wing	Males with white inner wing divided by two thin black bars; females have small white speculum.
Identification in Flight	Fast, low and direct; males with much less white on body than common merganser.
Common Range	Coastal.
1997 Harvest	823 (combined with common)

Sea Ducks

Sea ducks are rarely targeted by waterfowlers, but are sometimes killed incidentally on the coastal estuaries and lakes. Two scoters—the white-winged and the surf scoter—are common all along the Oregon coast. Black scoters are less abundant. Scoters are large, black, heavy-bodied ducks and are common inside bays and harbors, especially during stormy weather. The beautiful oldsquaw is an uncommon visitor to the Oregon coast, but a few are taken by hunters each year. The Harlequin—one of the world's most beautiful and striking ducks—winters along the coast in good numbers but is seldom available to hunters because of its preference for rocky surf zones and jetties. Harlequins nest along rushing mountain streams, then descend to the coast for the winter.

Hunting Methods

In Oregon, sea ducks are typically harvested incidentally by hunters targeting dabblers and divers on coastal bays and estuaries. See hunting methods for divers. Combined harvest of sea ducks in 1997 was 945.

Harlequin Duck—*Histrionicus histrionicus*

Local Names	"Lords and Ladies."
Size	14 to 19 inches.
Male	Spectacular and unmistakable pattern of white slashes and spots against a rich gray plumage with ruddy flanks; white teardrop-shaped crescent in front of eye.
Female	Grayish overall with dark gray head marked with white spots behind the eye and at the base of the bill.
Wings	Dark wings, male having small, inconspicuous white spots on inner half.
Identification in Flight	Male's gray white pattern is evident, including white stripes. extending down the length of the back; smallish and plump with long tail; flight usually fast and direct; small flocks.
Common Range	Winters along the coast; breeds along mountain streams.

White-winged Scoter—*Melanitta fusca*

Length	19 to 24 inches.
Male	Black with small white eye patch; red-orange bill with black knob.
Female	Dark brown with pale spots on sides of head
Wing	Dark with white speculum.
Identification in Flight	Low and direct flight, typically in lines; white speculum.
Common Range	Coastal but occasionally found on large bodies of fresh water (especially after severe coastal storms).

Black Scoter—*Melanitta nigra*

Local Names	Butterbill,, common scoter.
Length	17 to 21 inches.
Male	Large and all black; males have orange knob at base of bill.
Female	Dark gray brown with pale cheek patch.
Wing	All dark, but silvery underwing linings contrast with darker leading edge.
Identification in Flight	Silvery wing linings; flight is fast and direct.
Common Range	Coastal.

Surf Scoter—*Mellanita perspicillata*

Local Names	Skunkhead, goggle goose.
Length	17 to 21 inches.
Male	All-black body; black head with bright white patch on forehead and back of neck; large multicolored bill.
Female	Dark brown overall with pale spots on cheeks.
Wing	All dark with no white.
Identification in Flight	Strong, direct flight, often in lines low over the water; lands on water with wings extended up over the back.
Common Range	Coastal.

Oldsquaw—*Clangula hyemalis*

Length	16 to 21 inches.
Male	In winter, white head with darker marks; black-and-white back pattern; long, black, pointed tail; black wings.
Female	White head with darker patches; dark back; short, stubby bill.
Wing	All dark.
Identification in Flight	Quick and direct; all dark wings; male's long tail.
Common Range	Rare winter visitor to coastal waters.

GEESE

Of the 11 recognized subspecies of Canada goose, Oregon is home to seven, including wintering populations of the threatened dusky and Aleutian races. Others include the lesser, cackling, Western, Vancouver, and Taverner's Canada geese. The existence of dusky and Aleutian geese in western Oregon has a profound impact on the management of hunting seasons for the other, far more numerous subspecies.

Oregon's second most numerous goose is the snow goose, which is most abundant in eastern Oregon, where Summer Lake and Malheur Lake attract huge migrating flocks of these beautiful, white geese. Geese stage on these areas and each day, during their travels from feeding to staging and roosting locations, the massive flocks present one of nature's most stunning spectacles in the form of huge, undulating waves of elegant and noisy white geese. Mixed among the snow geese in eastern Oregon are a few very similar but noticeably smaller Ross' geese, a few of which are harvested each year by hunters.

The white-fronted goose occurs throughout much of the state in small, migrating flocks. They are more common east of the Cascades and are most often hunted in Klamath County, on Summer Lake and around Malheur Lake. White-fronted geese, often called "specklebellies," migrate through Oregon early, so best hunting opportunity occurs during the first half of October (be sure to check opening dates). White-fronted geese sometimes mix with flocks of Canada geese, so be sure of your target.

Black brant, medium-sized geese that are closely tied to estuarine environments, winter in small numbers at various locations along the Oregon coast. Best hunting opportunities are available on Netarts and Tillamook Bays, where the birds frequent exposed beds of eelgrass. Brant hunters are afforded a short November season and should scout flocks ahead of time to determine the birds' movements in relation to tide levels. Only 90 or so brant are harvested each year in Oregon. Consult the ODFW in Tillamook for further details and suggestions.

Hunting Methods

Goose hunting in Oregon takes many forms, but gunners who use decoys and calls experience the most consistent success, especially on snow geese, but also on Canada geese and other species. In agricultural areas, hunters can set up large spreads to attracts birds. Snow goose specialists use large numbers of decoys—often nothing more than "rag" decoys—to lure birds into range, especially on Summer Lake Wildlife Area in southeastern Oregon. Oregon hunters harvest about 4,000 snow geese per year along with several dozen Ross' geese.

The Canada goose harvest in Oregon averages about 35,000 birds annually and accounts for at least 85 percent of the state's yearly total for sport-killed geese. The best areas include parts of the Willamette Valley, the Columbia Basin, and the large wetlands of eastern Oregon (Summer Lake, Klamath Lake, Malheur Lake). Smaller concentrations of birds occur along major waterways, such as the Snake River in eastern Oregon and on Klamath Marsh.

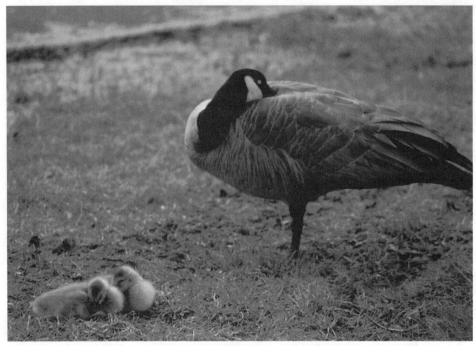

Sleeping Canada goose and chicks.

Gun and Shot Suggestions
Gauge—10 or 12.
Choke—Modified or improved/modified for doubles.
Shot—Only federally approved nontoxic shot may be used for waterfowl. Use heavy
loads: No. 1, BB, BBB, T or F.

Species and Identification

Canada Goose—*Branta canadensis*

Identification   All subspecies share a black neck and head with full or partial
white chinstrap; body deep rusty brown to light tan, depending
on subspecies. Range from very large (westerns) to slightly
larger than a mallard (cackling). Large western Canada geese
weigh up to 12 pounds. Distinct honking call, but the pitch
varies among species.

Snow geese near Burns, Oregon.

Lesser Snow Goose—*Chen caerulescens*

Identification   Adults are pure white with black wing tips; highly vocal—call is a high-pitched, raspy "uk-uk." Weighs from 6 to 8 pounds.

Ross' Goose—*Chen rossii*

Identification   Almost identical to the larger snow goose, but its bill is shorter and stubbier, lacking the black "lips" characteristic of the snow goose. Neck relatively shorter than that of the snow goose. Call similar to that of snow goose, but higher and less melodious. Weighs 4 to 6 pounds.

White-fronted goose and mallards.

White-fronted Goose ("Specklebelly")—*Anser albifrons*

Identification   An attractive brown goose with a white lower belly and dark blotches and bars on the upper belly and breast. Large pink bill outlined in white at its base. Adults have orange legs while juveniles have yellow legs. Average weight is about 6 pounds. The distinctive call is a melodious laughlike series of three or four high-pitched "kow-kow-kow-kows."

Black Brant—*Branta bernicla*

Identification   This medium-sized dark goose features a black breast, head, and neck. The neck is ringed with a broken white collar, and the flanks are streaked with white and brown. The undertail coverts are white; bill and legs are black. Range is limited to coastal bays and estuaries during winter.

The Complicated Game of Hunting Geese in Western Oregon

Waterfowl biologists in western Oregon face a thankless and complex task in managing Canada goose populations. On the one hand, exploding populations of locally produced geese wreak havoc on grain and grass crops in the Willamette Valley, while on the other hand, the valley serves as the wintering grounds for a threatened subspecies, the dusky Canada goose. On the north coast, meanwhile, there are wintering populations of rare Aleutian Island Canada geese. The solution to date has involved several strategies: 1) an early (September) hunt season aimed at culling resident geese and allowing an expansive sport-harvest opportunity; 2) a goose identification class that prospective goose hunters must pass before being issued a permit; 3) a harvest quota on dusky Canada geese that allows for limited accidental harvest of this subspecies; 4) carefully defined open and closed areas for goose hunting; and 5) the mandatory use of harvest reports and field check stations.

The Northwest Permit Goose Testing Sessions are scheduled for various locations throughout the state. Exact locations and times are listed in the game bird hunting synopsis. ODFW provides study materials for home study and then conducts the identification course. Prospective hunters are allowed three chances to pass the test.

The Oregon Department of Fish and Wildlife—specifically the Access and Habitat Board—announced in 1998 the initiation of a pilot program aimed at improving access to private lands for goose hunting. One of the traditional contradictions in western Oregon goose hunting is that landowners want something done about rapidly expanding populations of geese but have been hesitant to provide widespread access to private lands where the geese are so abundant and so damaging to agriculture. The new access program is designed to address this issue. Consult the current synopsis for details.

Northeast Region

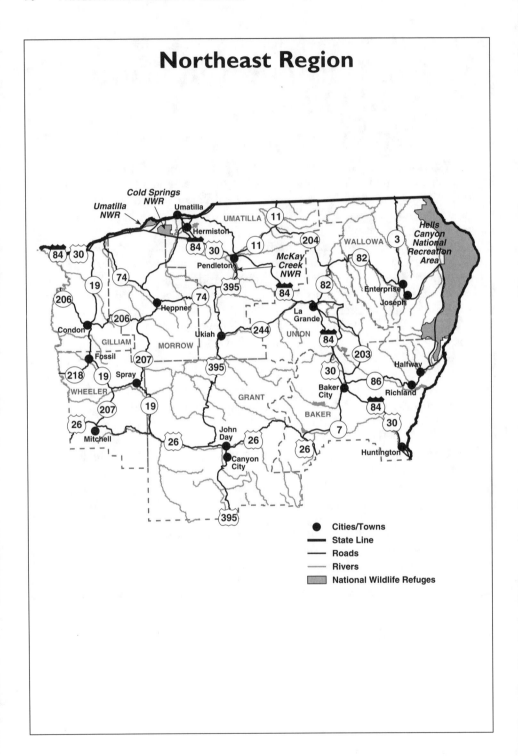

Cold Springs NWR
Umatilla NWR
Umatilla
Hermiston
UMATILLA
McKay Creek NWR
Pendleton
WALLOWA
Hells Canyon National Recreation Area
Enterprise
Joseph
Heppner
La Grande
UNION
Ukiah
MORROW
Condon
GILLIAM
Fossil
Spray
WHEELER
Halfway
Richland
Baker City
BAKER
GRANT
Mitchell
John Day
Canyon City
Huntington

84 30 11 11 204 3 82 82 395 74 74 244 84 84 203 30 86 19 206 206 207 218 19 207 19 26 26 26 26 7 30 395

Cities/Towns
State Line
Roads
Rivers
National Wildlife Refuges

Northeast Region

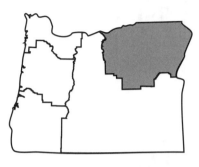

The northeast Region boasts perhaps the state's greatest diversity in wingshooting opportunity. The Columbia River Basin, which includes Umatilla, Morrow, and Gilliam Counties, offers some of Oregon's best waterfowling while extensive grain agriculture supports the state's highest and most expansive pheasant densities. Chukar abound in the John Day drainage and along the breaks of the Snake River and its tributaries; Hungarian partridge occur in appropriate habitat; and valley quail thrive in both agricultural and suburban tracts throughout the region. These same areas offer strong dove flights during September. Meanwhile, the extensive Blue and Wallowa Mountain Ranges offer underhunted populations of both blue and ruffed grouse, with the latter being closely tied to riparian habitats.

Such diversity in wingshooting opportunity underscores the geographic diversity of northeastern Oregon. The rugged Wallowa and Elkhorn ranges feature some of the state's highest and most picturesque peaks with pastoral valleys nestled at their feet. The Blue Mountains, which include the Elkhorn Range, cut a broad diagonal path through the region, yielding on the west to the precipitous sage-covered breaks of the John Day River (Oregon's longest free-flowing stream). The Wallowa Mountains rise suddenly from the Snake River on the east, where Hells Canyon cuts America's . deepest gorge.

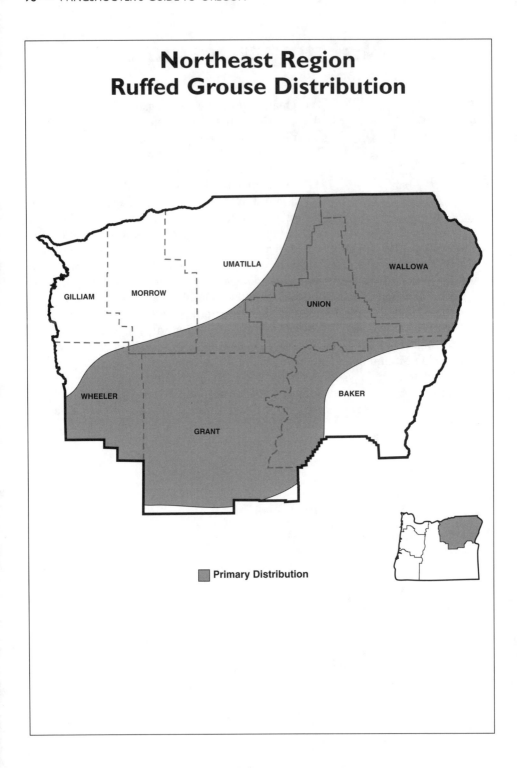

Northeast Region
Ruffed Grouse Distribution

Primary Distribution

Northeast Region
Blue Grouse Distribution

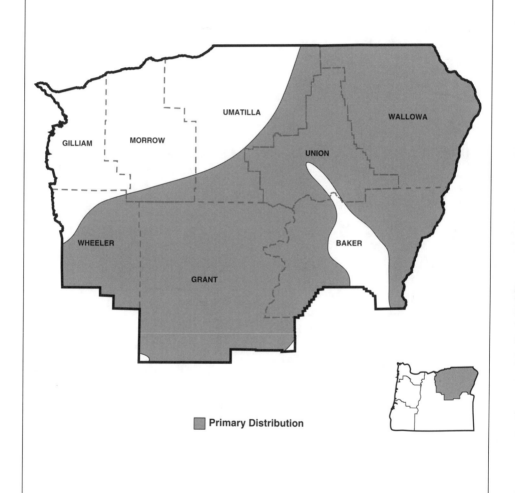

GILLIAM

MORROW

UMATILLA

WALLOWA

UNION

WHEELER

BAKER

GRANT

Primary Distribution

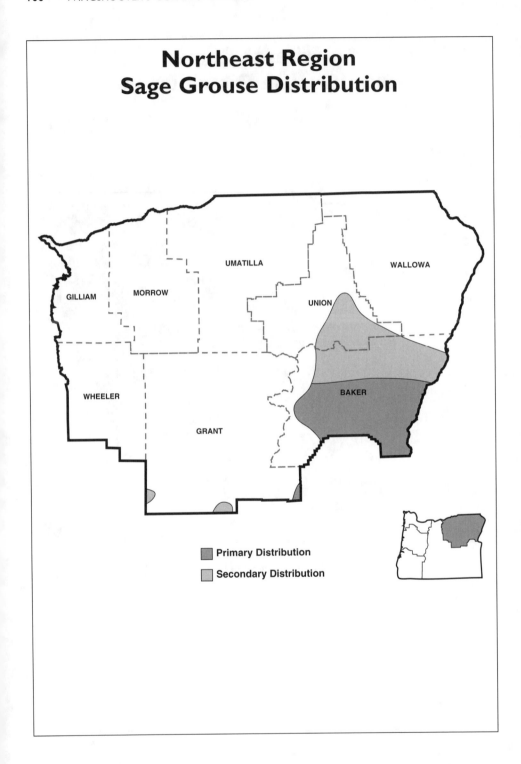

Northeast Region
Sage Grouse Distribution

UMATILLA

WALLOWA

GILLIAM

MORROW

UNION

WHEELER

BAKER

GRANT

■ Primary Distribution

■ Secondary Distribution

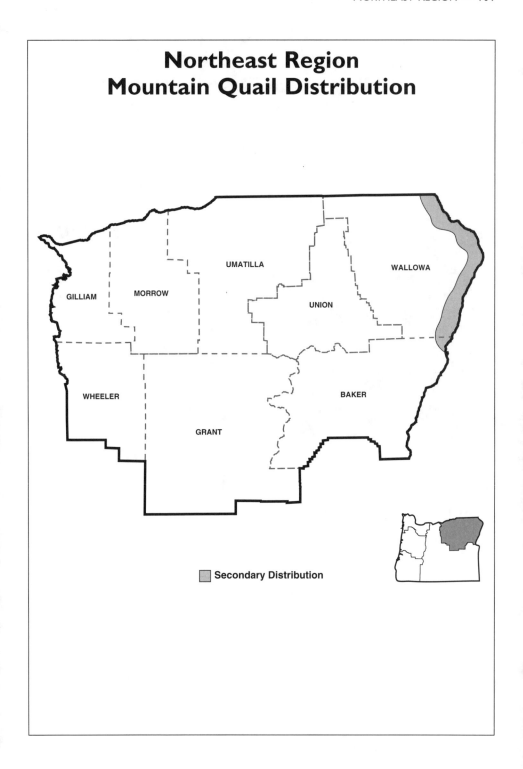

Northeast Region
Mountain Quail Distribution

Secondary Distribution

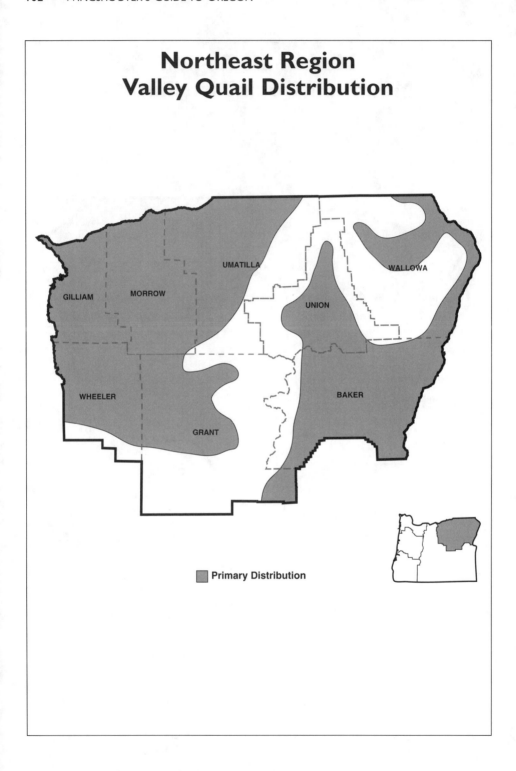

Northeast Region
Valley Quail Distribution

UMATILLA

WALLOWA

GILLIAM

MORROW

UNION

WHEELER

BAKER

GRANT

Primary Distribution

Northeast Region
Chukar Partridge Distribution

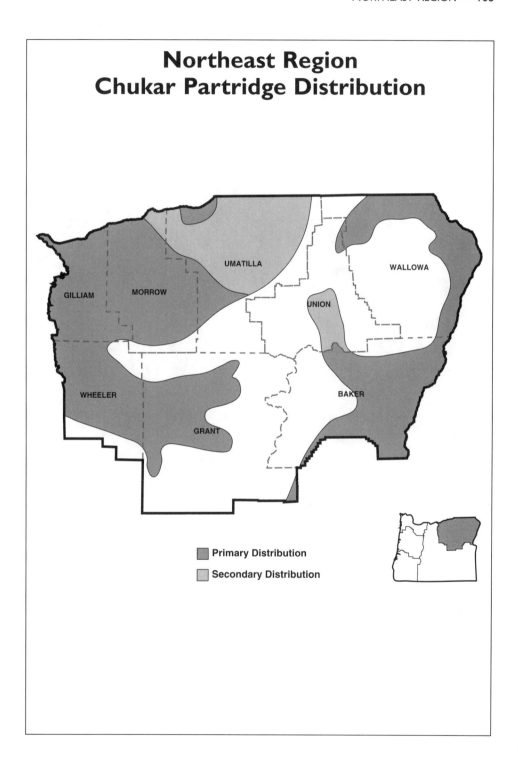

Primary Distribution

Secondary Distribution

Northeast Region
Hungarian Partridge Distribution

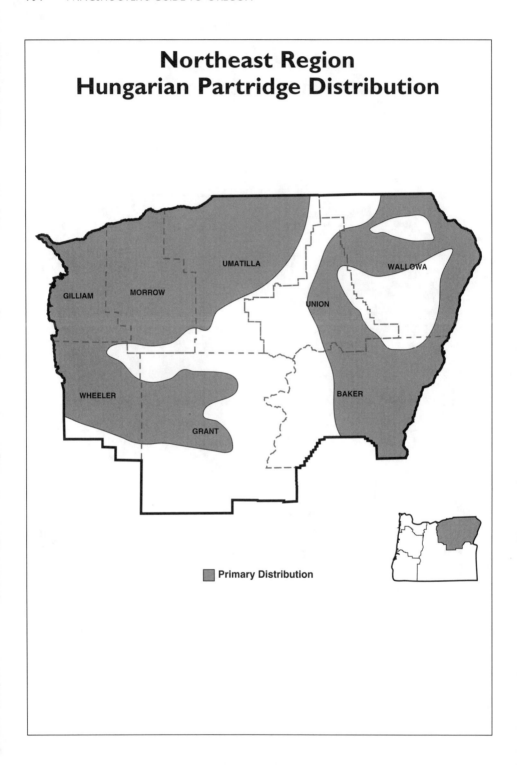

Primary Distribution

Northeast Region
Ring-necked Pheasant Distribution

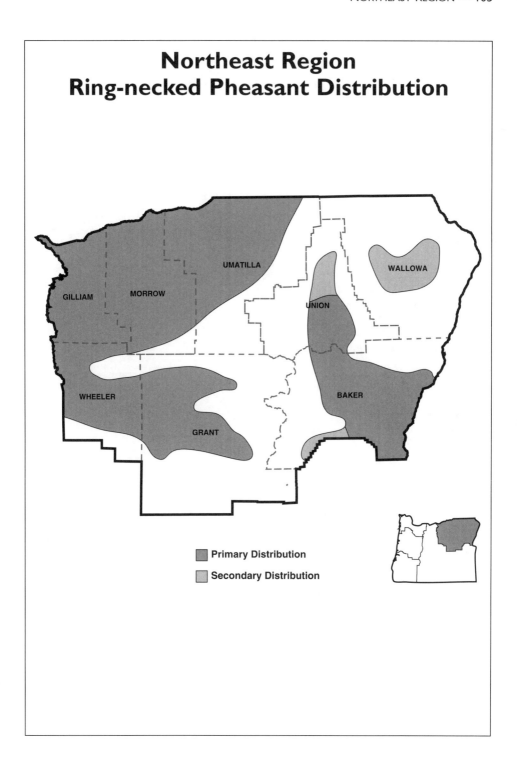

Primary Distribution

Secondary Distribution

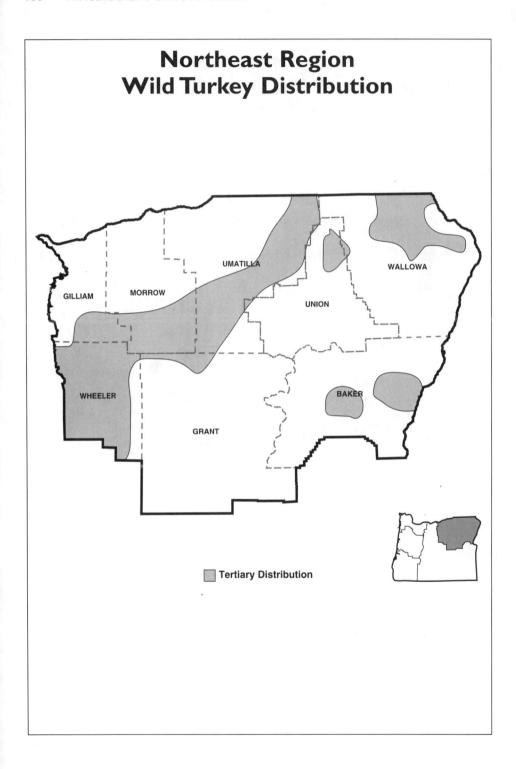

Northeast Region
Wild Turkey Distribution

UMATILLA

WALLOWA

GILLIAM

MORROW

UNION

WHEELER

BAKER

GRANT

▨ Tertiary Distribution

Joseph and Enterprise
Wallowa County

County Population–7,250	Joseph Population–1,255
County Area–3,153 sq. mi.	Enterprise Population–2,020
County Acres in CRP–14,209	Enterprise Elevation–3,757 feet
October Temperature–43°	

The snowcapped crags of the Wallowa Mountains dominate one of Oregon's most scenic counties. The Wallowa Mountains yield abruptly on the east to the Snake River and its awesome canyon (including Hells Canyon), where strong chukar populations challenge the hardiest wingshooters. During the early part of the chukar season, when the birds must find water each day, some shotgunners hunt by jetsled, motoring up or down the Snake and then hunting the side canyons. Later, after rain and snow allows the birds to stay high on the slopes, hunters must approach from the rim and walk a contour.

Wallowa County features several major rivers that are born in the Eagle Cap Wilderness, including the Minam, Wallowa, and Imnaha. The Grande Ronde—a major steelhead stream and important chukar-hunting drainage—cuts across the northwest corner of Wallowa County.

In addition to its chukar hunting, Wallowa County offers excellent blue grouse prospects along the steep, timbered ridges. Less plentiful, ruffed grouse occupy the riparian areas. Pheasant and quail are found in the valleys and irrigated crop lands.

Enterprise is the county seat, and nearby Joseph offers a small brewpub and other amenities. Postcard-perfect Wallowa Lake, just north of Joseph, attracts thousands of tourists each summer.

UPLAND BIRDS
Chukar Partridge, Hungarian Partridge, Ring-necked Pheasant, Valley Quail, Blue Grouse, Ruffed Grouse, Mountain Quail, Turkey, Mourning Dove

WATERFOWL
Ducks and Geese

ACCOMMODATIONS
Joseph
  Indian Lodge Motel, 201 South Main / 541-432-2651 / 16 units / Dogs allowed / $$
  Dragon Meadows Bed and Breakfast, 504 North Lake Street / 541-432-1027 / 2 units / Dogs allowed / No credit cards / $$$
Enterprise
  Ponderosa Motel, 102 Southwest Greenwood / 541-426-3186 / 25 units / Dogs allowed / $$–$$$

Wilderness Inn, 301 West North Street / 541-426-4535 / 29 units / Dogs allowed / $$–$$$

Stein's Cabins, 84681 Ponderosa Lane (Wallowa Lake) / 541-432-2391 / 11 units / Dogs allowed / $$–$$$

Cherokee Mingo Motel, 102 North Alder (Wallowa) / 541-886-2021 / 12 units / Dogs allowed / $–$$

CAMPGROUNDS AND RV PARKS (CALL FOR WINTER CLOSURES)
Joseph

Park at the River, 59888 Wallowa Lake Hwy / 541-432-8800 / 48 full hookups

Scenic Meadows RV Park, 59781 Wallowa Lake Hwy / 541-432-9285 / 16 full hookups, tent sites

Troy Wilderness Lodge and RV Park, 84570 Bartlett Road / 541-828-7741 / 20 full hookups

Wallowa Lake State Park, 722 Marina Lane / 800-452-5687 / 121 full hookups, 90 tent sites

Five Peaks RV Park, 508 North Mill Street / 541-432-4605 / 5 full hook-ups

Mountain View RV Park, 83459 Joseph Hwy / 541-432-2982 / 8 full; 19 electric/ water hookups; tent sites

Enterprise

Nez Perce Trailer and RV Park, 114 South River Street / 541-426-2501 / 8 full hookups

Outpost RV Park, 66258 Lewiston Hwy / 541-426-4027 / 48 full hookups

RESTAURANTS
Joseph

Cactus Jack's Cowboy Bar and Gold Room, 100 North Main Street / 541-432-5225 / Daily 11AM–10PM

The Embers, 206 North Main Street / 541-432-2739 / Daily 7AM–11PM / Brewpub

The Monarch Grill, 4 South Main Street / 541-432-7106 / Mon–Thur 11:30AM–8PM

LaRue's Cheyenne Café, 209 North Main Street / 541-432-6300 / Wed–Sat 6AM–2PM; Fri 5PM–8PM; Sun 7:30AM–2PM

Mariah's Cuisine, 12 South Main Street / 541-432-7035 / Mon–Sat 4PM–10PM; Sun 4PM–8PM

Renee's Gourmet Coffee & Heavenly Treats, 103 North Main / 541-432-5282 / 7AM–7PM daily / Dinner by reservation

Enterprise

Terminal Gravity Brewery, 803 School Street / 541-426-0158 / Wed–Sat 3:30PM–11PM; Sun 1PM–9PM / Microbrewery

Toma's, 309 South River Street / 541-426-4873 / Daily 6AM–10PM / 541-426-4873

Corner Restaurant, 501 West North / 541-426-2600 / Wed–Sun 6AM–8PM

Large Time Café, 307 West North / 541-426-9055 / Mon–Fri 6AM–2PM; Sun 8AM–2PM

Maye's Café, 309 West Main Street / 541-426-4241 / Mon–Sat 5AM–3PM

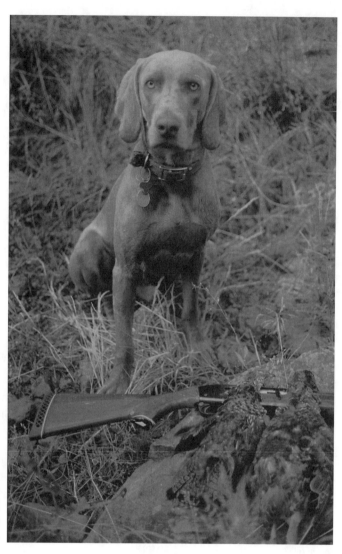

Jake, a Weimaraner, with blue and ruffed grouse from the Wallowa Mountains.

VETERINARY CLINICS

Enterprise

Double Arrow Veterinary Clinic, 66260 Lewiston Hwy / 541-426-4470; 24-hour emergency—listen to recording for number to call

Gerner Veterinary Clinic, 706 Depot Street / 541-426-3331 (24-hour emergency, same number)

Dog Boarding Services
Joseph
  Lin-Lee Kennels, 83456 Russell Lane / 541-432-8221 / Emergency: 541-426-4768
    or 432-2875
Enterprise
  Wyakin Shepards, 81667 Reavis Lane / 541-426-6407 / 3 exercise yards

Auto Repair
Joseph
  Heilmann 4-wheel Drive Center, 105 South Main Street / 541-432-0775
  Kilgore's Auto Parts & Service, 503 North Main Street / 541-432-3221
Enterprise
  Byrnes Chevron, 111 Northwest 1st / 541-426-3889
  Courtney Motors, 311 West Main Street / 541-426-3167 or 800-933-8888
  Summit Ford, 300 West Main / 541-426-4574 or 800-433-0702 /
    24-hour towing available, call one of the following: 541-426-4239, 426-3379,
    426-6007, 569-2482
  Milligan Motors Inc., 202 East North Street / 541-426-3129 or 800-421-3128

Auto Rental
Enterprise
  Courtney Motors, 311 West Main / 541-426-3167 or 800-933-8888
  Summit Ford, 300 West Main / 541-426-4574 or 800-433-0702

Sporting Goods Dealers
Joseph
  Sports Corral, 401 North Main Street / 541-432-4363 / Shotgun ammo and
    supplies
Enterprise
  Liquid Gas Company, 307 West Main Street / 541-426-3811 / Guns, ammo,
    reloading supplies
  Wallowa County Grain Growers, 911 South River Street / 541-426-3116 /
    Shotgun ammo

Air Service
Joseph
  Joseph State Airport / Contact: Spence Air Service, 541-426-3562
Enterprise
  Enterprise Municipal Airport / Contact: Spence Air Service, 541-426-3562

Medical
Enterprise
  Wallowa Memorial Hospital, 401 Northeast 1st Street / 541-426-3111

ATM MACHINES (ALL 24-HOUR ACCESS)

Joseph
  Community Bank, 609 North Main Street
Enterprise
  Community Bank, 300 Northwest 1st Street
                    202 Storie (Wallowa)
  Klamath First Federal, 106 Southwest 1st
  Pioneer Bank, 205 West Main Street

FOR MORE INFORMATION

Wallowa County Chamber of Commerce
107 Southwest 1st Street
Enterprise, OR 97828
541-426-4622 or 800-585-4121
email: wallowa@eoni.com

La Grande
Union County

County Population–24,500	LaGrande Population–12,415
County Area–2,038 sq. mi.	LaGrande Elevation–2,788 feet
County Acres in CRP–4,794	October Temperature–49°

The Union County Seat of La Grande occupies the pastoral Grande Ronde River Valley situated between the Wallowa Mountains to the east and the Blue Mountains that rise above town to the west and north. The presence of Eastern Oregon University assures that La Grande offers a fine assortment of restaurants and other amenities. Interstate 84 skirts the north and east edge of La Grande, following the Grande Ronde River for several miles just northwest of town.

Blue grouse thrive on the forested ridges of the Blue Mountains, and ruffed grouse occupy riparian zones and springs throughout the higher elevations. Wild turkeys have been established in the area, and hunting can be good for those who take the time to scout before the season opens in April.

Waterfowl and pheasant hunters flock to Ladd Marsh Wildlife Area just south of La Grande, while a few chukar hunters work the desert ridges in the southeast corner of the county.

UPLAND BIRDS
Chukar Partridge, Hungarian Partridge, Ring-necked Pheasant, Valley Quail, Blue Grouse, Ruffed Grouse, Turkey, Mourning Dove, Common Snipe

WATERFOWL
Ducks and Geese

ACCOMMODATIONS
Blue Mountain Motel, 2309 East Adams Avenue / 541-963-4424 / 65 units / Dogs allowed / Kitchenettes available / $$

Budget Inn, 2215 East Adams / 541-963-7116 / 34 units / Dogs allowed / Kitchenettes available / $$–$$$

Greenwell Motel, 305 Adams Avenue / 541-963-4134 or 800-772-0991 / 33 units / Dogs allowed with fee / $

Howard Johnson Inn, Hwy 82 and I-84 Interchange / 541-963-7195 or 800-446-4656 / 146 units / Dogs allowed / $$$

Moon Motel, 2116 Adams Avenue / 541-963-2724 / 9 units / Dogs allowed with fee / $–$$

Orchard Motel, 2206 Adams Avenue / 541-963-6160 / 12 units / Dogs allowed with fee / Nonsmoking / $–$$

Quail Run Motor Inn, 2400 Adams / 541- 963-3400 / 15 Units / Dogs allowed / $-$$

Royal Motor Inn, 1510 Adams Avenue / 541-963-4154 or 800-990-7575 / 44 units / Dogs allowed with fee / $$

CAMPGROUNDS AND RV PARKS

Hot Lake RV Resort, 65182 Hot Lake Lane / 541-963-5253 or 800-994-5253

La Grande Rendezvous Park, 2632 Bearco Loop / 541-962-0909 or 800-276-6873

RESTAURANTS

Ten Depot, 10 Depot Street, downtown / 541-963-8766 / Fine dining with varied menu / Steak, seafood, pasta and nightly specials / Full bar

Foley Station, 1011 Adams Avenue, downtown / Fine dining with creative northwest and continental cuisine / Breakfast and lunch Wed–Sun 7AM–3PM / Dinner Thurs–Sat 5PM–9PM

Mamacita's, 110 Depot Street, downtown La Grande / 541-963-6223 / Mexican / Daily lunch and dinner specials

El Bronco, 2102 Adams Avenue / 541-963-2534 / Authentic Mexican

Wrangler Family Steak House, 1914 Adams Avenue / 541-963-3131

Farmhouse Family Restaurant, 401 Adams Avenue 541-963-9318

Smokehouse Restaurant, 2208 East Adams Avenue / 541-963-9692

Cock and Bull Villa Roma, 1414 Adams Avenue (downtown mall) / 541-963-0573 / Italian

Klondike Pizza, 2104 Island Avenue / 541-963-4949

Flying J Restaurant, I-84 Exit 265 / 541-963-9762 / Open 24 hours

VETERINARY CLINICS

Animal Health Center, 10302 Wallowa Lake Hwy (Island City) / 541-963-6621

La Grande Small Animal Clinic, 1807 Cove Avenue / 541-963-8002

Mark Omann, 11401 Island Avenue / 541-963-2748

Bohden S. Demczynsky, 2303 Adams Avenue / 541-963-0287

DOG BOARDING SERVICES

Countryside Kennels, 62616 Fruitdale Lane / 541-963-3462

AUTO REPAIR

All Foreign Auto Center, 1610 Adams Avenue / 541-963-7566

Greg's Auto Repair, 1701 Adams Avenue / 541-963-7779

Joe's Auto Electric and Repair, 2213 Jefferson Avenue / 541-963-9345

La Grande Auto Repair, 1505 26th / 541-975-2000

Frontier Motors, 10705 Island Avenue (Island City) / 541-962-7099 / Jeep dealer

Goss Motor Company, 1415 Adams Avenue / 541-963-4161

Lynch Motor Company, 1602 Adams Avenue / 541-963-2104 / GMC, Buick, Pontiac dealer

Roberts Ford, 2906 Island Avenue (Island City) / 541-963-2161 / Ford dealer

SPORTING GOODS DEALERS
Rite Aid, Grand Ronde Plaza / 541-963-8318
Coast-to-Coast Hardware, 1700 Portland / 541-963-4372
Wal-Mart, 11619 Island Avenue / 541-963-6783
Bi-Mart, 2510 Adams / 541-963-2166

MEDICAL
Grande Ronde Hospital, 900 Sunset / 541-963-8421
Evergreen Health Care, 103 Adams Avenue / 541-963-4184

ATM MACHINES
US Bank, 1402 Adams Avenue
Bank of America, 1503 Washington Avenue

FOR MORE INFORMATION
LaGrande-Union County Chamber of Commerce
1912 Fourth Street, Suite 200
La Grande OR 97850
541-963-8588 or 800-848-9969
email: lagrande@uicnet.com

Baker City, Huntington, Richland, and Halfway
Baker County

County Population–16,500	Baker City Population–9,870
County Area–3,089 sq. mi.	Huntington Population–575
County Acres in CRP–792	Richland Population–185
October Temperature–49°	Halfway Population–355

Owing to the Snake River, which forms its eastern boundary, Baker County offers fine prospects for chukar, pheasant, waterfowl, quail, and Hungarian partridge. Near the little town of Huntington, the Snake enters the upstream end of Brownlee Reservoir, one of the river's many impoundments. Brownlee's steep, grassy slopes provide perfect chukar habitat. Hunters should carry a BLM map, however, as much of the land along Brownlee lies on private property. Doves and quail occur here as in the rest of the county. Baker County's southern half is dominated by agriculture, and the Huntington area is popular with pheasant and goose hunters.

Baker County reaches into the south half of the Wallowa Mountains north of the quaint little town of Halfway. Grouse hunters can find good numbers of both blue and ruffed grouse here and in the Blue Mountains along the western edge of the county, west and southwest of Baker City, the county seat. Interstate 84 bisects the county through some prime pheasant, quail, and dove habitat. Sage grouse occur in the arid regions of Baker County, especially where sagebrush plains meet irrigated alfalfa and grain fields along the Malheur County line.

UPLAND BIRDS
Chukar Partridge, Hungarian Partridge, Ring-necked Pheasant, Valley Quail, Blue Grouse, Ruffed Grouse, Sage Grouse, Turkey, Mourning Dove, Common Snipe

WATERFOWL
Ducks and Geese

ACCOMMODATIONS
Baker City

El Dorado Inn, 655 Campbell / 541-523-6494 or 800-537-5756 / Dogs allowed with $3 fee / 24-hour restaurant / $$

Quality Inn, 810 Campbell / 541-523-2242 or 800-228-5151 / Dogs allowed with $3 fee / $–$$

Baker City Motel, 880 Elm Street / 541-523-6381 or 800-931-9229 / Dogs allowed / $–$$

Oregon Trail Motel, 211 Bridge Street / 541-523-5844 / Dogs allowed with $5 fee / $$

The Western Motel, 3055 10th / 541-523-3700 or 800-481-3701 / Dogs allowed / $

Budget Inn, 3rd and Broadway / 541-523-6324 or 800-547-5827 / Dogs allowed with $3 fee / $–$$

Halfway

Halfway Motel, 170 South Main / 541-742-5722 / 26 units / Dogs allowed / $–$$

Pine Valley Lodge, 163 North Main / 7 units / $$$ / Continental breakfast included

Richland

Hitching Post Motel, Main Street / 541-893-6176 / Dogs allowed with $5 fee / $–$$

Huntington

Wayne's Motel, 110 West Washington Street / 541-869-2111

CAMPGROUNDS AND RV PARKS

Baker City

Mountain View Holiday Trav-L-Park and Mobile Manor, 2845 Hughes Lane / 541-523-4824

Oregon Trails West RV Park, I-84 at Richland Exit 302 / 541-523-3236 / 50 hookups plus tent sites

Baker City Motel and RV Park, 880 Elm Street / 541-523-6381

Richland

Eagle Valley RV Park, Highway 86 / 541-893-6161

Hewitt County Park, East of Richland on Brownlee Reservoir / 541-893-6147

Huntington

Limbaugh Trailer Spaces, 445 Lincoln Street / 541-869-2838

Rynearson Trailer Court, 150 East Fulton Street / 541-869-2463

RESTAURANTS

Baker City

The Phone Company, 1926 1st / 541-523-7997 / Fine dining

Geiser Grande Hotel, 1996 Main Street / 541-523-1889 / Fresh seafood and regional specialties / Extensive wine list / Northwest microbrews

Barley Brown's Brewpub, 2190 Main Street / 541-523-4266

Barry's Farmland Restaurant, 2175 Broadway / 541-523-8532

Oregon Trail Restaurant, 211 Bridge Street / 541-523-5844 / 24 hours

Baker Truck Corral, 515 Campbell (I-84 Exit 304) / 541-523-4318 / 24 hours

Halfway

Pine Valley Lodge Restaurant / 541-742-2027 / Breakfast (bakery) 6AM–3PM / Dinner 6PM–8PM Fri–Sat / Specializing in western, South American and '60s-style cuisine / Full bar

Stockman's Restaurant and Lounge / 541-742-2301 / Open in autumn 6AM–9PM and winter 7AM–8PM

Wild Bills and Co., 104 Main Street / 541-742-5833 / 6AM–9PM

Main Street Café / 541-742-7227

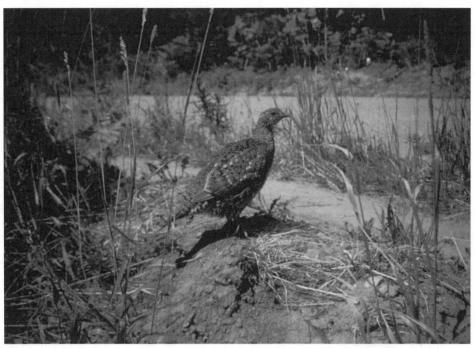

Blue grouse frequently dust and feed on logging roads.

Richland
Shorthorn Restaurant and Lounge / 541-893-6122 / Weekdays 6AM–8PM, weekends to 9PM
Cappuccino Corral, Main Street / 541-893-6167
Flip's Café, Main Street / 541-893-6192
Huntington
Streamliner-By-Candy Restaurant, 50 East Washington Street / 541-869-2322
Paul's Tavern, 20 East Washington Street / 541-869-2851

VETERINARY CLINICS
Baker City
Alpine Veterinary Hospital, 2925 10th Avenue / 541-523-5067
Animal Clinic, 2490 10th Avenue / 541-523-3611
Baker Veterinary Clinic, 3425 10th Avenue / 541-523-7772

DOG BOARDING SERVICES
Baker City
Donna's Dog Grooming, 1405 17th Street / 541-523-6080

AUTO REPAIR
Baker City
Broadway Garage, 2798 10th Street / 541-523-3203
Ken and Bink's Auto Repair, 3655 10th Street / 541-523-3444
Halfway Garage / 541-742-2136
Halfway
D and D Auto Supply / 541-742-7878

AUTO RENTAL
Practical Rent-A-Car, 800 Campbell / 541-523-6292 or 800-352-0739
Ford Rent-A-Car, 2300 Main Street / 541-523-3625

SPORTING GOODS DEALERS
Baker City
York's Sporting Goods, 1549 Campbell / 541-523-2577
Safari Gun Shop, 1826 Main Street / 541-523-1090
Rite Aid, 1217 Campbell Street / 541-523-3516
Coast-To-Coast Hardware, 2001 2nd Avenue / 541-523-3371

MEDICAL
Baker City
St. Elizabeth Health Services, 3325 Pocahontas Road / 541-523-6461
Halfway
Pine Eagle Clinic / 541-742-5023

ATM MACHINES
Halfway
US Bank

FOR MORE INFORMATION
Baker City Chamber of Commerce
490 Campbell Street
Baker City OR 97814-2206
541-523-5855
email: bakerchamber@bakercity.com

John Day and Canyon City
Grant County

County Population–8,100	John Day Population–2,015
County Area–4,528 sq. mi.	Canyon City Population–725
County Acres in CRP–758	October Temperature–50°

Grant County offers excellent opportunities for forest grouse and partridge, along with quail and dove. The expansive Blue Mountains dominate the county's east half and are the site of the John Day River' headwaters and two of its lengthy forks (the Middle and North Forks). Blue grouse occupy the timbered ridges above the river and its feeder streams throughout the Blue Mountains, and ruffed grouse live along the water and along the many springs found at higher elevations. The John Day mainstem flows mostly east to west through Grant County and is followed closely by US 26. Pheasant, quail, and dove occupy the valley near the towns of John Day and Mt. Vernon, but as one progresses west, elevation decreases as does rainfall. The irrigated valley eventually yields to arid canyonlands, and chukar become the dominant game bird along the west edge of the county.

UPLAND BIRDS
Chukar Partridge, Hungarian Partridge, Ring-necked Pheasant, Valley Quail, Blue Grouse, Ruffed Grouse, Turkey, Mourning Dove

WATERFOWL
Ducks and Geese

ACCOMMODATIONS
Best Western Inn, 315 West Main Street / Dogs allowed with fee / 541-575-1700 or 800-243-2628 / $$

Dreamers Lodge, 144 North Canyon Boulevard / 541-575-0526 or 800-452-4899 / Dogs allowed / $$

John Day Sunset Inn, 390 West Main Street / 541-575-1462 or 800-452-4899 / Dogs allowed / $$

Budget Inn, 250 East Main Street / 541-575-2100 or 800-854-8444 / Dogs in smoking rooms only, $3 fee / $$

Budget Motel, 711 West Main Street / 541-575-2155 / $$

CAMPGROUNDS AND RV PARKS
Grant County RV Park, 601 Northwest Bridge Street / 541-575-0110 / 25 full hookups

Hitching Post Trailer Court, P.O. Box 472, Long Creek (north of Mt. Vernon on Hwy 395) / 541-421-3043 / 16 full hookups.

RESTAURANTS
Birdhouse Café, 201 West Main Street / 541-575-1143
The Cave Inn, 830 South Canyon Boulevard / 541-575-1083
Gee's Family Restaurant, 241 West Main Street / 541-575-1683
Grubsteak Mining Co., 149 East Main Street / 541-575-1970
K.C.'s Grill, 316 South Canyon Boulevard / 541-575-1835
Squeeze-Inn Restaurant and Deck, 415 West Main Street / 541-575-1045
Stage West, 155 West Main Street / 541-575-0250

VETERINARY CLINICS
Gambler Vet Clinic / 541-932-4428 / Dog boarding available
Grant County Vet Clinic / 541-575-1597 / Dog boarding available

AUTO REPAIR
Les Schwab Tire Center, 551 West Main Street / 541-575-1346 / Tires, brakes, batteries, shocks, alignment
Auto Shop Quick Lube, 320 West Main / 541-575-1776
Byron's Auto, 193 Ford Road / 541-575-0828
Doug's Motor Vehicle Repair and Towing, 130 South Canyon Boulevard / 541-575-0544
JJ Custom Car Service, West Highway / 541-575-2977

AUTO RENTAL
Teague Motors, 516 South Canyon Boulevard / 541-575-1715

SPORTING GOODS DEALERS
Ace Hardware, 652 West Main / 541-575-0549
John Day True Value Hardware, 161 East Main / 541-575-0632
RJ Gunshop, 133 West Main / 541-575-2130

AIR SERVICE
John Day State Airport, Airport Road (no commercial flights) / 541-575-1151

MEDICAL
Blue Mountain Hospital, 170 Ford Road / 541-575-1311

HUNTING PRESERVES/CLUBS
Great Expectations Hunting Preserve, Star Rt. 2 (Kimberly) / 541-934-2395

FOR MORE INFORMATION
Grant County Chamber of Commerce
281 West Main Street
John Day OR 97845
541-575-0547
1-800-769-5664

Pendleton, Hermiston, and Umatilla
Umatilla County

County Population–65,500	Pendleton Population–15,900
County Area–3,231 sq. mi.	Hermiston Population–11,595
County Acres in CRP–85,744	Umatilla Population–3,515
October Temperature–52°	

Stretching from the Columbia River on the north to the Blue Mountains on the south, Umatilla County features huge expanses of grain agriculture where pheasants thrive. Private lands dominate Umatilla County's pheasant habitat, but a little pre-season door knocking can pay dividends. Public hunting is available in several places, including the Irrigon Wildlife Area, which stretches for 7 miles between the towns of Umatilla and Irrigon, and McKay Creek National Wildlife Refuge south of Pendleton. In addition to its pheasants, Umatilla County offers good prospects for valley quail and Hungarian partridge in appropriate habitat, and large flights of doves congregate around grain fields and watering areas during September.

Waterfowl hunting is a big draw on the Columbia River and in surrounding crop circles near the towns of Umatilla and Pendleton. McNary Dam blocks the Columbia north of Hermiston, creating the McNary Pool, where thousands of ducks stage during the fall. In this part of the Columbia Basin, hunters might see tens of thousands of mallards fly high overhead during the early morning hours. Canada Geese abound, too. Most serious duck hunters use boats to reach favorite areas. Columbia River launches are located at Irrigon, Umatilla, and Hat Rock (some 10 miles east of Umatilla on US 730).

UPLAND BIRDS
Chukar Partridge, Hungarian Partridge, Ring-necked Pheasant, Valley Quail, Blue Grouse, Ruffed Grouse, Turkey, Mourning Dove, Common Snipe

WATERFOWL
Ducks and Geese

ACCOMMODATIONS
Pendleton
Chaparral Motel, 620 Southwest Tutuilla / 541-276-8654 / Dogs allowed / Kitchenettes available / $–$$
Motel 6, 325 Southeast Nye / 541-276-3160 / Dogs allowed / $–$$
Tapadera Inn, 105 Southeast Court / 541-276-3231 / Dogs allowed / $–$$
Best Western Pendleton Inn, 400 Southeast Nye Avenue / 541-276-2135 or 800-528-1234 / $$–$$$
Traveler's Inn, 310 Southeast Dorion / 541-276-6231 / Dogs allowed / $–$$

Hermiston
  Sunset Motel, 425 North 1st / 541-567-5583 / Dog allowed / $–$$
  Sands Motel, 835 North 1st / 541-567-5516 / Dogs allowed / $–$$
  Best Western Hermiston Inn, 2255 South Hwy 395 / 541-564-0202 or 800-528-1234 / $$–$$$ / No dogs
  Oxford Suites, 1005 North 1st / 541-564-8000 / 91 units / Dogs allowed with $250 refundable deposit and $20 per day / $$–$$$
  Oxford Inn, 655 North 1st / 541-567-7777 / 90 units / Dogs allowed with $250 refundable deposit and $20 per day / $–$$$
Umatilla
  Tillicum Motor Inn, Hwy 730 / 541-922-3236 / Dogs allowed / 40 units / Kitchenettes available / $–$$
  Rest-A-Bit Motel, Hwy 730 / 541-922-3271 / Dogs allowed / 36 units / Kitchenettes available / $–$$

CAMPGROUNDS AND RV PARKS
Pendleton
  Arrowhead RV Park, I-84 and Exit 216 / 541-276-8484
  Mountain View RV Park, 1375 Southeast 3rd / 541-276-1041 / 70 hookups
Hermiston
  Able Farms Tom RV Park, 1845 South Hwy 395 / 541-564-2394
Umatilla
  Shady Rest RV Park, Hwy 730 / 541-922-5041 / 18 full hookups, 6 partial hookups
  Umatilla Marina Park, 1710 Quincy / 541-922-3939 / 20 hookups, 6 tent sites

RESTAURANTS
Pendleton
  Raphael's Restaurant, 233 Southeast 4th / 541-276-8500 / One of the region's best restaurants / Reservations recommended
  Como's Italian Eatery, 39 Southeast Court Avenue / 541-278-9142 / Lunch and dinner / Quaint, authentic Italian
  El Charrito, 322 South Main / 541-276-2038 / Mexican cuisine
  Mazatlan Mexican Restaurant, 1408 Southwest Court Avenue / 541-276-2646
  Steele's Bar and Grill, 103 Southeast Court / 541-276-3288
  Big John's Hometown Pizza, 225 Southwest 9th / 541-276-0550
  Cimmiyotti's, 137 South Main / 541-276-4314 / A local favorite since 1959
  Ranch Café, I-84 Exit 202 / 541-278-2233 / Open 24 hours
Hermiston
  Shari's Restaurant, 800 South Hwy 395 / 541-567-1808 / Open 24 hours
  Fontaine's, 845 North 1st / 541-567-9544 / Open 4PM–11PM
  El Cazador, 1240 North 1st / 541-567-2804 / Mexican cuisine / Open for lunch and dinner Sun–Thurs until 10PM; Fri–Sat until 11PM
  Hale's Restaurant and Tavern, 174 East Main / 541-567-7975

Two male ruffed grouse with their tails fanned.

Umatilla
Bo-Jacks Landing Restaurant, 1226 6th / 541-922-3708
Chappy's Restaurant and Lounge, 705 Willamette Avenue / 541-922-5647
Crossroads Restaurant and Service Station, 2020 Hwy 730 / 541-922-3297 / 24 hours
Nick's Italian Restaurant, 610 6th Avenue / 541-922-2572

VETERINARY CLINICS
Pendleton
Riverside Veterinary Clinic, 330 Northeast Hwy 11 / 541-276-4270 or 800-404-4270 / 24-hour emergency service / Dog boarding
Pendleton Veterinary Clinic, 1901 Southwest Court Avenue / 541-276-3141 / 24-hour emergency service / Dog boarding
Hermiston
Oregon Trail Veterinary Clinic, Hwy 395, north of Hermiston / 541-567-1138 / 24-hour emergency service
Hermiston Veterinary Clinic, 1995 South Hwy 395 / 541-567-6466 / 24-hour emergency service

DOG BOARDING
Hermiston
  Homestead Boarding Kennel, 1850 Greer Road / 541-567-5478

AUTO REPAIR
Pendleton
  Les Schwab Tire Center, 1550 Southwest Southgate / 541-276-1571 / Tires, brakes, alignment, shocks, batteries
  Andy's Auto Clinic, 375 Northeast Hwy 11 / 541-276-1030
  Comrie Auto and Truck Repair, 1510 Southgate / 541-276-1921
  West Side Repair, 124 Southeast Byers Avenue / 541-276-7164
Hermiston
  Les Schwab Tire Center, 830 North 1st / 541-567-8528 / Tires, brakes, alignment, shocks, batteries
  Cascade Automotive, 1335 North 1st / 541-567-8265
  Lopez Automotive, 1055 North 1st / 541-567-1698
  Ron's Auto and Truck Repair, 845 East Ridgeway / 541-567-8040

AUTO RENTAL
Pendleton
  Ugly Duckling Rent-A-Car, 309 Southwest Emigrant / 541-276-1498
  Hertz Rent-A-Car, 2016 Airport Road / 541-276-3183
Hermiston
  Ford Rentals (Rohrman Ford), 555 South Hwy 395 / 541-567-3291
  Rent-A-Wreck, 1835 North 1st Place / 541-567-6685

SPORTING GOODS DEALERS
Pendleton
  Barnum's Trading Post, 28 Southeast Emigrant / 541-276-3151
  Garner's Guns and Sporting Goods, 2214 Southeast Court / 541-276-7552 / Open 7 days, 7AM–11PM
  Rite Aid, 1900 Southwest Court / 541-276-7300
  Wal-Mart, 2203 Southwest Court / 541-966-9970
  Bi-Mart, 901 Southwest Emigrant / 541-276-7850
Hermiston
  Columbia Outdoor and Surplus, 395 East Main / 541-567-2080 / Guns, shotgun ammo, hunting supplies
  Wal-Mart, 1350 North 1st / 541-567-4854
  Bi-Mart, 200 South 1st Place / 541-567-6493

AIR SERVICE
  Eastern Oregon Regional Airport at Pendleton, Airport Road / 541-276-7754

MEDICAL
Pendleton
   St. Anthony Hospital, 1601 Southeast Court / 541-276-5121 or 800-826-6908
Hermiston
   Good Shepherd Community Hospital, 610 Northwest 11th / 541-567-6483

24-HOUR GAS STATIONS
Pendleton
   Indian Hills B.P., Exit 210 off I-84

TAXIDERMISTS
Pendleton
   Authentic Taxidermy Service, 214 Southwest 6th / 541-276-8331.

ATM MACHINES
Pendleton
   Bank of America, 301 South Main
   Inland Empire Bank, 125 Southeast Court
   US Bank, 105 Southwest Court
   Western Bank, 1701 Southwest Court
Hermiston
   Bank of America, 306 East Main
   US Bank, 245 Southeast 2nd

FOR MORE INFORMATION
Pendleton Chamber of Commerce
501 South Main
Pendleton OR 97801
541-276-7411 or 800-547-8911
email: pendleton@pendleton-oregon.org

Greater Hermiston Chamber of Commerce
415 South Hwy 395
P.O. Box 185
Hermiston OR 97838
541-567-6151
email: ghcc@ucinet.com

Umatilla Chamber of Commerce
1530 6th Street
Umatilla OR 97882
541-922-4825

Heppner, Condon, Mitchell, Fossil, and Spray
Morrow, Gilliam, and Wheeler Counties

County Population:
  Morrow–9,000
  Gilliam–1,900
  Wheeler–1,600
County Area:
  Morrow–2,040 sq. mi.
  Gilliam–1,223 sq. mi.
  Wheeler–1,713 sq. mi.

Heppner Population –1,500
Condon Population–830
Mitchell Population–200
Fossil Population–530
Spray Population–165
October Temperature–50°
County Acres in CRP:
  Morrow–104,501
  Gilliam–66,083
  Wheeler–6,907

Morrow and Gilliam Counties border the Columbia River on the north and then extend south into the John Day River drainage. Extensive grain agriculture provides prime habitat for pheasant, quail, and Hungarian partridge. Chukar abound as well, often feeding in the wheat stubble where fields meet canyon breaks. The John Day and its tributaries flow through desert canyons guarded by rimrock—perfect chukar habitat. Wheeler County borders the south edge of Gilliam County and lies almost entirely within the John Day drainage. Chukar are the most significant game bird in Wheeler County, but pheasant, quail, and Huns occupy appropriate habitat. Throughout this tri-county area, mourning dove flights can provide fast shooting for hunters who find the right combination of dove feeding, roosting, and watering areas.

Gilliam County offers the most acreage dedicated to the state's Upland Cooperative Access Program (UCAP), wherein private landowners allow reasonable access to their property and provide upland bird habitat in exchange for per-acre payments. The money comes from Oregon's Upland Bird Stamp program. To date, some 42,000 UCAP acres are available to hunters in Gilliam County and more still in the other Columbia Basin counties. Most of this land is the domain of pheasants, valley quail, and Hungarian partridge. Access to UCAP properties is available in two forms: Some lands are posted with "Welcome to Hunt" signs, while others bear signs indicating that interested parties must first obtain the landowner's written permission. On these latter tracts, hunters should consider visiting the owner well ahead of the forthcoming season because landowners often limit the number of permit holders to keep pressure at manageable levels.

For most Oregonians, Interstate 84 provides the quickest access to the John Day drainage and these three counties. State Route 19 heads south from I-84 at the little town of Arlington and bisects Gilliam and Wheeler Counties, while State Route 207 departs I-84 near Hermiston and leads north to Lexington and Heppner and eventually Spray and Mitchell. Several secondary highways and myriad county roads branch out across the area. The scenic Painted Hills, part of the John Day Fossil Beds National

*Jake pointing Hungarian partridge near Heppner,
with Mt. Hood in the background.*

Monument, occupy the southwest corner of Wheeler County, just north of US 26, which comes from Prineville. No large towns exist here—it is more a collection of tiny communities scattered about the high plains and canyonlands, connected by lonesome, narrow highways.

UPLAND BIRDS
Chukar Partridge, Hungarian Partridge, Ring-necked Pheasant, Valley Quail, Blue Grouse, Ruffed Grouse, Turkey, Mourning Dove, Common Snipe

WATERFOWL
Ducks and Geese

ACCOMMODATIONS
Heppner
  Northwestern Motel and RV Park, 389 North Main / 541-676-9167 / Dogs
    allowed with $5 fee / $–$$
Mitchell
  Sky Hook Motel / 541-462-3569 / Dogs allowed with $5 fee / $–$$
Fossil
  Fossil Motel and Trailer Park, 105 1st Street / 541-763-4075 / Kitchen units
    available / Dogs allowed / $

Spray
  Spray Asher Motel, Hwy 19 / 541-468-2053 / Dogs with manager's approval / $
  River Ridge Resort, Hwy 19 / 541-468-2001

RESTAURANTS
Heppner
  Kate's Pizza, 164 North Main / 541-676-5017
  Yaw's Restaurant, 176 North Main / 541-676-9489
Mitchell
  Blueberry Muffin Café, Hwy 26 / 541-462-3434
  The Sidewalk Café / 541-462-3459
Fossil
  Chica's Country Inn / 541-763-4328
  Service Creek Trading Post, Service Creek (north of Fossil) / 541-468-3331 /
    Open 7 days
  Shamrock / 541-763-4896
Spray
  Rimrock Room and Café / 541-468-2861

VETERINARIANS
Heppner
  J.W. Norene, 860 Heppner-Spray Hwy / 541-676-9656

AUTO REPAIR
Heppner
  Les Schwab Tire Center, 124 North Main / 541-676-9481 / Tires, brakes, batteries, shocks, alignment
  Dependable Auto Repair, 213 Linden Way / 541-676-9946
  Skagg's Auto Clinic, 126 East May / 541-676-5102
Spray
  Bud's Auto Repair, Hwy 19 / 541-468-2986

SPORTING GOODS
Fossil
  Wasmundt's Gun Shop, Main Street / 541-763-3041

MEDICAL
Heppner
  Pioneer Memorial Hospital, 564 North Pioneer Drive / 541-676-91337

ATM MACHINES
Heppner
  First Interstate Bank of Oregon, 111 North Main
Fossil
  First Interstate Bank of Oregon, First Street

HUNTING PRESERVES
Heppner
Treo Corporation (Heppner) / 541-676-5840

FOR MORE INFORMATION
Heppner Chamber of Commerce
111 North Main Street
Heppner, OR 97836
541-676-5536

High Desert Region

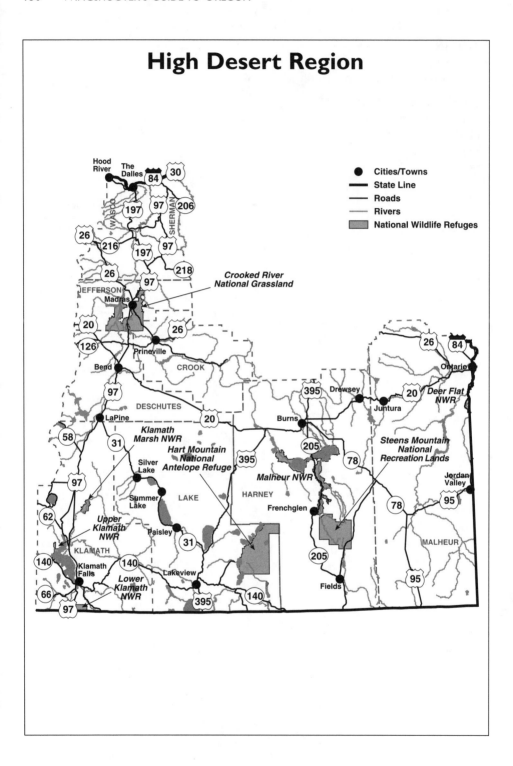

Cities/Towns
State Line
Roads
Rivers
National Wildlife Refuges

Hood River
The Dalles
84
30
197
97
SHERMAN
206
26
216
197
97
26
218
97
Crooked River National Grassland
JEFFERSON
Madras
20
26
126
Prineville
Bend
CROOK
97
DESCHUTES
395
Drewsey
26
84
Ontario
20
Deer Flat NWR
Juntura
LaPine
20
Burns
58
31
Klamath Marsh NWR
Silver Lake
Hart Mountain National Antelope Refuge
395
205
78
Steens Mountain National Recreation Lands
Jordan Valley
97
Summer Lake
LAKE
HARNEY
Malheur NWR
95
62
Upper Klamath NWR
Paisley
31
Frenchglen
78
95
KLAMATH
140
MALHEUR
140
Klamath Falls
140
Lakeview
205
66
Lower Klamath NWR
395
Fields
95
97
140

High Desert Region

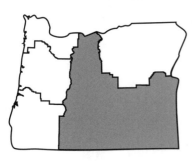

The expansive High Desert Region reaches from the Columbia River (Wasco and Sherman Counties) south to the California border and east to the Idaho border. As one would expect from such a huge geographical division, the High Desert Region offers myriad wingshooting opportunities, including some of the state's best chukar, quail, and waterfowl hunting.

The southeast corner of the state—Lake, Malheur, and Harney Counties—is especially noted for it wingshooting opportunities. Chukar thrive in the numerous remote desert canyons and along the impressive fault-block rims of the Steens Mountains, Hart Mountain, and Abert Rim. Chukar hunters, in fact, can explore long popular and productive places such as Succor Creek, the Lower Owyhee Canyon, and along the Malheur River. The more adventurous can seek their quarry in countless remote and seldom visited canyons where small streams feed their meager flows to larger rivers that supply the lifeblood of the region's grazing and agricultural economy.

Far to the northwest, the Deschutes River and John Day River carve massive canyons out of the sage desert, providing further chukar habitat. In fact, the Lower Deschutes River speeds through its precipitous canyon for nearly 100 miles, from its confinement at Pelton Dam to its confluence with the Columbia. In addition to some of the state's—and the country's—finest chukar hunting, the High Desert Region offers a bounty of valley quail, along with pheasants, Hungarian partridge, doves, and sage grouse.

Nowhere in Oregon, in fact, are sage grouse populations as strong as those in the remote reaches of Lake, Harney, and Malheur Counties. Traditionally, Oregon's sage grouse season is arranged as a tag-draw system, wherein successful applicants abide by a season running only a few days and carrying a bag limit, typically, of two birds. The wings must be turned in to collection centers so biologists can further study these unique indigenous game birds.

In addition to widespread opportunities for upland bird hunting, the High Desert Region offers some of the state's best waterfowling at Summer Lake Wildlife Area in Lake County, Upper Klamath Lake in Klamath County, and Malheur National Wildlife Refuge in Harney County. All of these wetlands boast a large list of duck and goose species, including Canada geese, white-fronted geese, and snow geese.

High Desert Region
Ruffed Grouse Distribution

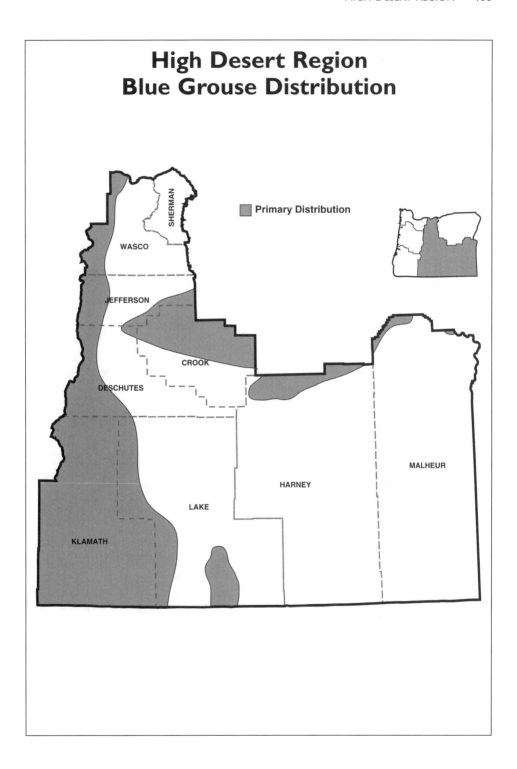

High Desert Region
Blue Grouse Distribution

Primary Distribution

SHERMAN

WASCO

JEFFERSON

CROOK

DESCHUTES

MALHEUR

HARNEY

LAKE

KLAMATH

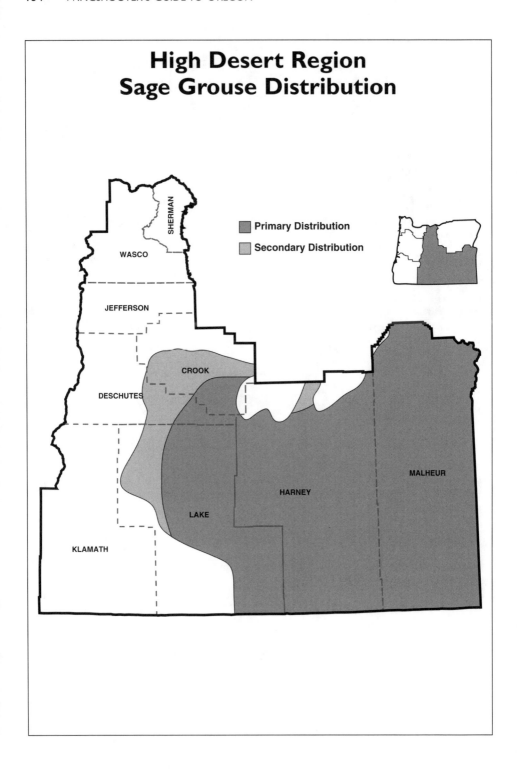

High Desert Region
Sage Grouse Distribution

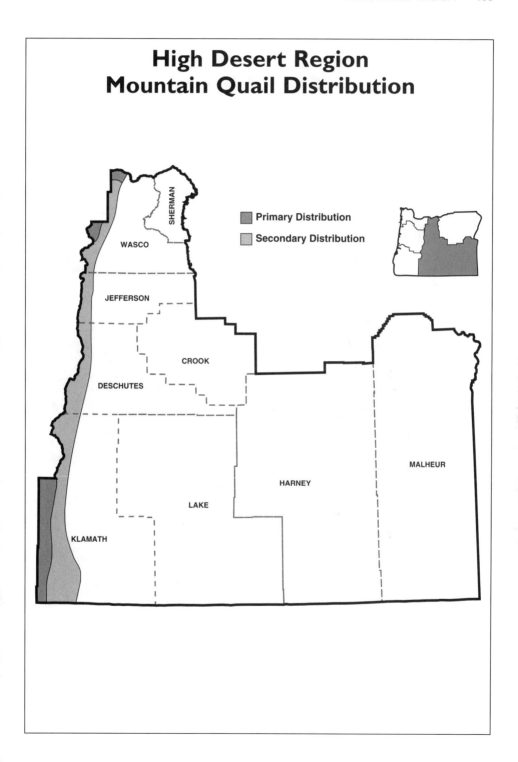

High Desert Region
Mountain Quail Distribution

High Desert Region
Valley Quail Distribution

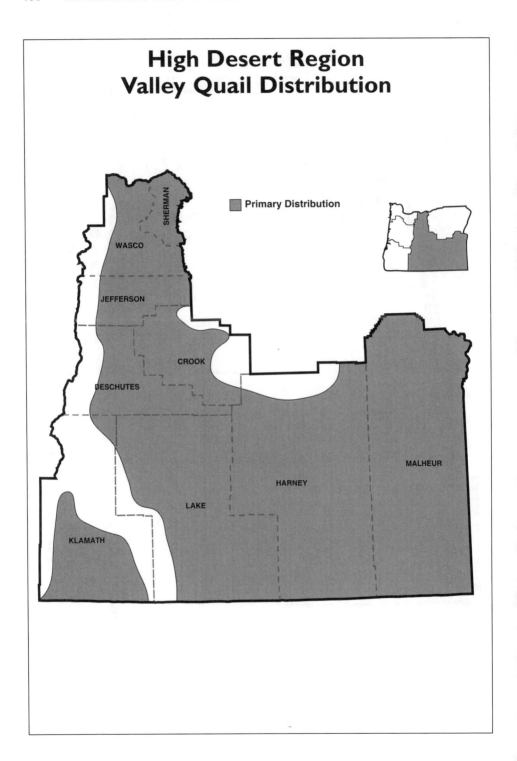

Primary Distribution

SHERMAN

WASCO

JEFFERSON

CROOK

DESCHUTES

MALHEUR

HARNEY

LAKE

KLAMATH

High Desert Region
Chukar Partridge Distribution

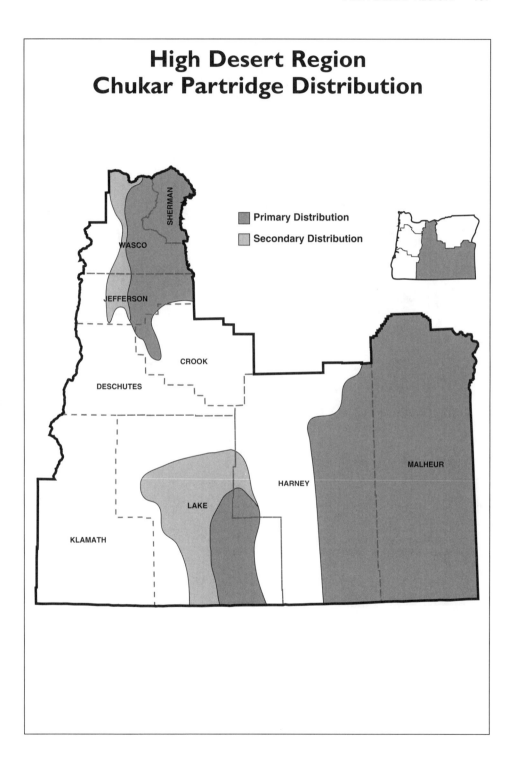

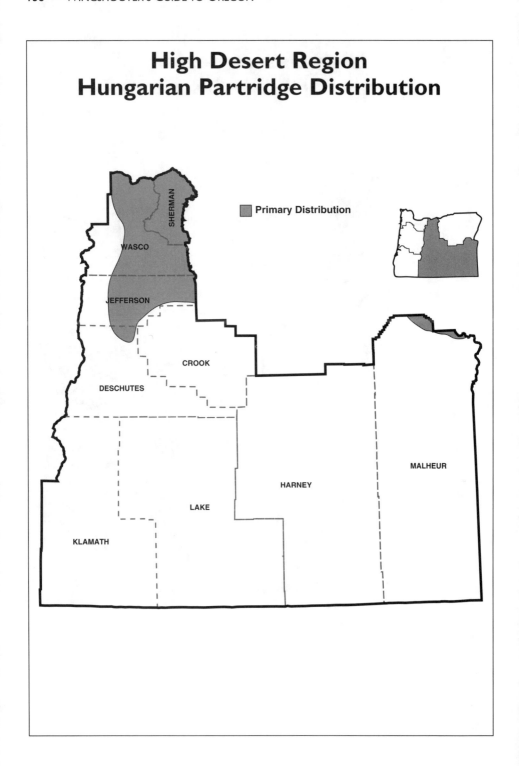

High Desert Region
Hungarian Partridge Distribution

Primary Distribution

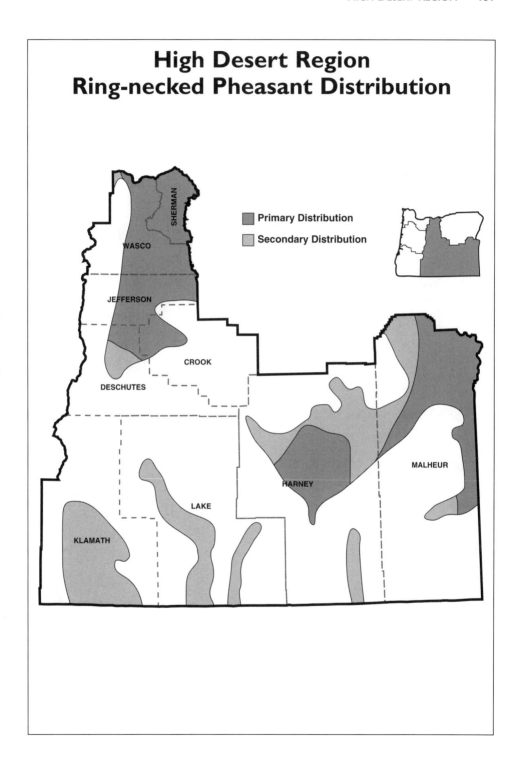

High Desert Region
Ring-necked Pheasant Distribution

High Desert Region
Wild Turkey Distribution

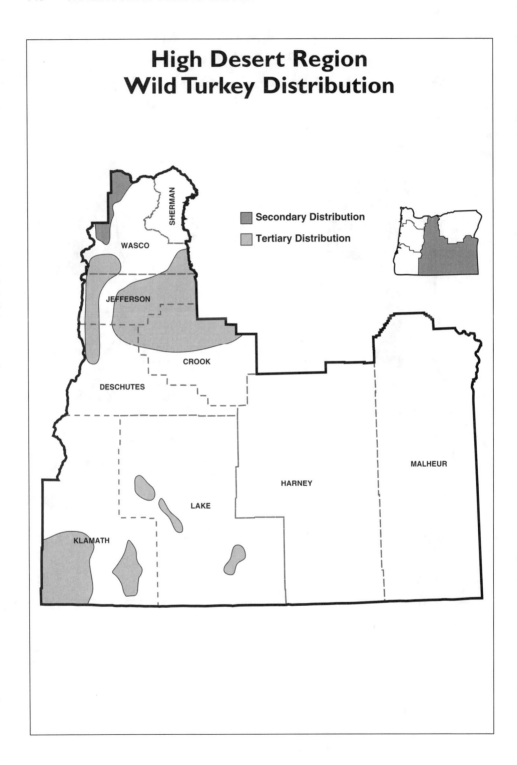

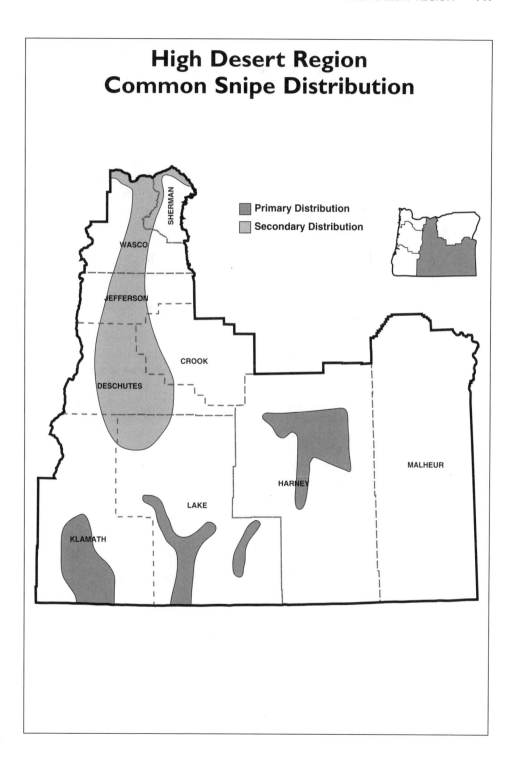

High Desert Region
Common Snipe Distribution

Primary Distribution
Secondary Distribution

SHERMAN

WASCO

JEFFERSON

CROOK

DESCHUTES

MALHEUR

HARNEY

LAKE

KLAMATH

Ontario/Juntura and Jordan Valley
Malheur County

County Population–28,700	Ontario Population–10,680
County Area–9,926 sq. mi.	Jordan Valley Population–390
County Acres in CRP–0	October Temperature–50°

Oregon's second-largest county forms a lengthy boundary with Idaho, from the Nevada line all the way to the Snake River at Farewell Bend north of Ontario. The county's geography varies considerably, from the intensely farmed agricultural lands in the Malheur Valley around Vale and Ontario to the dramatic desert gorges of the expansive Owyhee River drainage in the south. Bird hunting is equally diverse and includes some of the state's best opportunity for chukar, pheasant, valley quail, and doves.

Malheur County also boasts what is arguably the state's most remote hideaway: the extreme southeast corner of Oregon, drained by the little known West Little Owyhee and East Fork Owyhee Rivers, whose sheer canyons defy all but the hardiest and most adventurous of desert travelers. These two branches of the Owyhee converge some 50 miles south of the little town of Jordan Valley.

Eventually, the Owyhee River is backed up by a dam into 40-mile-long Owyhee Reservoir, where chukar enthusiasts, traveling by boat, can reach remote side canyons. Below Owyhee Dam, the river flows through a dozen more miles of prime and popular chukar habitat. Succor Creek, which flows south to north near the Idaho border (east of the Owyhee), provides an additional popular and easily accessible haunt for chukar hunters. Meanwhile, the Malheur River bisects the north half of the county, providing significant habitat for chukar, quail, pheasant, and waterfowl.

French trappers, whose furs and supplies were stolen from their riverside camp, applied the name "Riviere au Malheur" (Unfortunate River), which later became Malheur River and provided the county its name. Today, some 94 percent of Malheur County is classified as rangeland, some two-thirds of which is administered by BLM.

UPLAND BIRDS
Chukar Partridge, Valley Quail, Ring-necked Pheasant, Hungarian Partridge, Sage Grouse, Blue Grouse, Mourning Dove, Common Snipe

WATERFOWL
Ducks and Geese (Canada, Snow, White-fronted, Ross')

ACCOMMODATIONS
Ontario
  Best Western Inn, 251 Goodfellow Street / 541-889-2600 or 800-828-0364 / 61 units / Dogs allowed / $$
  Budget Colonial Inn, 1395 Tapadera Avenue / 541-889-9615 / 84 units / Dogs allowed / $–$$

Budget Inn, 1737 North Oregon Street / 541-889-3101 or 800-905-0024 / 26 units / Dogs allowed / $$–$$$

Carlile Motel, 589 North Oregon Street / 541-889-8658 / 19 units / Dogs allowed / $–$$

Holiday Inn, 1249 Tapadera Avenue / 541-889-8621 / 100 units / Dogs allowed / $$$

Holiday Motor Inn, 615 East Idaho Avenue / 541-889-9188 / 73 units / Dogs allowed / $–$$

Motel 6, 275 Northeast 12th Street / 541-889-6617 / 126 units / Dogs allowed / $–$$

Oregon Trail Motel, 92 East Idaho Avenue / 541-889-8633 / 30 units / Dogs allowed / $–$$$

Plaza Motel, 1144 Southwest 4th Avenue / 541-889-9641 / 20 units / $–$$

Stockman's Motel, 266 Goodfellow Street / 541-889-8282 / 28 units / $$

Oasis Motel, Hwy 20 (Juntura) / 541-277-3605 / Dogs allowed in kennels with manager's approval and $3 fee / $

Jordan Valley

Sahara Motel, Hwy 95 / 541-586-2500 or 2501 / Dogs allowed with $5 fee / $–$$

Basque Station Motel, Hwy 95 / 541-586-2373

CAMPGROUNDS AND RV PARKS

Ontario

Country Campground, 2 miles west of Airport Corner / 541-889-6042

Malheur County Fairgrounds, 795 Northwest 9th Street / 541-889-3431

Oasis Campground, 6170 Hwy 201 / 541-262-3365

RESTAURANTS

Ontario

Casa Jaramillo, 157 Southeast 2nd / 541-889-9258 / Lunch and dinner Tues–Sun / Authentic Mexican cuisine

Alexander's on the River, 1930 Southeast 5th Street / 541-889-8070 / Steak and seafood

Cheyenne Social Club, 111 Southwest 1st Street / 541-889-3777 / Steak and seafood

Country Kitchen, 1249 Tapadera Avenue / 541-889-3941 / Family dining

Denny's Restaurant, 76 Goodfellow / 541-889-7802 / Open 24 hours

Fiesta Guadalaraja, 336 South Oregon Street / 541-889-8064 / Mexican cuisine

Rusty's Pancake and Steak House, 14 Northwest 1st Street / 541-889-2700

Sizzler, 830 Southeast 1st Avenue / 541-889-5005

Jordan Valley

Old Basque Inn, Hwy 95 / 541-586-2298 / Specializing in Basque cuisine

JV Café and Bar, Hwy 95 / 541-586-7982

Oasis Restaurant, Hwy 20 (Juntura) / 541-277-3605 / Open 7AM–9PM

VETERINARY CLINICS
Ontario
  The Pet Care Center, 2280 Southwest 4th Avenue / 541-889-7776 /
    24-hour emergency number same / Dog boarding available
  Ontario Animal Hospital, 2514 Southwest 4th Avenue / 541-889-2333 / 24-hour
    emergency number same / Dog boarding available

DOG BOARDING SERVICES
Ontario
  Atherton Kennels, 3616 Hwy 201 / 541-889-5045
  Calhoun Kennels, 2814 Alameda Drive / 541-889-4646

AUTO REPAIR
Ontario
  Art's Service, Inc., 1585 Southwest 4th / 541-889-5811 or 800-697-2494 / Towing
    service
  Gentry Ford, Inc., 1802 Southwest 4th / 541-889-9694 or 800-767-4510
  Ady Chevrolet, 1701 Southwest 4th / 541-889-7272
  Claire's Automotive, 78 Southwest 5th / 541-889-2664
  Dennis Dillon Auto and Truck Center, 1805 Southwest 4th / 541-889-1391
Jordan Valley
  Jim's Texaco, Hwy 95 / 541-586-2373

AUTO RENTAL
Ontario
  Gentry Ford, Inc., 1802 Southwest 4th / 541-889-5811 or 800-697-2494

24-HOUR GAS STATIONS
Ontario
  Ontario Chevron, 1218 Southwest 4th

SPORTING GOODS DEALERS
Ontario
  Cambo's Outdoorsman, 532 East Idaho Avenue / 541-889-3135
  Rite Aid, 1430 Westpark Plaza / 541-889-3184
  Bi-Mart, 2283 Southwest 4th Avenue / 541-889-2141

AIR SERVICE
Ontario
  Cirrus Air LLC / 541-889-4120

MEDICAL
Ontario
  Holy Rosary Medical Center, 351 Southwest 9th / 541-881-7000
  Physicians Primary Care Center, 335 Southwest 13th / 541-889-8410
Jordan Valley
  Jordan Valley Health Clinic, Hwy 95 / 541-586-2422 / Open Tues–Thurs

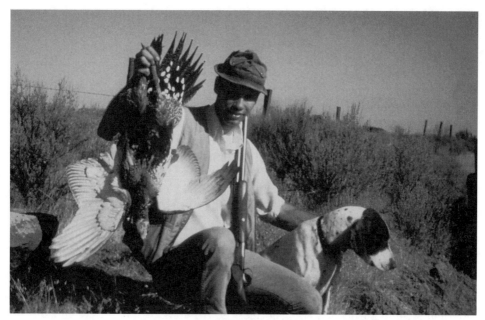

Hunter with sage grouse.

24-HOUR GAS STATIONS
Ontario
Pilot Travel Center, 653 East Idaho Avenue / 541-889-9070
Jackson's Food Store, Inc., 1320 West Idaho Avenue / 541-889-5015

ATM MACHINES
Ontario
Wells Fargo, 189 Southwest 1st
US Bank, 281 Southwest 1st
Western Bank, 319 Southwest 4th
Malheur Federal Credit Union, 505 Sunset Drive
Bank of America, 1094 Southwest 4th
Pioneer Bank, 225 Southwest 4th

LOCAL/REGIONAL BIRD-HUNTING GUIDES
Ontario
High Lonesome Hunts (Mike Schaffeld), 4733 John Day Hwy (Vale) / 541-473-2916

FOR MORE INFORMATION
Ontario Chamber of Commerce
88 Southwest 3rd Avenue
Ontario, OR 97914-2722
541-889-8012
email: ontvcb@micron.net

Burns (Frenchglen, Fields, and Drewsey)
Harney County

County Population–7,500	Burns Population–3,015
County Area–10,228 sq. mi.	October Temperature–47°
County Acres in CRP–0	

The largest and least-populated county in Oregon, Harney boasts a ratio of less than one person per square mile of land. Harney County also offers a preponderance of public lands where chukar and quail abound. The county's arid geography includes sprawling Harney and Malheur Lakes—huge, shallow desert sump lakes whose water level varies considerably from decade to decade. Malheur National Wildlife Refuge encompasses much of these lakes, which support huge numbers of nesting and migrating waterfowl and wading birds.

Massive fault-block mountain ranges dominate the south half of the county. The Steens Mountains rise gradually from the west only to fall abruptly away to the east, leaving an awe-inspiring 5,000-foot escarpment shadowing the mirage-filled Alvord Desert. Just south of the Steens, whose highest reach measures 9,670 feet, the Pueblo Mountains climb to heights of 8,500 feet. Both mountain ranges are marked by numerous side canyons where chukar abound.

The county seat of Burns straddles US 20 in the northern tier of Harney County, providing all necessary services. Otherwise, travelers to this county must rely on the scant services available in tiny villages such as Fields, Frenchglen, and Drewsey.

UPLAND BIRDS
Chukar Partridge, Valley Quail, Ring-necked Pheasant, Sage Grouse, Blue Grouse, Mourning Dove, and Common Snipe

WATERFOWL
Ducks and Geese (Canada, Snow, White-fronted, Ross')

ACCOMMODATIONS
Ponderosa Best Western, 577 West Monroe / 541-573-2047 / 52 Units / Dogs allowed with $10 refundable deposit / Continental breakfast / $$–$$$

Royal Inn, 999 Oregon Avenue / 541-573-5293 / 44 units / Dogs allowed with $20 refundable deposit / $$–$$$

✓**Bontemps Motel**, 74 West Monroe / 541-573-2037 or 800-229-1394 / 15 units, 4 kitchenettes / Dogs allowed with $10 refundable deposit / $$–$$$

Orbit Motel, Hwy 20/395 North / 541-573-2034 / 31 units, 1 kitchenette / Dogs allowed / $–$$

Horton House Guest House, 191 West C Street / 541-573-1687 / 2 units / No dogs / Continental breakfast / Kitchen facility / $$

Hershey and Daryl locked on a covey of birds.

✓ **Sage Country Inn Bed and Breakfast**, 351½ West Monroe / 541-573-7243 / 4 units / Dogs allowed in kennel only / Full country gourmet breakfast included / $$$

✓ **Lone Pine Guest Ranch**, Lone Pine Road / 541-573-2103 / 2 rooms with private baths, fireplace, kitchenettes, queen beds / Dogs allowed at discretion of proprietor / Breakfast included / $$$

✓ **Blue Bucket Inn Bed and Breakfast**, HCR 68 537 (Drewsey) / 541-493-2240 / 2 rooms / No dogs / Full country breakfast included; other meals available / $$$

FRENCHGLEN ACCOMMODATIONS/RESTAURANTS/SUPPLIES

Frenchglen Hotel / 541-493-2825 / 8 units / $$–$$$ / Open through Nov. 15 / Reservations recommended / Dinner served family style, 6:30 nightly / Breakfast, 6AM–9:30AM / Lunch seated or packed

Steens Mountain Resort and RV Park, Frenchglen / 541-493-2415 / 98 units (full, partial and tent-sites) / 5 cabins/1 trailer / $–$$ / Open all year / Laundry facilities / General store (shotgun ammo available)

Page Springs Campground (BLM)

Frenchglen Mercantile / 541-493-2738

Fields Accommodations/Restaurants/Supplies

Fields Store and Restaurant / 541-495-2275 / Restaurant and store open 8AM–6PM after end of October; 9AM–5PM on Sunday / Gas, diesel and propane available / 3 motel units, each with two double beds ($), plus one 5-bed room ($75 night) / Alvord Hot Springs located 24 miles north

Campgrounds and RV Parks

RV Village, 1273 Seneca Drive / 800-573-7640 / 47 trailer sites; no tents / Small dogs only / Open through November 15

Harney County Fairgrounds, South Egan Street (Fairgrounds Road) / 541-573-6852 or 541-573-6166 / 13 RV hookups plus tent sites / Open all year

Malheur Field Station, 28 miles south of Burns off Hwy 205 near the Malheur Refuge Headquarters / 541-493-2629 / 9 RV sites, no tent camping / Open through November

Crystal-Crane Hotsprings, 25 miles east of Burns on Hwy 78 / 541-493-2312 / 5 cabins ($30/night); 6 RV sites with partial hookups; 5 tent sites; 6 private hot tubs

Restaurants

Pine Room Restaurant and Lounge, 543 West Monroe / 541-573-6631 / Open 5PM–10PM; lounge until 2AM / Specializing in steak and seafood dishes

Apple Peddler Restaurant, 540 Hwy 20 North / 541-573-2820 / Open 24 hours

The Elk Horn Restaurant and Linda's Thai Food, 457 North Broadway / 541-573-3201 / Open 9AM–2PM and 4:30PM–10PM (closed Tuesdays) / Thai food menu served Mondays and Thursdays

Worst Food in Oregon, Hwy 20 (Hines) / 541-573-3760 / Open Mon–Sat 6AM–2PM / Big, hearty breakfasts and lunches at 1970s prices

Broadway Deli, 530 North Broadway / 541-573-7020 / Mon–Sat 8AM–4PM / Deli sandwiches made to specs

Veterinarians/Dog Boarding

Harney County Veterinary Clinic, 1050 Crane Boulevard / 541-573-6450 / 24-hour emergency pager number: 573-0101 / Mon–Fri 8:30AM–5:30PM, Sat 9AM–12NOON / Dog boarding available

Auto Repair

Ruel Teague Motors, 82 South Harney / 541-573-2863 / Open Mon–Fri 8AM–5:30PM, Sat 8AM–12:30pm / GMC, Chrysler, Plymouth, Dodge, Jeep sales and service

Burns Ford, Inc., 188 North Broadway / 541-573-6014 / Open Mon–Fri 8AM–6PM, Sat 8AM–1PMt

L.R. Swarthout, 19 West Monroe / 541-573-6316 / Open Mon–Fri 8AM–6PM

Auto Rental

Ruel Teague Motors, 82 South Harney / 541-573-2863

24-HOUR GAS STATIONS
The Truck Stop, Hwy 20 (Hines) / Auto diesel available

SPORTING GOODS DEALERS
B and B Sporting Goods, Inc., 104 Conley Avenue, Hwy 20 (Hines) / 541-573-6200 / Shotgun supplies, some gun dog supplies

AIR SERVICE
Burns Airport, Airport Road off Hwy 78 south of town / 541-573-6139 / No airlines; for charter service, contact Ruel Teague Charter Service / 541-573-2863

MEDICAL
Harney District Hospital, 557 West Washington / 541-573-7281

ATM MACHINES
Klamath First Federal Bank, 293 North Broadway
US Bank, 493 North Broadway (and U-bank inside Safeway at 246 West Monroe)
The Truck Stop, Hwy 20 (Hines)

SHOTGUN RANGES
Burns Butte Sportsman Range, 2.5 miles on Forest Road 47 from US 20 in Hines / 541-573-7122 / Trap, sporting clays

REGIONAL BIRD HUNTING GUIDES/OUTFITTERS
Broken Trails Guide Service, P.O. Box 386, Burns 97720 / 541-573-7262 / Broken265@aol.com
Steens Mountain Packers, Hwy 205, Frenchglen, 97736 / 800-977-3995 / Info@steensmountain.com

Lakeview and Paisley (Summer Lake/Silver Lake)
Lake County

County Population–7,550	Lakeview Population–2,640
County Area–8,359 sq. mi.	Paisley Population–365
County Acres in CRP–3,907	October Temperature–48°

Wingshooters flock to Lake County to hunt Summer Lake, one of Oregon's premier waterfowl hotspots. Summer Lake Wildlife Area borders the larger Summer Lake National Wildlife Refuge, an important breeding and staging area for ducks, geese, swans, and shorebirds. Shallow throughout, sprawling Summer Lake occupies a broad basin guarded on the west by dramatic Winter Ridge. The springfed Ana River and many smaller springs feed Summer Lake, which has no outside drainage. The water simply evaporates. Drought cycles substantially reduce the surface area of the lake, and wet seasons have the opposite effect.

The Summer Lake Basin is but one of several dramatic desert landscapes in Lake County. Abert Rim, another of southeast Oregon's huge fault-block escarpments, rises thousands of feet above the desert north of Lakeview. Abert Rim slopes away gently to the east, yielding to the Warner Valley, where a series of large sump lakes rise and fall with the whims of seasonal water cycles and to the east of this valley, 8,065-foot Warner Peak and 7,710-foot Hart Mountain climb high above the surrounding desert, most of which is encompassed by the Hart Mountain National Antelope Refuge.

Chukar inhabit all of this country where suitable habitat exists, and valley quail occupy suburban and agricultural areas. Though not particularly numerous, pheasants live in the agricultural areas of Summer Lake and around Lakeview. The eastern half of the county features some of the state's most productive sage grouse hunting units, and forest grouse (blue and ruffed) occupy the timbered slopes of Lake County's western edge.

UPLAND BIRDS
Chukar Partridge, Valley Quail, Ring-necked Pheasant, Sage Grouse, Blue Grouse, Ruffed Grouse, Mourning Dove, Turkey, and Common Snipe

WATERFOWL
Ducks and Geese (Canada, Snow, White-fronted, Ross')

ACCOMMODATIONS
Lakeview

Best Western Skykine Motor Lodge, 414 North G Street / 541-947-2194 / Dogs allowed / $$–$$$

Lakeview Lodge Motel, 301 North G Street / 541-947-2181 / 40 units / Dogs allowed / $–$$

Summer Lake Wildlife Area during "bluebird" weather.

Interstate-8 Motel, 354 North K Street / 541-947-3341 / Dogs allowed / $$
AA Motel, 411 North F Street / 541-947-2201 / Dogs allowed / $$
Rim Rock Motel, 727 South F Street / 541-947-2185 / Kitchen units available /
   Dogs allowed / $–$$
Paisley
Miles Motel, 302 Hwy 31 / 541-943-3148 / No Dogs / Kitchenettes available / $
Summer Lake Motel, 37580 Hwy 31 (Summer Lake) / 541-943-3164 / Dogs
   allowed / $–$$
Summer Lake Bed and Breakfast Inn, 31501 Hwy 31 (Summer Lake) /
   541-943-3983 or 800-261-2778 / Dogs allowed / $$–$$$
Silver lake Mercantile and Motel, Hwy 31 (Silver Lake) / 541-576-2131 / Dogs
   allowed / $

RV PARKS/CAMPGROUNDS
Lakeview
Hunter's Hot Springs Resort, Hwy 395 N / 541-947-2125
Mile High Trailer and RV Park, 764 North H Street / 541-947-2232

Paisley
  Summer Lake Hot Springs, Hwy 31 / 541-943-3931
  Horse Ranch RV Park, HC61, Box 1463 (Silver Lake) / 541-576-2488
  Summer Lake Wildlife Management Area (Summer Lake) / No hookups

RESTAURANTS
Lakeview
  Hunter's Hot Springs Resort, Hwy 395 North / 541-947-2125
  Jerry's Restaurant, 508 North 2nd / 541-947-2600 / 24-hour
  The Landing, Hwy 395 North / 541-947-5225
  Mom's Corner Café, 930 South F Street / 541-947-5044
  Papa Dan's Pizza and Mexican Food, 1217 North 4th / 541-947-2248
Paisley
  Cowboy Dinner Tree Restaurant, South Hager Mt. Road (Silver Lake) /
    541-576-2426 / Open Fri–Sun 5PM–9PM / Regionally renowned for hearty
    ranch-style dinners
  Desert Café and Bar, Hwy 31 (Silver Lake) / 541-576-2221 / Lake County's
    largest beer list
  Dinner Bell Deli, Hwy 31 (Silver Lake) / 541-576-2379
  Summer Lake Restaurant, 36980 Hwy 31 (Summer Lake) / 541-943-3994

VETERINARIANS
Lakeview
  Lakeview Animal Hospital, 1733 North 4th / 541-947-3383 / Mon–Fri
    8:30AM–5:30PM, Sat 9AM–11AM / 24-hour emergency service available
  Nunn Veterinary Clinic, Hwy 395 South / 541-947-4946

SPORTING GOODS
Paisley
  Summer Lake Store, 37580 Hwy 31 (Summer Lake) / 541-943-3164 / Shotgun
    ammo

AUTO REPAIR
Lakeview
  Les Schwab Tire Center, 422 North F / 541-947-3388 / Tires, brakes, alignment,
    shocks, batteries
  Auto Works, 921 North 4th / 541-947-4748
  JB's Transmission and Auto Repair, 1206 South G Street / 541-947-2790
  Max's Garage, 276 North P Street / 541-947-3550
  Mike's Automotive Service, 231 North V Street / 541-947-3970
Paisley
  Chewaucan Garage, 433 Hwy 31 / 541-943-3124

AIR SERVICE
Lakeview
  Lake County Airport/Goose Lake Aviation / 541-947-4222

MEDICAL
Lakeview
Lake District Hospital, 700 South J Street / 541-947-2114

TAXIDERMISTS
Lakeview
Great Basin Taxidermy, 314 South H Street / 541-947-4271

ATM MACHINES
Lakeview
Klamath First Federal Bank, 1 Southeast First Street
U.S. National Bank, 518 North First Street
South Valley Bank and Trust, 215 North G Street

FOR MORE INFORMATION
Lake County Chamber of Commerce
126 North E Street
Lakeview, OR 97630
(541) 947-6040
email: lakeview@triax.com

Klamath Falls
Klamath County

County Population–61,600	Klamath Falls Population–18,940
County Area–6,135 sq. mi.	October Temperature–49°
County Acres in CRP–213	

Dominated by massive Upper Klamath and Agency Lakes, Klamath County understandably boasts some of the state's best waterfowl hunting. The Klamath Basin National Wildlife Refuge Complex encompasses some 144,700 acres in California and Oregon. On the Oregon side, the Upper Klamath and Klamath Marsh National Wildlife Refuges span 14,400 acres and 37,600 acres, respectively. Much of the available hunting area is accessible only by boat. The Klamath Basin also offers plenty for the upland hunter. Pheasant exist in fair numbers wherever suitable habitat occurs, and valley quail are common. Blue grouse and ruffed grouse occupy the mountains surrounding the basin. Mourning doves and common snipe provide additional opportunities.

The town of Klamath Falls offers a wide array of services and accommodations, including some first-class restaurants, a natural result of having a college located within the city (Southern Oregon University). US 97 runs north to south through the basin, skirting the lengthy eastern shoreline of sprawling Upper Klamath Lake. Several major rivers drain the area, including the Williamson and Wood Rivers, which feed Klamath Lake.

UPLAND BIRDS
Chukar Partridge, Valley Quail, Ring-necked Pheasant, Hungarian Partridge, Sage Grouse, Blue Grouse, Ruffed Grouse, Mourning Dove, Turkey, and Common Snipe

WATERFOWL
Ducks and Geese (Canada, Snow, White-fronted, Ross')

ACCOMMODATIONS
A-1 Budget Motel, 3844 Hwy 97 North / 541-884-8104 / Dogs allowed / $$
Cimarron Motor Inn, 3060 South 6th / 541-882-4601 / Dogs allowed / $–$$
Econo Lodge, 75 Main Street / 541-884-7735 / Dogs allowed / $–$$
Golden West Motel, 6402 South 6th / 541-882-1758 / Dogs allowed with manager's approval / Weekly rates available / $–$$
High Chaparral Motor Lodge, 5440 Hwy 97 North / 541-882-4675 / Dogs allowed
La Vista Motel, 3939 Hwy 97 North / 541-882-8844 / Dogs allowed
Motel 6, 5136 South 6th / 541-884-2110 / Dogs allowed / $–$$

*Male ruffed
grouse on his
"drumming stump."*

RV Parks/Campgrounds

Greensprings RV Park, Greensprings Drive / 541-882-0823
Lakeside Mobile Home and RV Park, 4885 Wocus Road / 541-884-1724
Oregon 8 RV Park, 5225 Hwy 97 North / 541-882-0482 / Tent sites

Restaurants

Chez Nous, 3927 South 6th / 541-883-8719 / Continental cuisine
Schatzie's Gasthof, 3200 Hwy 97 North / 541-883-8650 / German cuisine
Sergio's, 430 Main Street / 541-883-8454 / Mexican
Fiorella's Italian Ristorante, 6139 Simmers Avenue / 541-882-1878
Saddle Rock Café and Pub, 1012 Main Street / 541-883-3970
Mollie's Restaurant and Lounge, 3817 Hwy 97 North / 541-882-9591 / 24-hour

Veterinary Clinics

Companion Pet Clinic, 2343 Gettle Street / 541-882-7674
Klamath Animal Clinic, 2726 South 6th / 541-882-8854 / 24-hour emergency
service available / Dog boarding available

Everett Animal Hospital, 632 Oak Avenue / 541-884-2926 / 24-hour emergency service available

Basin Animal Clinic, 1776 Washburn Way / 541-884-4558 / 24-hour emergency: 882-9005 / Dog boarding available

DOG BOARDING SERVICES

Double C's K9 Bed and Breakfast, 4141 Washburn Way / 541-882-5959

Klamath Critter Sitter, 2147 Arthur / 541-884-1640

AUTO REPAIR

Les Schwab Tire Center, 5757 South 6th / 541-882-6623 / Tires, brakes, alignment, shocks, batteries

ATW Automotive and Transmission, 3425 Homedale Road / 541-884-2208 or 885-8008

Beacon Auto and Truck Repair, 1201 East Main / 541-884-8304

East Main Auto and 4X4 Repair, corner of Main and Darrow / 541-882-4850

Ground Effects Auto Repair, 1616 Ivory / 541-884-3462

K-Falls Auto Service, Inc., 2108 Washburn Way / 541-883-7676

AUTO RENTAL

Budget Car Rental, Klamath Falls Airport / 541-885-5421 or 800-527-0700

Harvest Ford Rent-A-Car, Klamath Falls Airport / 541-850-8252

Hertz, Klamath Falls Airport / 541-882-0220 or 800-654-3131

Avis, Klamath Falls Airport / 541-882-7232 or 800-831-2847

Toyota Rent-A-Car, 3267 Washburn Way / 541-882-8837

SPORTING GOODS

All Season's Sports, 714 Main Street / 541-884-3863

Big R Ranch, Farm and Home Supply, 6225 South 6th / 541-882-5548

Chris' Gun Den, 1124 East Main Street / 541-884-1642

Parker's Rod and Gun Rack, 7364 South 6th Street / 541-883-3726

Bi-Mart, 1920 Washburn Way / 541-884-1751

AIR SERVICE

Klamath Falls Municipal Airport / 541-883-5372

MEDICAL

Merle West Medical Center, 2865 Daggett Avenue / 541-882-6311

FOR MORE INFORMATION

Klamath County Chamber of Commerce
701 Plum Avenue
Klamath Falls OR 97601-6031
(541) 884-5193
email: klamcham@cdsnet.net

Bend, Prineville, and Madras
Deschutes, Jefferson, and Crook Counties

County Population:	Bend Population–35,635
Deschutes–98,000	Prineville Population–6,920
Jefferson–16,900	Madras Population–5,005
Crook–15,900	County Acres in CRP:
County Area:	Deschutes–0
Deschutes–3,055 sq. mi.	Jefferson–11,481
Jefferson–1,791 sq. mi.	Crook–721
Crook–2,991 sq. mi.	October Temperature–48°

Deschutes and Jefferson are transition counties, their western boundaries running along the crest of the Cascade Range, where steep, timbered ridges provide ideal blue grouse habitat. Ruffed grouse live along the stream bottoms and springs. As the elevation drops going east, however, the rain-shadow effect of the mountains becomes increasingly evident. Ponderosa pines replace the Douglas fir / true fir / hemlock forests of the higher slopes and in turn the sagebrush / juniper steppe habitat predominates as you move east past the Metolius River drainage.

Most of Deschutes, Jefferson, and Crook Counties fall within this habitat, dominated—in its natural state—by sagebrush and juniper. Extensive irrigated agriculture, however, has replaced much of the range and at the same time provided habitat for valley quail, pheasant, Hungarian partridge, and doves. Chukar inhabit the canyons of the Crooked River near Prineville.

Deschutes County is growing faster than any other county in Oregon, with most of the population increase occurring in and around Bend and Redmond. Because of its booming tourism industry, Bend offers numerous fine restaurants, along with a multitude of lodging options. US 97 traverses the area from north to south and, through Bend, is said to be Oregon's busiest street.

UPLAND BIRDS
Chukar Partridge, Valley Quail, Ring-necked Pheasant, Hungarian Partridge, Sage Grouse, Blue Grouse, Ruffed Grouse, Mourning Dove, Turkey, and Common Snipe

WATERFOWL
Ducks and Geese (Canada, Snow, White-fronted, Ross')

ACCOMMODATIONS
Bend

Alpine West Lodge, 61440 South Hwy 97 / 541-389-0250 / Dogs allowed / $–$$
Westward Ho Motel, 904 South Hwy 97 / 541-382-2111 / Dogs allowed / $–$$
Plaza Motel, 1430 Northwest Hill / 541-382-1621 / Dogs allowed / $–$$

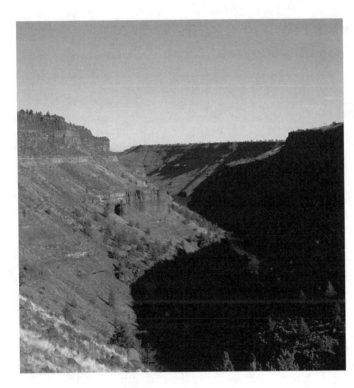

The Deschutes River Canyon is good chukar country.

Chalet Motel, 510 Southeast 3rd / 541-382-6124 / Dogs allowed / $–$$

Bend Riverside Motel, 1565 Northwest Hill / 541-389-2363 / Dogs allowed / $$–$$$

There are many more hotels and motels available in Bend.

Prineville

Carolina Motel, 1050 East 3rd / 541-447-4152 / 26 units / 10 full kitchen units / Small dogs with fee / $–$$$

City Center Motel, 509 East 3rd / 541-447-5522 / 20 units / Small dogs allowed / $–$$

Ochoco Inn, 123 East 3rd / 541-447-6231 / 47 units / 4 kitchen units / Small dogs with fee / $–$$

Rustlers Roost, 960 West 3rd / 541-447-4185 / 20 units / 8 kitchen units / Small dogs with fee / $$

Madras

Best Western Rama Inn, 12 Southwest 4th / 541-475-6141 or 800-528-1234 / Dogs allowed with $10 fee / $$–$$$

Budget Inn, 133 Northeast 5th / 541-475-3831 / Dogs allowed with $5 fee / $$

Juniper Motel, 414 North Hwy 26 / 541-475-6186 / Dogs allowed

Hoffy's Motel, 709 Northeast Hwy 26 / 541-475-4633 / Small dogs only with $5 fee / $–$$

Madras Hotel and Motel, 171 Southwest C Street / 541-475-2345 / No dogs / $

Royal Dutch Motel, 1101 Southwest Hwy 97 / 541-475-2281 / Dogs allowed / $–$$

RV PARKS/CAMPGROUNDS

Bend

Bend Kampground, 63615 Hwy 97 / 541-382-7738

Bend Keystone RV Park, 305 Northeast Burnside Avenue / 541-382-2335

Crown Villa RV Park, 60801 Brosterhous Road / 541-388-1131

Prineville

Sun Rocks RV Park, 14900 South Juniper Canyon Road / 541-447-6540 or 800-771-0941 / 38 full hookups / 10 partials / Tent sites

The Trees Mobile Park, 960 West 2nd / 541-447-6854 / 7 full hookups

Crook County RV Park, 1040 South Main / 541-447-2599 / 80 hookups

Madras

Deschutes Canyon Campground, 7228 Northwest Hwy 26 / 541-553-1011

Lake Simtustus RV Park and Campground, 2750 Pelton Dam Road / 541-475-1085

Trails West, 159 Southwest Bard Lane / 541-475-6062

RESTAURANTS

Bend

McKenzie's, 1033 Northwest Bond / 541-388-3891 / 5pm-9pm daily / Steaks, seafood, pasta

Bend Woolen Mill, 1854 Northeast Division / 541-317-1061 / Brewpub with full lunch/dinner menu

Ernesto's Italian Restaurant, 1203 Northeast 3rd Street / 541-389-7274 / Traditional Italian cuisine and Northwest wines

Han's, 915 Northwest Wall / 541-389-9700 / One of Bend's best dinner restaurants, also lunch / Open Tues–Sat

Honker's Restaurant, 805 Industrial Way / 541-389-4665

Mexicali Rose, Corner of Hwy 97 and Franklin / 541-330-5885

Pine Tavern Restaurant, Brooks Street, downtown / 541-382-5581

Rosette, 150 Northwest Oregon Avenue / 541-383-2780 / Fine Pacific Northwest cuisine

Denny's Restaurant, 805 Northeast 3rd / 541-382-4635 / Open 24 hours

Shari's Restaurant, 3098 North Hwy 97 / 541-382-0674 / Open 24 hours

61155 South Hwy 97 / 541-389-2405 / Open 24 hours

Prineville

The Apple Peddler, 1485 East 3rd / 541-416-5075

Barr's Café, 887 North Main / 541-447-5897

Dad's Place, 229 North Main / 541-447-7059

Morgan's Restaurant and Lounge, 123 East 3rd / 541-447-3888

Ranchero's Mexican Restaurant, 960 West 3rd / 541-416-0103

Madras

Ding Ho Family Restaurant, 36 Southwest I Street / 541-475-4610

Grandma Hoffy's Restaurant, 675 Northeast Hwy 26 / 541-475-7369

Jerry's Restaurant, 37 Southwest 4th / 541-475-6632 / 24-hour

Madras J and L Café, 992 South Hwy 97 / 541-475-3598 / 24-hour

Mexico City, 48 Southwest 4th / 541-475-6078

VETERINARIANS

Bend

Alpine Veterinary Clinic, 61230 South Hwy 97 / 541-382-8930

Deschutes Veterinary Clinic, 1474 Northwest Hill Street / 541-382-2481 /
24-hour emergency service

Family Pet Hospital, 425 Northeast Windy Knolls Drive, Suite 4 / 541-388-2075

Bend Veterinary Clinic, 360 Northeast Quimby Avenue / 541-382-0741 /
24-hour emergency service

The Ark Animal Clinic, 706 Northeast Greenwood / 541-389-6111 / 24-hour
emergency service

Bush Animal Clinic, 806 Northwest Brooks / 541-382-7671 / 24-hour emergency
service

Prineville

Prineville Veterinary Clinic, 1535 East 3rd / 541-447-2179 or
447-5051 / Mon–Fri 8:30AM–5:30PM, Sat 9AM–1PM

Madras

Cascade East Veterinary Clinic, 1689 Southwest Hwy 97 / 541-475-7226 / 24-hour
emergency service

Madras Animal Hospital, 401 Southwest Fairgrounds Road /
541-475-2283 / 24-hour emergency service

DOG BOARDING

Bend

Kennels Von Duffin, 64155 North Hwy 97 (2 miles north of Mt. View Mall) /
541-388-3739

Bend Pet Resort, 60909 Southeast 27th Street / 541-388-0435

Ranch Kennels, 22040 Nelson Road / 541-382-3634

Prineville

Pampered Pets, 280 Northeast 13th / 541-416-1653

AUTO REPAIR

Bend

Les Schwab Tire Center, 61085 Hwy 97 / 541-385-4702 / Tires, brakes, alignment, shocks, batteries

Thompson Import Specialties, 20417 Cady Way / 541-388-0429

Bend Automotive Center, 20449 Cady Way / 541-389-3815
B and B Automotive Service, 924 Southeast Wilson, Suite A / 541-389-4999
Eddie's Auto Repair, 2100 Northeast Hwy 20 / 541-388-4001
Pilot Butte Auto Repair, 62080 Dean Swift Road., Suite 150 / 541-388-4645
Prineville
Bear Auto Repair, 985 North Madras Hwy / 541-447-6561
Becerra's Tune-up, 1155 Harwood Street / 541-447-6490
Steve's Automotive Repair, 430 North Main Street / 541-447-1103 / Emergency: 541-447-1665
Stipe Engine Specialists, 1717 Industrial Park Road / 541-447-2330
Madras
Les Schwab Tire Center, 1412 Southwest Hwy 97 / 541-475-3834 / Tires, brakes, batteries, shocks, alignment
Affordable Auto Repair, 96 Southeast 6th / 541-475-1802
Cliff's Repair, 330 Southwest Culver Hwy / 541-475-6618
Juniper Auto Repair, 431 Southeast 5th / 541-475-4669
Midstate Auto Repair, 916 South Hwy 97 / 541-475-6585 or 800-661-6585

AUTO RENTAL
Bend
Avis Rent-A-Car, Redmond Airport, 2522 Southeast Airport Way, Redmond / 541-923-3750
Budget Rent-a-Car, 519 Northeast 3rd / 541-383-2642 or at Redmond Airport / 541-923-0699
Sears Rent-a-Car, 519 Northeast 3rd / 541-383-2643 or at Redmond Airport / 541-923-0706
Hertz, South Hwy 97 / 541-388-1535 or at Redmond Airport / 541-923-1411
Enterprise Rent-a-Car, 315 Northeast Clay Avenue / 541-383-1717
Madras
Ford Rent-a-Car, 681 Northeast Hwy 97 / 541-475-7204

SPORTING GOODS DEALERS
Bend
G. I. Joe's, 63455 North Hwy 97 / 541-388-3773
Wal-Mart, 20120 Pinebrook Boulevard / 541-389-8184
Frontline Guns and Supplies, 160 Southeast 3rd Street, Suite 1 / 541-382-9377
Bi-Mart, 351 Northeast 2nd / 541-389-5505
Prineville
Prineville Sporting Goods, 346 North Deer / 541-447-6883
Prineville Hardware, 1515 East 3rd / 541-447-3383
McCarthy's True Value, 227 East 3rd / 541-447-7041
Madras
Madras Gun and Tackle, 1810 Southwest Hwy 97 / 541-475-2044
Oscar's Sporting Goods, 380 Southwest 5th / 541-475-2962
Bi-Mart, 1575 Southwest Hwy 97 / 541-475-1394

AIR SERVICE
Bend
  Redmond Municipal Airport / 541-548-6059 / Serviced by Horizon and United
    Express
Prineville
  Prineville/Crook County Airport, 4585 Airport Road / 541-447-1118

MEDICAL
Bend
  St. Charles Medical Center, 2500 Northeast Neff Road / 541-382-4321
  Central Oregon District Hospital, 1253 North Canal Boulevard, Redmond /
    541-548-8131
Prineville
  Pioneer Memorial Hospital, 1201 North Elm / 541-447-6254
Madras
  Mountain View Hospital, 470 Northeast A Street / 541-475-3882

SHOTGUN RANGES
Bend
  Central Oregon Sporting Clays / 541-382-5663

TAXIDERMISTS
Prineville
  Jim's Taxidermy, 3190 Northwest Gumport Road / 541-447-2725 or 800-898-2725

ATM MACHINES
Prineville
  Wells Fargo, 3rd and Beaver
  US National Bank, 3rd and Belknap
  Bank of the Cascades, 3rd and North Main

FOR MORE INFORMATION
Bend Chamber of Commerce
63085 North Hwy 97
Bend, OR 97701
(541) 382-3221
email: bend@bendchamber.org

Prineville/Crook County Chamber of Commerce
390 Fairview Street
Prineville OR 97754
(541) 447-6304
email: pchamber@coinet.com

The Dalles
Wasco and Sherman Counties

County Population:
    Wasco–22,500
    Sherman–1,900
County Area:
    Wasco–2,396 sq. mi.
    Sherman–831 sq. mi.
	The Dalles Population–11,765
	County Acres in CRP:
	    Wasco–38,482
	    Sherman–75,711
	October Temperature–56°

The Lower Deschutes River plunges through its massive canyon on a south to north journey through the heart of the Wasco/Sherman County area. The canyon's rimrock-lined sides and steep, grassy slopes create ideal chukar habitat, and indeed, the Lower Deschutes is one of the traditional hot spots for Oregon chukar hunters. Above the canyon rims, Wasco and Sherman Counties fan out into mile after mile of grain fields where pheasant, quail, Hungarian partridge, and dove become the quarry.

US 97 runs north-south through the southeast portion of Wasco County and through the heart of Sherman County. North of the Wasco/Jefferson County line and west of the historical town of Shaniko, US 197 departs US 97 and winds its way down into the Deschutes Canyon at the town of Maupin. From Maupin, bird hunters can drive down the canyon to hunt the popular areas along the 17-mile stretch of gravel road leading down to Macks Canyon. From Macks Canyon to the mouth of the Deschutes—a stretch of 25 miles—access to the river and canyon is almost entirely by boat (jetsled up or drift down), foot, or bicycle.

UPLAND BIRDS
Chukar Partridge, Valley Quail, Ring-necked Pheasant, Hungarian Partridge, Blue Grouse, Ruffed Grouse, Mourning Dove, Turkey, and Common Snipe

WATERFOWL
Ducks and Canada Geese

ACCOMMODATIONS
Shamrock Motel, 118 West 4th / 541-296-5464 / Dogs allowed / $–$$
Best Western Umatilla House, 2nd and Liberty / 541-296-9107 or 800-722-8277 / 65 units / Dogs allowed / $$–$$$
Days Inn, 2500 West 6th / 541-296-1191 / Dogs allowed / $$
Shilo Inn, 3223 Bret Clodfelter Way / 541-298-5502 / Dogs allowed / $$–$$$
The Inn at The Dalles, 3550 Frontage Road / 541-296-1167 / Dogs allowed / $$–$$$
Lone Pine Motel, 351 Lone Pine Drive / 541-298-2800 / Dogs allowed / $–$$

CAMPGROUNDS AND RV PARKS
Lone Pine Village RV Park, I-84 East Exit 87 / 541-298-2000 or 800-955-9626

RESTAURANTS
The Baldwin Saloon, First and Court Streets / 541-296-5666 / Fresh seafood and oyster dishes, steaks, sandwiches
Casa El Mirador, 302 West 2nd / 541-298-7388 / Sun–Thur 11AM–10PM (11AM–9PM winter), Fri–Sat 11AM–11PM (11AM–10PM winter) / Mexican cuisine
Ole's Supper Club, 2620 West 2nd / 541-296-6708
Umatilla House, 112 West 2nd / 541-296-5404
Cousin's Restaurant, 2411 West 6th / 541-298-2771 / 6am-10pm daily

VETERINARY CLINICS
The Dalles Veterinary Clinic, 408 West 3rd / 541-296-9191
Columbia Veterinary Hospital, 1000 West 6th / 541-296-5059
Pet Associates Veterinary Clinic, 513 West 10th / 541-298-6888

AUTO REPAIR
Les Schwab Tire Center, 2645 East 2nd / 541-296-6134 / 8AM–6PM, Sat 8AM–5PM / Tires, brakes, alignment, shocks, batteries
Ace Automotive and Transmission, 1206 West 2nd / 541-298-2886 / Mon–Sat 8:30AM–6PM
Certified Auto and Transmission, 1800 West 2nd / 541-296-1330
Fast Auto Service, 111 West 1st / 541-298-3877 / Mon–Fri 8AM–5PM, Sat 9AM–3PM
K and H Specialties Napa Auto Care Center, 3226 West 2nd / 541-296-6817
Precision Auto Repair, 825 East 2nd / 541-296-5153

AUTO RENTAL
Brace Bros Rent-A-Car, 1119 West 2nd / 541-296-3761
Enterprise Rent-a-Car, 100 East 2nd / 541-506-5007 or 800-736-8222
Ford Rent-a-Car, 2400 West 6th / 541-296-6191
Toyota Rent-a-Car, 523 East 3rd / 541-296-2271

SPORTING GOODS DEALERS
Old Mill Bargain Store, 2917 East 2nd / 541-296-6706
Fred Meyer, 1215 West 6th / 541-296-1700
Bi-Mart, 3300 West 6th Avenue / 541-298-1155

MEDICAL
Mid-Columbia Medical Center, 1700 East 19th / 541-296-1111

ATM MACHINES
US Bank, 401 Washington
Bank of America, 115 East 4th
Washington Federal Savings, 235 East 3rd

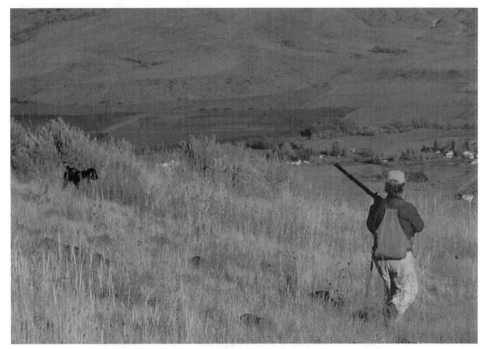

Huns in the foothills.

FOR MORE INFORMATION
The Dalles Area Chamber of Commerce
404 West 2nd Street
The Dalles, OR 97058
(541) 296-2231
email: tdacc@gorge.net

Columbia Region

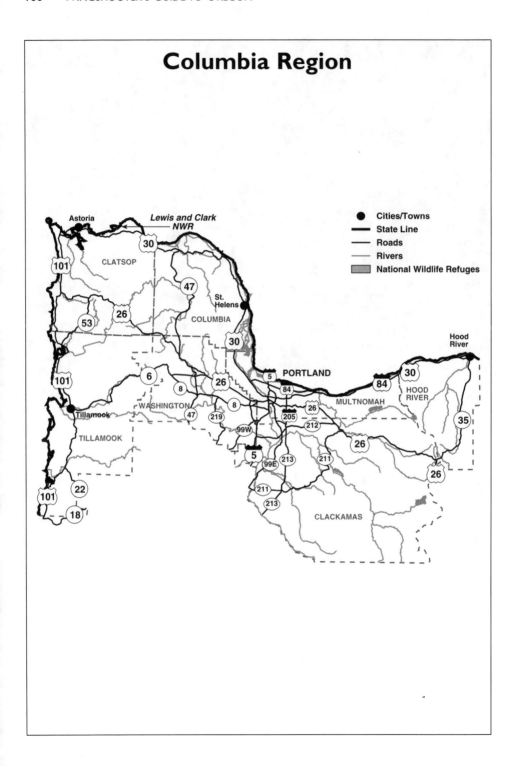

Columbia Region

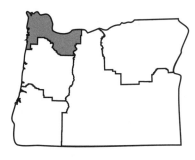

The Columbia Region, as its name implies, stretches along the Columbia River from the river's mouth near Astoria to the Bonneville Dam reach in Hood River County. In between lies the Portland Metropolis, Oregon's most densely populated region. Portland and its satellite communities account for more than a third of the state's 3.1 million citizens. As one might expect, the crowded metro counties—Multnomah and Washington—offer very limited wingshooting opportunities. Oddly enough, however, the state's most popular public duck hunting destination, Sauvie Island, lies only minutes north of Portland.

Throughout the rest of the Columbia Region, wingshooting opportunities abound. The Coast Range west of Portland along with the forested reaches of Clackamas and Hood River Counties provide ample habitat for ruffed and blue grouse, as well as mountain quail and band-tailed pigeon. To locate access routes and likely hunting areas, one need only consult maps of the Mt. Hood National Forest and Clatsop and Tillamook State Forests on the north coast.

This diverse region also offers some of the state's best estuary duck hunting, with Young's Bay at Astoria ranking as a favorite and highly productive destination. Likewise, Tillamook Bay, Nehalem Bay, and Netarts Bay all offer fine waterfowling prospects, including the best opportunity in Oregon for pursuing the elusive black brant. Hunters should also consider pursuing common snipe on the north coast. These speedy migrants arrive in good numbers by mid-autumn and are partial to dairy pastures, stream margins, and vegetated estuary flats.

US 101 runs along the entire Oregon coast and is joined at Astoria by US 30, at Seaside by US 26, and at Tillamook by SR 6, all of which connect to Portland. The journey from Portland to the coast takes about an hour or a little more. To the east of Portland, Interstate 84 heads about 63 miles to the town of Hood River, where underhunted populations of grouse await those willing to explore the forested regions south of town. Blue grouse hunting in this area can be especially addicting owing to the spectacular views of massive Mt. Hood afforded the wingshooter who walks the area's many high ridges.

In the Columbia Region, best hopes for pheasant and valley quail lie in the agricultural lands south and west of Portland. Pheasant also inhabit Sauvie Island. Preseason scouting, of course, pays dividends, especially for those who—long before the opener— seek permission to hunt private lands.

Columbia Region
Ruffed Grouse Distribution

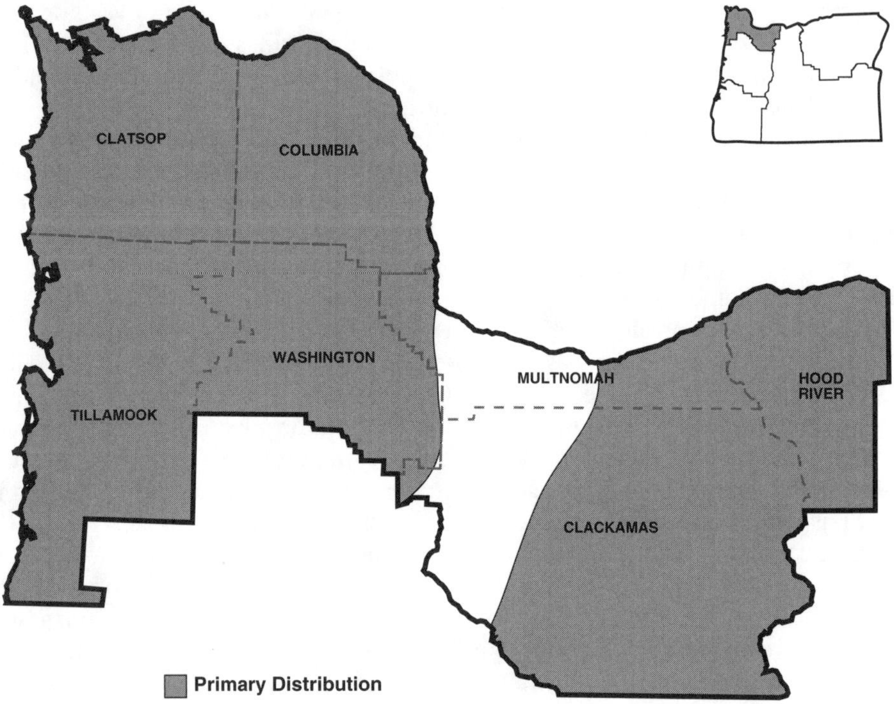

CLATSOP

COLUMBIA

WASHINGTON

MULTNOMAH

HOOD RIVER

TILLAMOOK

CLACKAMAS

■ Primary Distribution

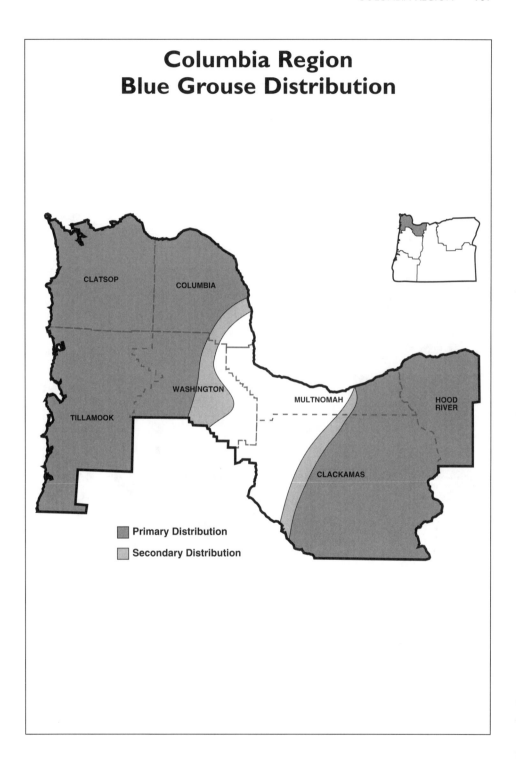

Columbia Region
Blue Grouse Distribution

CLATSOP

COLUMBIA

WASHINGTON

TILLAMOOK

MULTNOMAH

HOOD
RIVER

CLACKAMAS

■ Primary Distribution
▢ Secondary Distribution

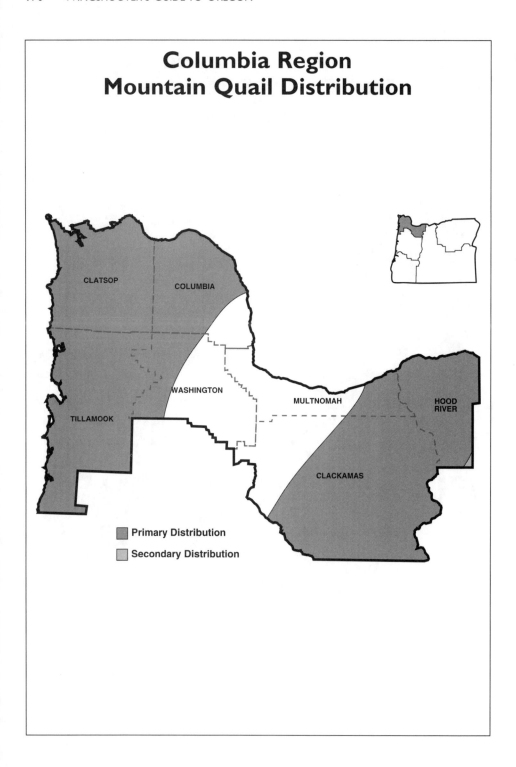

Columbia Region
Mountain Quail Distribution

CLATSOP

COLUMBIA

WASHINGTON

MULTNOMAH

HOOD RIVER

TILLAMOOK

CLACKAMAS

Primary Distribution
Secondary Distribution

Columbia Region
Valley Quail Distribution

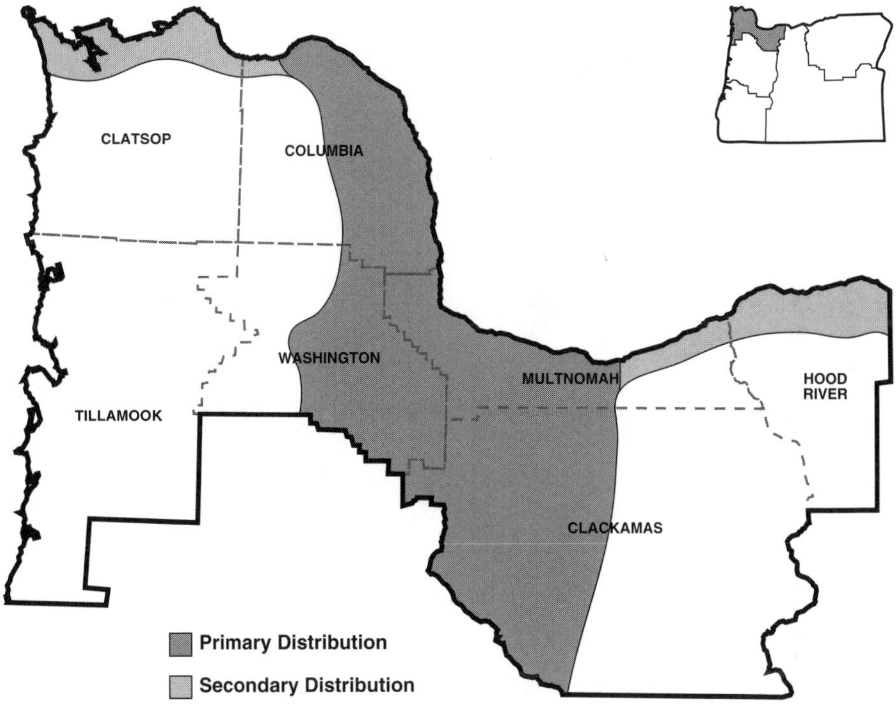

CLATSOP

COLUMBIA

WASHINGTON

TILLAMOOK

MULTNOMAH

HOOD
RIVER

CLACKAMAS

Primary Distribution
Secondary Distribution

Columbia Region
Ring-necked Pheasant Distribution

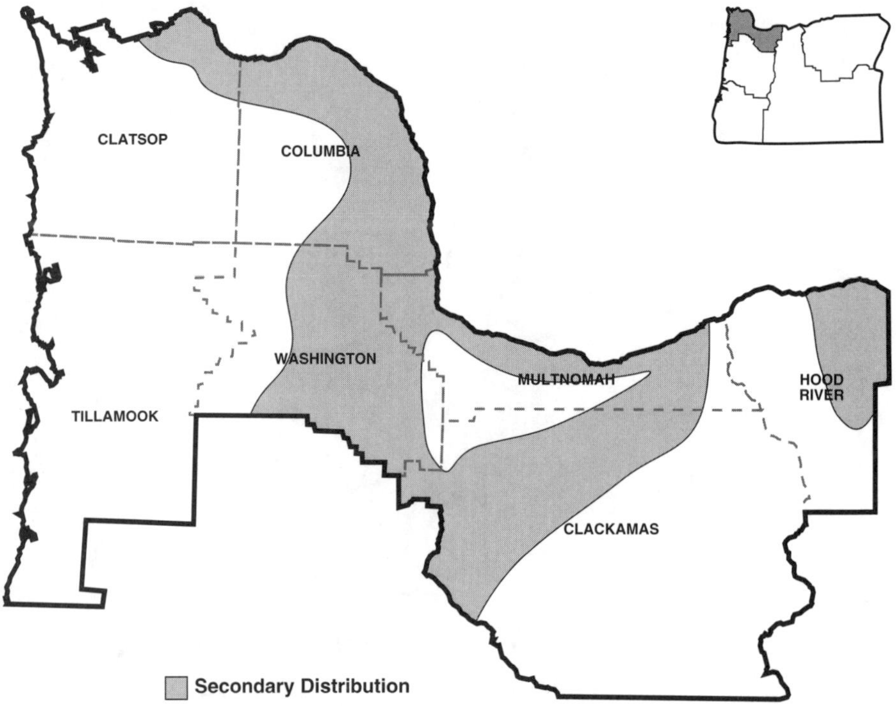

CLATSOP

COLUMBIA

WASHINGTON

TILLAMOOK

MULTNOMAH

HOOD
RIVER

CLACKAMAS

Secondary Distribution

Columbia Region
Wild Turkey Distribution

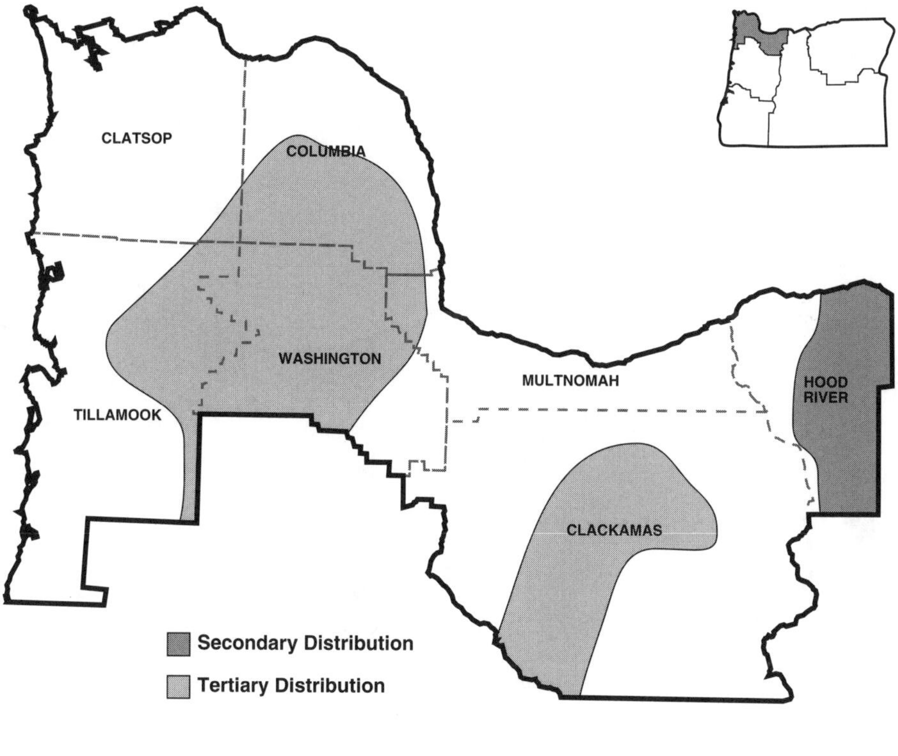

CLATSOP

COLUMBIA

WASHINGTON

MULTNOMAH

HOOD
RIVER

TILLAMOOK

CLACKAMAS

Secondary Distribution

Tertiary Distribution

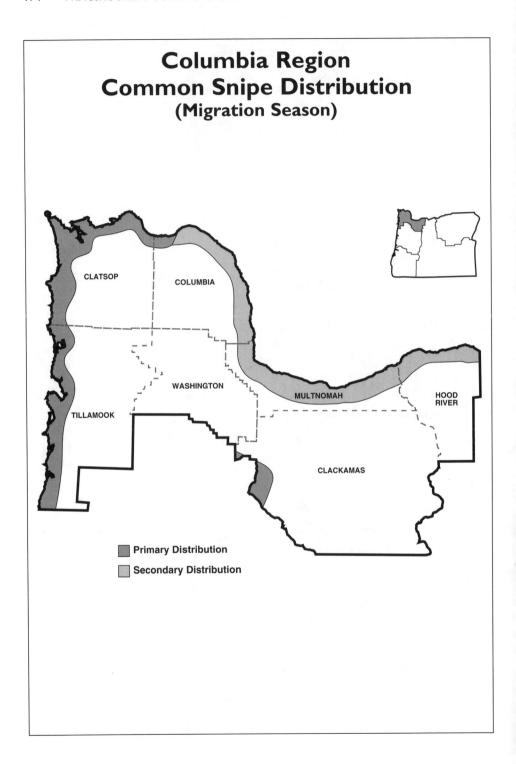

Columbia Region
Common Snipe Distribution
(Migration Season)

Astoria
Clatsop County

County Population–34,600	Astoria Population–10,090
County Area–873 sq. mi.	October Temperature–53°
County Acres in CRP–0	

For the Lewis and Clark expedition, Astoria marked the end of a remarkable journey, and today the region offers much to the history buff, including a museum/interpretive center dedicated to the Corps of Discovery. The Corps reached Astoria in December of 1805 and immediately set about establishing winter quarters. Almost as quickly, they were greeted by a very wet Oregon coast winter.

Those same wet winters provide many days of perfect waterfowling weather, and it is the duck hunting that today draws sportsman to Astoria during the fall and winter. Chief among the region's several prime waterfowling locales is Young's Bay, a large shallow expanse located immediately west of Astoria. Young's Bay attracts ducks by thousands, both dabblers and divers. Mallards, pintail, wigeon, and green-winged teal abound; scaup raft by the hundreds; and good numbers of canvasback and redheads arrive each fall. A boat is a good idea in Young's Bay because you can hunt many areas that are impossible or difficult to reach otherwise. However, hunters afoot will find good access along the dikes and shorelines on the bay's west side.

UPLAND BIRDS
Blue Grouse, Ruffed Grouse, Mountain Quail, Valley Quail, Ring-necked Pheasant, Mourning Dove, Band-tailed Pigeon, and Common Snipe

WATERFOWL
Ducks, Canada Geese, and Black Brant

ACCOMMODATIONS
Bay Shore Motor Inn, 555 Hamburg Street / 503-325-2205 or 800-621-0641 / Dogs allowed / $$

Crest Motel, 5366 Leif Erickson Drive / 503-325-3141 or 800-421-3141 / Dogs allowed / $$

Lamplighter Motel, 131 West Marine Drive / 503-325-4051 or 800-845-8847 / Dogs allowed / $$

Red Lion Inn, 400 Industry Street / 503-325-7373 or 800-547-8010 / Dogs allowed / $$–$$$

CAMPGROUNDS AND RV PARKS
Rogers RV Park and Campground, Highway 202 / 503-325-8595 / 25 spaces

Kampers West Kampground, 1140 Northwest Warrenton Drive (Warrenton) / 503-861-1814 / 221 spaces

KOA Campground, 1100 Ridge Road (Warrenton) / 503-861-2606 or 800-562-8506 / 310 spaces

Sunset Lake Resort and RV Park, 850 Lewis Avenue (Warrenton) / 503-861-1760 / 55 spaces

Fort Stevens State Park, Ridge Road in Warrenton / 503-861-1671 or 800-452-5687 / 617 spaces

RESTAURANTS

Andrew and Steve's Cafe, 1196 Marine Drive / 503-325-5762 / 7AM–9PM

Cafe Uniontown, 218 West Marine Drive / 503-325-8708 / Open Tues–Sat for lunch and dinner

Cannery Cafe, One Sixth Street / 503-325-8642 / Tues–Sat 11AM–8:30PM

Pig 'n Pancake, 146 West Bond Street / 503-325-3144

Shark Rock Cafe, 577 14th Street / 503-325-7720 / Mon–Sat 8AM–8:30PM

The Ship Inn, One Second Street / 503-325-0033 / Open 7 days

Wet Dog Cafe, 144 11th Street / 503-325-6975 / Open daily from 11AM / Brewpub

Hometown Pizza Company, 212 8th Street / 503-325-4927 / Free delivery

VETERINARY CLINICS

Astoria Animal Hospital, 309 Alt. Highway 101 / 503-325-1581

Columbia Veterinary Hospital, 576 31st Street / 503-325-2250

DOG BOARDING

Bay Breeze Boarding, 1480 Southeast 9th Street (Warrenton) / 503-861-9817

AUTO REPAIR

North Coast Auto Service, 2060 Marine Drive / 503-325-3282

AUTO RENTAL

Enterprise Rent-A-Car / 503-325-7500 or 800-736-8222

Hertz Rent-A-Car, 1492 Duane / 503-325-7700 or 800-654-3131

SPORTING GOODS

Link's Outdoor, 1254 Commercial / 503-325-5931 / Extensive inventory of bird hunting supplies

Coast to Coast Stores, 1665 East Harbor Street, Warrenton / 503-861-1161

MEDICAL

Columbia Memorial Hospital, 2111 Exchange / 503-325-4321

24-HOUR GAS STATIONS

Mini-Mart, 95 West Marine Drive / also an ATM machine

58 Southeast Harbor Drive (Warrenton) / also an ATM machine

Two ruffed grouse and a mountain quail from the Coast Range.

ATM MACHINES
Bank of America, 977 Commercial Street
U.S. National Bank, 987 Duane Street
Wells Fargo Bank, 1218 Commercial Street
Western Bank, 303 11th Street

MORE INFORMATION:
Astoria-Warrenton Chamber of Commerce
P.O. Box 176
Astoria, OR 97103
503-325-6311 or 800-875-6807
e-mail: awacc@seasurf.com

Tillamook
Tillamook County

County Population–23,800	Tillamook Population–4,310
County Area–1,125 sq. mi.	October Temperature–53°
County Acres in CRP–0	

Hunters interested in black brant should head for Tillamook County, where a majority of Oregon's small wintering population occurs on the extensive tidewater environs of Tillamook and Netarts Bays. These same areas, along with the other Tillamook County estuaries (especially Nehalem Bay and Nestucca Bay), offer extensive and productive opportunities for duck hunting. Boat ramps are available at all these locations, but hunters afoot can find lots of good areas from which to shoot. The Coast Range, which dominates the county, includes ample habitat for ruffed grouse, blue grouse, and mountain quail. Tillamook County also features expansive habitat for common snipe, which migrate through the area in substantial numbers. Look for them along the vegetated fringes of the estuaries and in the county's many dairy pastures (you'll need landowner permission to hunt the pastures).

The county seat of Tillamook offers all necessary services and includes several worthwhile amenities, especially the Tillamook Cheese Factory. The town of Tillamook and its small valley overlook the southwest corner of sprawling Tillamook Bay, famous for its runs of chinook salmon that ascend five major rivers that feed the bay. Several small towns, stretched out along US 101, occupy the east and northeast shores of the bay. These include Bay City and Garibaldi. From Portland, the most direct route to Tillamook is SR 6, but check on road conditions during wet winter weather because mudslides occur here regularly.

UPLAND BIRDS
Blue Grouse, Ruffed Grouse, Mountain Quail, Mourning Dove, Band-tailed Pigeon, and Common Snipe

WATERFOWL
Ducks, Canada Geese, and Black Brant

ACCOMMODATIONS
Mar Clair Inn, 11 Main Avenue / 503-842-7571 or 800-331-6857 / 47 units /
  Dogs with extra fee and credit card / $$–$$$
Shilo Inn, 2515 Hwy 101 North / 503-842-7971 or 800-222-2244 / 100 units /
  Dogs with fee / $$–$$$
Western Royal Inn, 1125 North Main Avenue / 503-842-8844 or 800-624-2912 /
  For units / Small dogs with fee / $$–$$$
Red Apple Inn, 815 Main Avenue / 503-842-7511 or 800-257-1185 / 22 units /
  Dogs allowed / $$

Mountain quail.

CAMPGROUNDS AND RV PARKS
Trask River Mobile Home and RV Park, 3370 Geinger Road / 503-842-6142 / 10 full hookups, 4 partials
Tillamook Bay City RV Park, Hwy 101 (Bay City) / 503-377-2124 / 30 full hookups
Big Barn Marina and RV Park, 85 3rd Street West / 503-842-8596 / 26 partial hookups, 30 tent sites

RESTAURANTS
Beach Pancake and Dinner House, 3670 Hwy 101 / 503-842-8898
Cedar Bay Restaurant and Lounge, 2015 1st Street / 503-842-8288
El Gallito Restaurante, 5535 C Street (Bay City) / 503-377-4405
Fei Ying Restaurant, 2106 1st. Street / 503-842-2190
La Casa Medello, 1160 Hwy 101 North / 503-842-5768
The Locomotion Restaurant, 1145 North Main Avenue / 503-842-1960
Rendezvous Restaurant and Lounge, 214 Pacific / 503-842-5453
Schooner Restaurant, 2065 Netarts Bay Road / 503-842-1455
Shilo Restaurant and Lounge, 2535 North Main Street / 503-842-5510

VETERINARY CLINICS

Pioneer Veterinary Hospital, 801 Main / 503-842-8411
Reigning Cats and Dogs Animal Hospital, 1109 Main / 503-842-2322
The Tillamook Veterinary Hospital, 1095 North Main / 503-842-7552

DOG BOARDING

Iantha Hart House, P.O. Box 853 / 503-842-8012

AUTO REPAIR

Bayside Repair, 13400 Trask River Road / 503-842-1100
Gary's Automotive, 1867 North Main / 503-842-6267
K and M Automotive, 3740 Hwy 101 North / 503-842-4132
Mechtronics, 4360 3rd Street / 503-842-4361
Russell Chevrolet, 1 Main / 503-842-25420

SPORTING GOODS

Richard's Gun Shop, 4225 Hwy 101 North / 503-842-4678

MEDICAL

Tillamook County General Hospital / 503-842-4444

FOR MORE INFORMATION

Tillamook Chamber of Commerce
3705 Hwy 101 North
Tillamook OR 97141-7773
503-842-7525

St. Helens
Columbia County

County Population–40,100	St. Helens Population–9,060
County Area–687 sq. mi.	October Temperature–55°
County Acres in CRP–0	

Only minutes north of Portland, the town of St. Helens occupies the west bank of the Columbia River immediately north of the tip of Sauvie Island. Waterfowling comprises the main attraction in Columbia County, whose extensive Columbia River frontage includes many sloughs, islands, and channels that attract ducks and geese by the thousands.

Columbia County also stretches south into the Coast Range, where ruffed grouse, blue grouse, and mountain quail thrive on countless acres of timberlands. Included are many extensive alder stands preferred by ruffed grouse. US 30 departs northwest Portland and heads first to Scappoose and then to St. Helens before continuing on to Astoria. Otherwise, access to Columbia County is entirely by county and local roads.

UPLAND BIRDS
Blue Grouse, Ruffed Grouse, Mountain Quail, Mourning Dove, Band-tailed Pigeon, and Common Snipe

WATERFOWL
Ducks, Canada Geese, Black Brant, Snow Geese, and White-fronted Geese

ACCOMMODATIONS
Best Western Oak Meadows Inn, 585 South Columbia River Hwy / 503-397-3000 or 800-528-1234
The Village Inn, 535 South Columbia River Hwy / 503-397-1490

CAMPGROUNDS AND RV PARKS
St. Helens Marina, 134 North River / 503-397-4162
Violette's Villa, 495 South Columbia River Hwy / 503-397-0821

RESTAURANTS
Dockside Steak and Pasta, 343 Souh 1st / 503-366-0877
Kuy's Oriental Cuisine, 524 Milton Way / 503-397-0946 / Thai and Cambodian cuisine
Klondike Restaurant and Saloon, 71 Cowlitz Street / 503-397-4297
Mo's Thai Kitchen, 56821Columbia River Hwy / 503-366-0672
Muchas Gracias Mexican Food, 155 Columbia River Hwy / 503-366-1075 / Open 24 hours
St. Helens Café, 298 South 1st / 503-397-1692 / Open at 5 a.m

VETERINARY CLINICS
Valley Veterinary Clinic, 203 South Columbia River Hwy / 503-397-4190 /
　Emergency service available
Columbia Veterinary Clinic, 35645 Firlok Park Boulevard / 503-397-1928

DOG BOARDING
Vonnie's Dog House, 244 North Columbia River Hwy / 503-397-6684
Caledon Kennels, 27428 Gibb Road (Scappoose) / 503-543-7556

AUTO REPAIR
Anderson Automotive Inc., 164 South 15th Street / 503-397-9113
Jim's Auto and Truck Repair, 144 Marshall / 503-366-0893
Auto Tech, 711 North Columbia River Hwy / 503-366-2717

AUTO RENTAL
Enterprise Rent-A-Car, 57895 Columbia River Hwy / 503-397-6328
Midway Fleet Rental Cars and Trucks, 305 South Columbia River Hwy /
　503-366-1090

SPORTING GOODS
Rivercity Sporting Goods, 145 North 19th / 503-366-0904
Rite-Aid, 785 South Columbia River Hwy / 503-397-6785

MEDICAL
St. John Medical Center, 1614 East Kessler (Longview, Washington) / 360-423-
　1530 or 800-438-7562

AIR SERVICE
Portland International Airport, approximately 1 hour east

FOR MORE INFORMATION
St. Helens Chamber of Commerce
1934 Columbia Boulevard
St. Helens, OR 97051
503-397-0685

Hood River
Hood River County

County Population–19,000	Hood River Population–5,130
County Area–533 sq. mi.	October Temperature–51°
County Acres in CRP–0	

Hood River, located in the heart of the scenic Columbia River Gorge, serves as the seat for a county whose elevations range from 150 feet on the banks of the big river to 11,235 feet at the summit of Mt. Hood, Oregon's highest point. In between are found excellent prospects for grouse, quail, and wild turkey, the latter of which flourish here and in neighboring Wasco County. Hood River County is widely known for its production of apples, and the fringes of apple orchards offer good prospects for ruffed grouse. Most such grouse coverts in the region—those places where the apple orchards yield to stands of mixed forest and brushy riparian zones—lie on private property, so hunters must seek permission. A few ring-necked pheasants, along with coveys of valley quail, occupy the county's agricultural lands where appropriate habitat exists.

Better still, however, are the prospects for blue grouse and mountain quail. Both species are quite common on steep, forested terrain within the Mt. Hood National Forest, whose boundaries include a substantial chunk of Hood River County. Habitat for both birds begins on the precipitous slopes immediately above the Columbia and extends south across all but the Hood River Valley itself. The breaks of the Columbia Gorge harbor lots of blue grouse, along with ruffed grouse where appropriate habitat exists. However, hunters must exercise caution owing to numerous steep slides, sudden breaks, and cliffs hidden among the timber.

Waterfowl hunting is limited despite the presence of the massive Columbia River. Duck hunters can explore the margins of the river, especially upstream from Cascade Locks, where good numbers of mallards, wigeon, pintail, and teal assemble during late fall and winter. Scaup often form large rafts on the Columbia, but few hunters make a serious effort at pursuing them. In any case, a boat is a virtual requirement for waterfowl hunting along the Columbia River in Hood River County. Public launches are available at the Hood River Marina and at the Port of Cascade Locks.

UPLAND BIRDS
Blue Grouse, Ruffed Grouse, Mountain Quail, Valley Quail, Ring-necked Pheasant, Mourning Dove, Band-tailed Pigeon, Common Snipe

WATERFOWL
Ducks and Canada Geese

ACCOMMODATIONS

Vagabond Inn, 4070 Westcliff Drive / 541-386-2992 / Dogs allowed / $–$$
Best Western Hood River Inn, 1108 East Marina Way / 541-386-2200 or
800-828-7873 / 149 units / Dogs allowed / $$–$$$
Columbia Gorge Hotel, 4000 Westcliff Drive / 541-386-5566 / 42 units / Dogs
allowed / $$$

CAMPGROUNDS AND RV PARKS

Memaloose State Park, I-84, 11 miles east of Hood River / 541-478-3008 /
43 hookups; 67 tent sites
Tucker County Park, State Highway 281, 5 miles south of Hood River /
541-386-4477 / 14 RV sites; tent sites
Sunset RV Park, 2300 West Cascade / 541-386-6027

RESTAURANTS

Stonehedge Inn, 3405 Cascade Street / 541-386-3940 / Open for dinner Wed–
Sun / Fine dining
Pisquale's Ristorante, 102 Oak Street / 541-386-1900 / Daily 8AM–9PM / Italian
and Pacific Northwest cuisine
Sixth Street Bistro and Loft, 509 Cascade Street / 541-386-5737 / Open for
breakfast, lunch, dinner
The Crazy Pepper, 101 4th Street / 541-387-2454 / 11AM–10:30PM
Bette's Place, 416 Oak Street / 541-386-1880 / Mon–Sat 5:30AM–5PM,
Sun 6AM–4PM
Shari's, 1803 12th Street / 541-386-3394 / Open 24 hours

VETERINARY CLINICS

Columbia Gorge Veterinary Clinic, 1208 Belmont Drive / 541-386-7773 /
8AM–5:30PM, Sat 8:30–NOON
Upper Valley Vet Clinic, 6809 Hwy 35 (Mt. Hood) / 541-352-7446 / Mon, Tue,
Thur, Fri 8AM–5PM, Sat 9AM–1PM
Tucker Road Animal Hospital, 1125 Tucker Road / 541-386-1566 / 8:30AM–5:30PM,
Sat 9AM–NOON
Alpine Veterinary Hospital, 300 Frankton Road / 541-386-6658 / 9AM–5:30PM,
Sat to 4PM

DOG BOARDING

Spoiled Boys Kennel, P.O. Box 202 (Underwood, WA, across the river from Hood
River) / 509-493-4150
Columbia Gorge Veterinary Clinic, 1208 Belmont Drive / 541-386-7773
The Laughing Cavalier Kennels, 7060 Hwy 35 (Mt. Hood) / 541-352-6419

GUN DOG TRAINERS

Spoiled Boys Kennel, P.O. Box 202 (Underwood, WA, across the river from Hood
River) / 509-493-4150

AUTO REPAIR
Cliff Smith Motors, 3100 West Cascade / 541-386-3311
Hood River Ford-Mercury, 1802 12th Street / 541-386-5277
John's Equipment Repair, 4301 Barrett Drive / 541-386-5517
Gorge Automotive, 1200 Industrial Loop Road / 541-386-5030

SPORTING GOODS
The Gun Shop, 1302 12th Street / 541-386-3266
Rite Aid, 2049 West Cascade / 541-387-2424

MEDICAL
Hood River Memorial Hospital, 13th and May Streets / 541-386-3911 or
    800-955-3911

TAXIDERMISTS
Wild Country Studios / 541-352-6225

24-HOUR GAS STATIONS
Exxon Hood River, 214 Front Street / 541-386-2220
Marina Chevron, 949 East Marina Way / 541-386-7887

ATM MACHINES
U.S. National Bank, corner of Oak and 3rd Streets
U.S. National Bank, 1309 12th Street
Key Bank, 1920 12th Street
Columbia River Bank, 2650 West Cascade Avenue
Bank of America, 115 Oak Street

AIR SERVICE
Portland International Airport, one hour west via Interstate 84

FOR MORE INFORMATION
Hood River County Chamber of Commerce
405 Portway Avenue
Hood River, OR 97031
541-386-2000
email: hrccc@gorge.net

Portland and the Metro Area

Fully a third of Oregon's 3.2 million people reside in Portland and the myriad surrounding communities that comprise the metro area and the northern Willamette Valley. Such a population density assures that Portland offers an abundance of amenities and services. Fine restaurants abound and those listed here reflect the three- and four-star rated establishments listed by Stephanie Irving in her book, *Northwest Best Places* (1998 edition). These are just a few of the very best; many other great restaurants await culinary enthusiasts.

True to its Northwest heritage, Portland boasts numerous popular coffee houses and brewpubs. In fact, the McMenamin brothers operate some 30-odd breweries and pubs in the Portland area, including such remarkable establishments as The Edgefield, a 25-acre property in Troutdale offering a brewery, fine-dining restaurant, pub restaurant, winery, distillery, cigar bars and a bed and breakfast. Services in the Portland area are so numerous that a complete listing herein would be impossible. Instead we have elected to list airport hotels, a few kennels, sporting goods dealers, and the aforementioned restaurants.

The Willamette River divides Portland in half before reaching the Columbia. Just minutes northwest of the city on the Columbia, sprawling Sauvie Island offers some of the state's best waterfowling (see entry under state wildlife areas). Otherwise, the metro offers little in the way of bird hunting opportunity. Portland does, however, offer the state's only international airport, which is serviced by all the major airlines.

ACCOMMODATIONS NEAR PORTLAND AIRPORT (DOGS ALLOWED)
Days Inn Airport, 3828 Northeast 82nd Avenue / 503-256-2550 or 800-329-7466 / $$-$$$

Howard Johnson, 7101 Northeast 82nd Avenue / 503-255-6722 or 800-345-3896 / $$$

Madison Suites, 3620 Northeast 82nd Avenue / 503-257-4981 or 800-945-4425 / $$-$$$

Quality Inn Airport, 8427 Northeast Sandy Boulevard / 503-256-4111 or 800-221-2222 / $$$

Travelodge Portland Airport, 9727 Sandy Boulevard / 503-255-1400 or 800-556-0006 / $$-$$$

BREW PUB RESTAURANTS
Bridgeport Brew Pub, 1313 Northwest Marshall / 503-241-3612

Bridgeport Ale House, 3632 Southeast Hawthorne / 503-233-6540

Lucky Labrador Brewpub, 915 Southeast Hawthorne / 503-236-3555

Widmer Gasthaus, 955 North Russell / 503-281-3333

McMenamin's Cornelius Pass Roadhouse, Sunset Hwy and Cornelius Pass Road / 503-640-6174

McMenamin's Edgefield, 2126 Southwest Halsey (Troutdale) / 503-669-8610

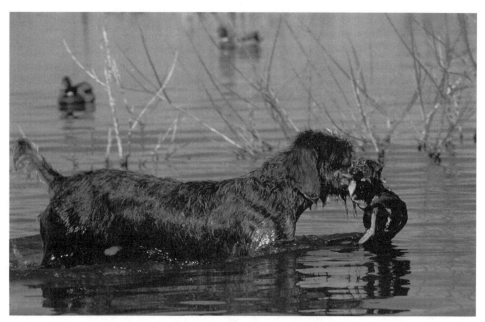

Duke retrieves a duck on an early morning hunt.

McMenamin's Pubs, approximately 30 venues in Portland metro area / Call 503-223-0109 for locations

Portland Brewing Company Taproom and Grill, 2730 Northwest 31st Avenue / 503-228-5269

RESTAURANTS

Genoa, 2832 Southeast Belmont Street / 503-238-1464

The Heathman Restaurant and Bar, 1009 Southwest Broadway / 503-241-4100

Zefiro, 500 Northwest 21st / 503-226-3394

Atwater's, 111 Southwest 5th Avenue / 503-275-3600

Avalon Grill, 4630 Southwest Macadam Avenue / 503-227-4630

Café des Amis, 1987 Northwest Kearney Street / 503-295-6487

Couvron, 1126 Southwest 18th Avenue / 503-225-1844

Esparza's Tex-Mex Café, 2725 Southeast Ankeny Street / 503-234-7909

Fiddleheads, 6716 Southeast Milwaukie / 503-233-1547

Higgins, 1239 Southwest Broadway / 503-222-9070

L'Auberge, 2601 Northwest Vaughn Street / 503-223-3302

Lemongrass, 1705 Northeast Couch / 503-231-5780

McCormick and Schmick's Seafood Restaurant, 235 Southwest 1st Avenue / 503-224-7522

Murata, 200 Southwest Market / 503-227-0080
Paley's Place, 1204 Northwest 21st Avenue / 503-243-2403
Papa Hayda, 701 Northwest 23rd Avenue / 503-232-9440
Pazzo Ristorante, 627 Southwest Washington Street / 503-228-1515
3 Doors Down, 1429 Southeast 37th Avenue / 503-236-6886
Wildwood, 1221 Northwest 21st Avenue / 503-248-9663

SPORTING GOODS
G.I. Joe's, 3485 Southwest Cedar Hills Boulevard (Beaverton Mall) / 503-644-9932
       17799 Southwest Boores Ferry Road (Tualatin) / 503-635-5433
       1140 North Hayden Meadows (Delta Park) / 503-283-0312
       7280 Northwest Butler Avenue (Hillsboro) / 503-846-1914
       3900 Southeast 82nd Avenue (Eastport Plaza) / 503-777-4528
       15600 Southeast McGlaughlin Boulevard (Oak Grove) / 503-653-5618
       700 Northeast Eastman Parkway, Gresham / 503-667-3122
Andy and Bax Sporting Goods and GI Surplus, 324 Southeast Grand Avenue /
   503-234-7538
Bwana Junction, 322 Southwest 3rd / 503-228-0783
The Gun Broker, 14981 Southeast 82nd Drive (Clackamas) / 503-657-7203
Rite Aid , 10108 Southeast Washington / 503-252-4636 / 11 additional Portland-
   area locations
Northwest Armory, 12632 Southeast McLaughlin Boulevard / 503-654-7974
The Gun Room, Inc., corner of 56th and Foster Road / 503-777-3931
Three Bears Guns, 11374 Southeast 82nd Avenue / 503-786-7167
Keith's Sporting Goods, 95 Northeast Victory (Gresham) / 503-492-6999
Bi-Mart, 17108 Southeast Powell Boulevard / 503-667-5494
       12321 Northeast Halsey / 503-257-3007
       4315 Southeast Woodstock / 503-771-1001
       13500 Southwest Pacific Way (Tigard) / 503-624-0103
       2800 Northeast Hogan Drive (Gresham) / 503-661-2366

AUTO RENTAL
Advantage Rent-a-Car / 1-800-777-5500
Alamo / 1-800-327-9633
Avis Rent-a-Car / 1-800-831-2847
Enterprise / 1-800-736-8222
Budget / 1-800-527-0700
Dollar Rent-a-Car / 1-503-249-4792 or 1-800-800-4000
National / 1-800-227-7368
Thrifty Car Rental / 1-503-254-6563 or 1-800-367-2277
Hertz / 1-503-249-8216 or 1-800-654-3131

DOG BOARDING

Charlton Kennels, 13825 Northwest Charlton Road, Sauvie Island / 503-621-3675
/ Boarding and retriever training

Fletcher's Boarding Kennels, 12959 Southeast Powell Boulevard / 503-761-2091

Minoggie Kennels, 19322 Northwest Sauvie Island Road / 503-621-3597 /
Boarding and retriever training

Twin Willows Kennel, 320 Northeast Gertz Road / 503-285-3669

Sauvie Island Kennels, 23200 Northwest Reeder, Sauvie Island / 503-621-3204 /
Boarding and pointer training

FOR MORE INFORMATION

Portland Metropolitan Chamber of Commerce
221 Northwest Second Avenue
Portland, OR 97209-3999
503-228-9411
503-228-5126 Fax

The Super Hot Duplex Loads

Timmy's first efforts at hand loading met with resounding success. He just followed the instructions and was instantly saving money on the price of shotgun shells. Soon he started experimenting and I was the first of his hunting partners to witness the field-testing of what he told me was his new "super-hot duplex load."

At the time, I'd have been happy to try a few myself. In retrospect, however, I'm glad that I was shooting an old Remington 870 20-bore. Timmy was reloading 12-gauge, so I had to stick with the Federal Premium #4s that had always served me so well prior to the steel shot laws.

One fine winter day we ventured to the Oregon coast to hunt the saltwater sloughs of a favorite estuary. The typical mix of dabblers and divers was assembled, and we settled into the tall marsh grass, hoping for some pass shooting that would prevent us the ordeal of sloshing around in low-tide mud to set out two dozen decoys. Shooting hours arrived with a west wind that ruffled the tawny marsh. The morning sun threatened to penetrate low, gray clouds but was finally beaten into submission by perfect waterfowling weather.

The first birds of the day, a brace of greenheads with the wind at their backs, came on us so quickly that they nearly escaped unharassed. Timmy was far more ready than I. He whipped around for a going-away shot of about 35 yards and let fly over the bulrushes with his new super-hot duplex load. Wholly unimpressed, the two drakes continued their exit unabated, and Timmy stood there staring as if he expected, at any moment, one of the two to swing back around, circle once, and then drop stone dead at his feet.

The morning passed too quickly. I killed three green-winged teal and missed several more, then added a drake mallard to the bag. Timmy fired only three or four times and had not a duck to show for his efforts. His targets were those erratic little hell-bent-for-leather teal, so one could hardly fault his marksmanship. Still, I recall some sense of wonderment at the quiet little "bang" that made Timmy's 12-gauge waterfowling piece sound more like my 20-bore firing dove loads.

The tidal push finally filled our narrow slough, and we elected to set out the decoys. Soon thereafter, our first takers arrived—a pair of hooded mergansers. They came in low and fast, sailing past the decoys and heading up the slough. Tim was right on the drake, whose elegant plumage Tim wanted displayed in the form of a nice mount. The first shot "banged" rather quietly with no results; the second sort of popped, not unlike the sound made by .22 caliber birdshot.

Curiously, as Tim let fly with that second shot, a scattering of pellets gently sprayed the front of our decoy spread not 15 yards distant. His first shot

A drake American wigeon from western Oregon.

charge had barely enough energy to clear the barrel. Immediately after the second shot, I saw the telltale rings of pellets entering the water just six feet in front of Timmy.

Those "super-hot duplex loads" were so hot that he had to turn the gun's barrel down to dump the remaining shot from the second round. I might have fired on the drake myself had I not been bent over double with a belly full of laughter. Timmy, now laughing himself, threatened me with a belly full of lead. "You'd better use my gun if you intend any damage," I retorted.

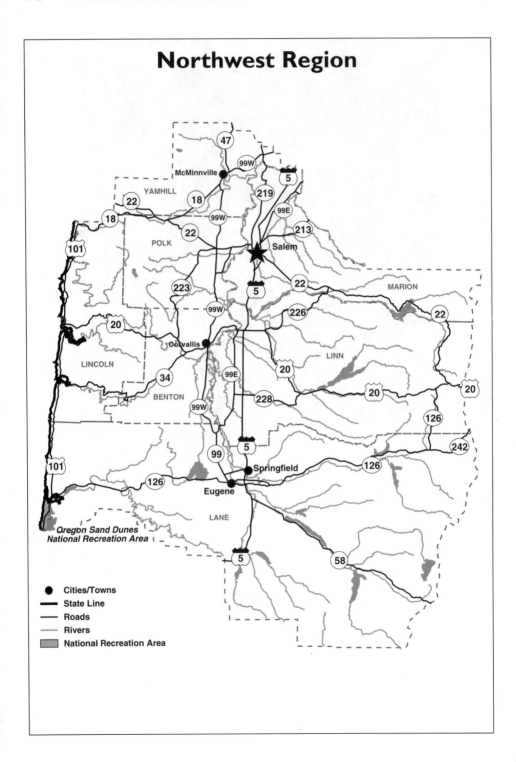

Northwest Region

Northwest Region

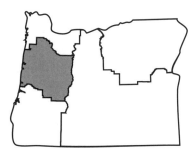

Stretching from the crest of the Cascade Range, across the broad Willamette Valley, and over the Coast Range to the white sand beaches of Lincoln County, Oregon's Northwest Region offers top-flight hunting opportunities for wingshooters of every bent. The central Oregon coast features several highly productive estuaries, where water-fowlers enjoy fine shooting over decoys and where common snipe abound, providing some of the best longbill hunting in the West. One of the favorite duck-hunting locales is sprawling and scenic Siletz Bay, south of Lincoln City. Meanwhile, the Coast Range and the Cascades abound with perfect grouse and mountain quail habitat and band-taileded pigeon migrate through both ranges. The fringes of the Willamette Valley offer the best of western Oregon's remaining pheasant populations along with strong densities of valley quail. The river for which the valley is named attracts strong flights of both locally produced and migrating ducks, geese, and doves.

Salem, Oregon's capital city, straddles the Willamette River on the western edge of Marion County. To the south, and on the opposite bank, lies Corvallis, the hub of the central valley. Just north is Albany, the county seat of Linn County. The valley fringe is ringed with small towns, most of whose economies are tied to the land in the form of timber and agriculture. These small towns—Stayton, Mill City, Silverton, Lebanon, Sweet Home, Amity, Dallas, Valley Junction, *et al.*—offer the major services required by travelers. All, however, are located but a short drive from the large cities of the valley floor, where hunters can find every imaginable service, including many varied and exceptional restaurants.

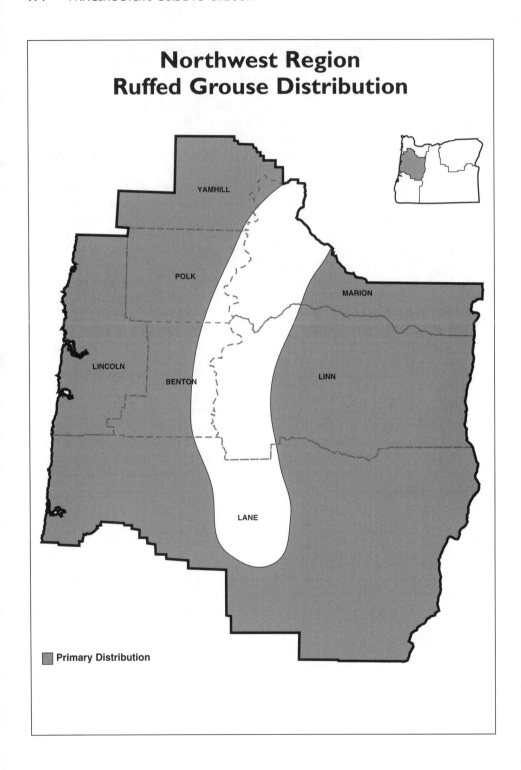

Northwest Region
Ruffed Grouse Distribution

YAMHILL

POLK

MARION

LINCOLN

BENTON

LINN

LANE

■ Primary Distribution

Northwest Region
Blue Grouse Distribution

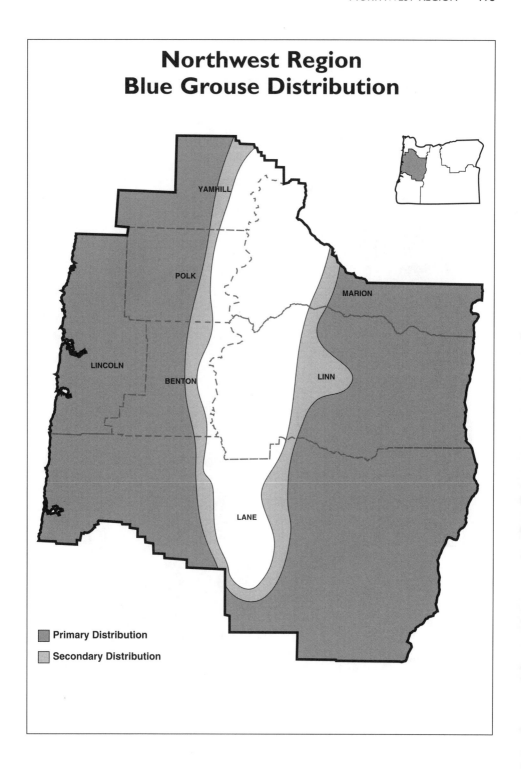

YAMHILL

POLK

MARION

LINCOLN

BENTON

LINN

LANE

Primary Distribution
Secondary Distribution

Northwest Region
Mountain Quail Distribution

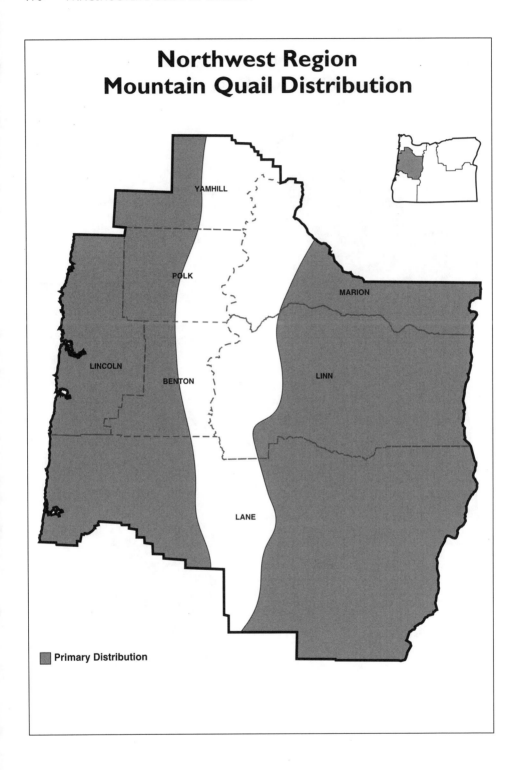

Primary Distribution

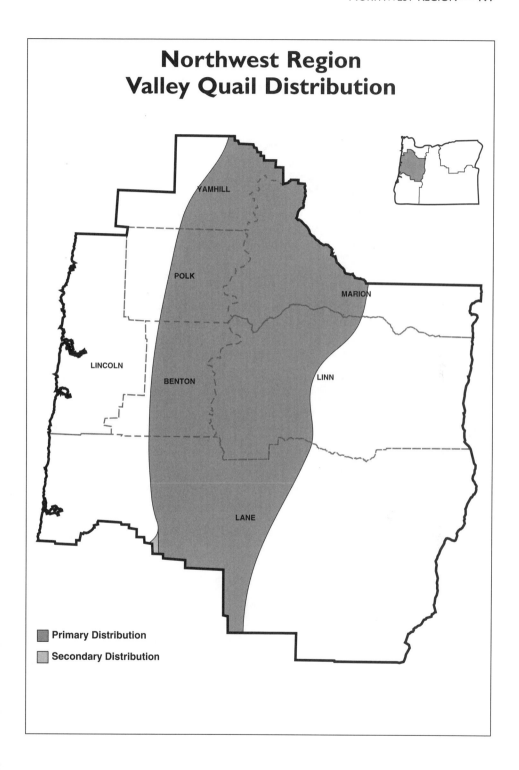

Northwest Region
Valley Quail Distribution

YAMHILL

POLK

MARION

LINCOLN

BENTON

LINN

LANE

Primary Distribution
Secondary Distribution

Northwest Region
Ring-necked Pheasant Distribution

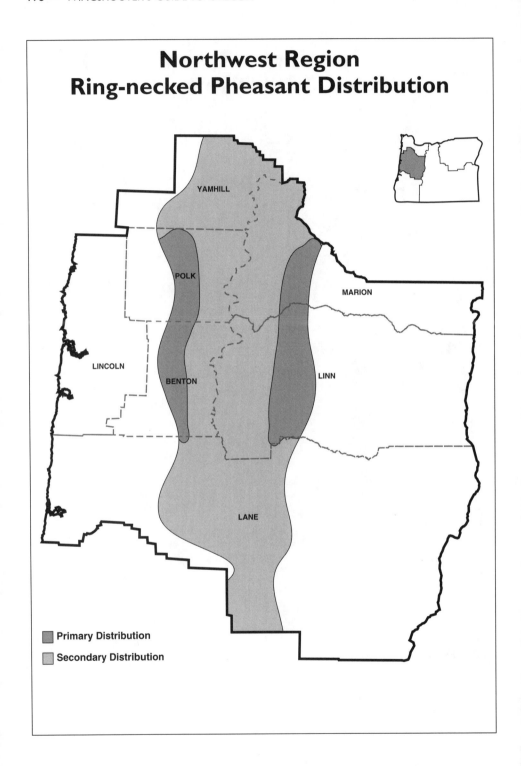

Primary Distribution
Secondary Distribution

Northwest Region
Wild Turkey Distribution

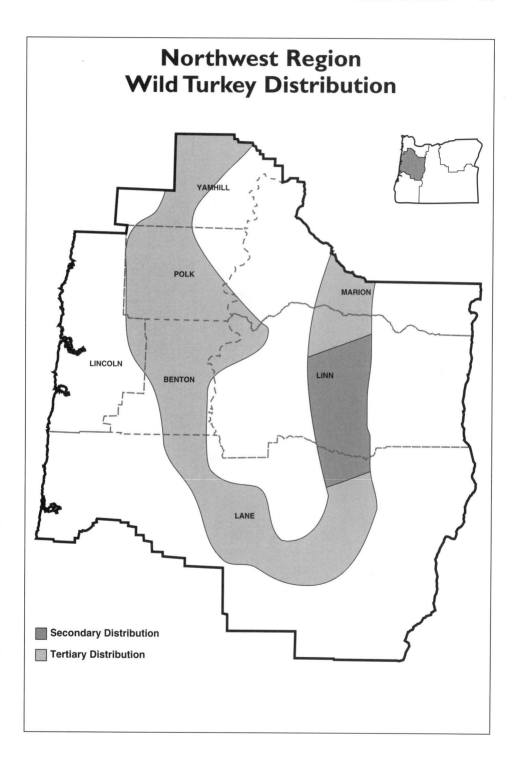

YAMHILL

POLK

MARION

LINCOLN

BENTON

LINN

LANE

Secondary Distribution
Tertiary Distribution

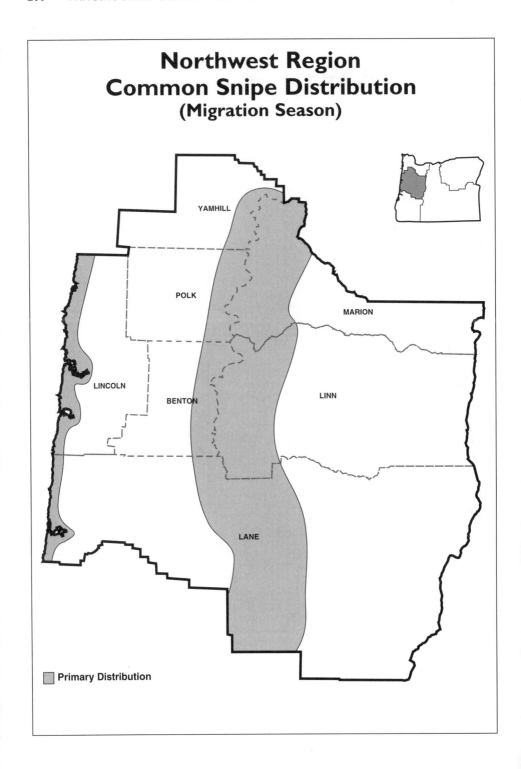

Northwest Region
Common Snipe Distribution
(Migration Season)

YAMHILL

POLK

MARION

LINCOLN

BENTON

LINN

LANE

Primary Distribution

McMinnville
Yamhill and Polk Counties

County Population:	McMinnville Population–24,265
Yamhill–77,500	County Acres in CRP:
Polk–56,300	Yamville–1,545
County Area:	Polk–847
Yamhill–718 sq. mi.	October Temperature–54°
Polk–745 sq. mi.	

Because they offer a distinct transition from the east slope of the Coast Range to the bottom of the Willamette Valley floor, Yamhill and Polk Counties offer much of interest to bird hunters. The forested slopes on the west halves of both counties provide lots of productive grouse and mountain quail cover. As you approach the valley floor, forest bird cover yields to some of western Oregon's better pheasant and valley quail cover in the form of small and medium-sized parcels of fallow land and grazing land where brush rows, blackberries, and hardwood stands remain intact. The valley floor itself is dominated in places by grass seed farms, where Canada geese provide the major sport. The Willamette River itself offers good prospects for duck hunting (see section on Willamette River Greenway).

McMinnville is the largest town in both counties, which are otherwise serviced by a number of small communities, including Monmouth, Independence, Sheridan, Dayton, Amity, and Willamina. This region also boasts some of the Northwest's best wine country, where important varietals include the Willamette Valley's famed pinot noirs. SR 99W traces a north-south path through both counties, leading north to the Portland Metro area and south to Corvallis. SR 22 departs Salem after crossing the Willamette River and heads west across Polk County on its way to the coast.

UPLAND BIRDS
Blue Grouse, Ruffed Grouse, Valley Quail, Mountain Quail, Ring-necked Pheasant, Mourning Dove, Band-tailed Pigeon, and Common Snipe

WATERFOWL
Ducks and Canada Geese

ACCOMMODATIONS
Best Western Vineyard Inn Motel, 2035 South Hwy 99W / 503-472-4900 or
800-285-6242 / Dogs allowed / $$–$$$
Paragon Motel, 2065 South Hwy 99W / 503-472-9493 / Dogs allowed / $–$$$
Safari Motor Inn, 345 North Hwy 99W / 503-472-5187
Orchard View Inn, 16540 Northwest Orchard View Road / 503-472-0165

Campgrounds and RV Parks
Mulkey RV Park, 14325 Southwest Hwy 18 / 503-472-2475
Old Stone Village Mobile Home and RV Park, 4155 Three-Mile Lane / 503-472-4315

Restaurants
Arbor Inn Restaurant, 2045 South Hwy 99W / 503-434-5151 / Sun–Thur
6AM–8PM, Fri–Sat 6AM–9PM
Dragon Gate Restaurant, 1310 North Baker Street / 503-472-6629 / Tues–Thur
11AM–9PM, Fri–Sat 11AM–11PM, Sun 11AM–9PM / Chinese cuisine
Golden Valley Brewery and Pub, 980 East 4th Street / 503-472-2739 / Mon–Thur
11:30AM–11:30PM, Fri–Sat 11:30AM–12:30, Sun 11:30AM–10PM
Hotel Oregon McMenamin's, 310 Northeast Evans / 888-472-8427 / Microbrewery, wine bar, pub food
Nick's Italian Restaurant, 521 East 3rd Street / 503-434-4471 / Tues–Thur
5:30–9PM, Fri–Sat 5:30–10PM, Sun 5–8:30PM
Roger's Seafood, 2121 East 27th Street / 503-472-0917
3rd Street Grill, 729 East 3rd Street / 503-435-1745 / Mon–Sat 5–9PM

Veterinary Clinics
Baker Street Animal Hospital, 1715 South Baker Street / 503-434-7263 /
8:30AM–6PM, Sat 9AM–1PM
McMinnville Veterinary Hospital, 2001 Northeast Lafayette / 503-472-6184

Dog Boarding
Best Friends Boarding Kennels, 17425 Southwest Masonville Road / 503-434-5088
Baker Street Animal Hospital, 1715 South Baker Street / 503-434-7263 /
8:30AM–6PM, Sat 9AM–1PM
McMinnville Veterinary Hospital, 2001 Northeast Lafayette / 503-472-6184

Auto Repair
Juniper Auto, 906 East 11th Street / 503-435-0409
Dwight's Auto Service, 640 Northeast 3rd Street / 503-472-2934
Riverside Auto, 3325 Northeast Riverside Drive / 503-472-4024
Ray's Auto Service, 710 Northeast 3rd Street / 503-472-3483

Auto Rental
Enterprise Rent-A-Car, 2670 North Hwy 99W / 503-472-4010
Ford Rent-A-Car, 1925 Northeast Hwy 99W / 503-472-6124 or 800-223-5099

Sporting Goods
Rite Aid, 1201 North Hwy 99W / 503-472-5910
R.J.'s Guns and Supplies, 1226 North Adams / 503-472-4511
Bi-Mart, 1635 South Baker / 503-472-8466

Medical
Willamette Valley Medical Center, 2700 Three-Mile Lane / 503-472-6131

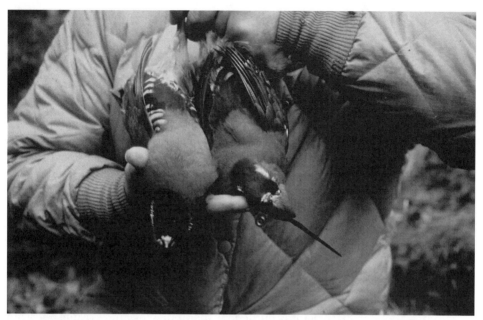

Mountain quail abound in the forested uplands of western Oregon.

AIR SERVICE
Portland International Airport, one hour northeast

FOR MORE INFORMATION
McMinnville Chamber of Commerce
417 North Adams Street
McMinnville, OR 97128
503-472-6196

Salem
Marion County

County Population–262,800	Salem Population–126,635
County Area–1,194 sq. mi.	October Temperature–53°
County Acres in CRP–17	

Marion County, which includes Oregon's capital city of Salem, stretches from the east bank of the Willamette River to the crest of the Cascade Mountains near 10,495-foot Mt. Jefferson. Its major drainage is the North Santiam River, whose rapid plunge from the mountains carves first a narrow, forested canyon and then a broadening valley as the river approaches its confluence with the Willamette.

Beginning in the foothills east of Salem, Marion County offers abundant farmland that once hosted a sizable population of ring-necked pheasants. The advent of the grass seed industry spelled doom for these populations, however, and they now survive in low densities in what little good habitat remains. Grass seed farming is characterized in part by expansive clean-swept fields devoid of brushy edges, vegetated fencelines and standing crop rows. Moreover, after the seed grass is cut, the remaining stubble in these fields is burned, further removing any possible pheasant cover. Marion County's pheasants now survive best in the foothills, generally on small tracts of fallow land with blackberry growth, native and introduced grasses, and perhaps the cover of open woodlots.

Far more common than pheasants, valley quail occupy the same types of habitat and are also quite common in residential areas. Mountain quail, blue grouse, and ruffed grouse abound from the foothills east of Salem deep into the Cascade Mountains. East of the Santiam Canyon town of Mill City (pop. 1,640), the Cascade Range is dominated by public lands administered by the Willamette National Forest and in places by the state of Oregon.

Duck and goose hunters find excellent sport along the Willamette River near Salem. Mallards, wigeon, green-winged teal, wood ducks, and ring-necked ducks are all quite common. Most of the river hunting is done by boat, with the launch at Salem's Wallace Marine Park being a popular and convenient access point.

Salem offers countless fine restaurants and every other imaginable service. Interstate 5 provides primary access from the north and south, while SR 22 heads up the Santiam Canyon to the east and west toward the coast (a one-hour drive takes you to Lincoln City).

UPLAND BIRDS
Blue Grouse, Ruffed Grouse, Valley Quail, Mountain Quail, Ring-necked Pheasant, Mourning Dove, Band-tailed Pigeon, Common Snipe

WATERFOWL
Ducks and Canada Geese

ACCOMMODATIONS
Phoenix Inn, 4370 Commercial Street Southeast / 800-445-4498 / 88 units / Dogs allowed / $$–$$$

Phoenix Inn, 1590 Weston Court Northeast / 888-239-9593 / 80 units / Dogs allowed / $$–$$$

Quality Inn Hotel, 3301 Market Street Northeast / 800-248-6273 / 150 units / Dogs allowed / $$$

City Center Motel, 510 Liberty Street Southeast / 503-364-0121 / Dogs allowed / $–$$

Motel 6, 2250 Mission Street Southeast / 503-588-7197 / Dogs allowed / $
1401 Hawthorne Avenue Northeast / 503-371-8024 / Dogs allowed / $

Motel Orleans, 1875 Fisher Road / 503-588-5423 / Dogs allowed / $–$$

Super 8 Motel, 1288 Hawthorne Northeast / 800-800-8000 / Dogs allowed / $$

Eagle Crest Bed and Breakfast, 4401 Eagle Crest Northwest / 503-364-3960 / Dogs allowed / $$

CAMPGROUNDS AND RV PARKS
Eola Bend RV Resort, 4700 Salem-Dallas Hwy 22 / 503-364-7714 / 180 spaces

Salem RV Park, 4490 Silverton Road Northeast / 800-937-4166 / 158 spaces

Salem Campgrounds and RVs, 3700 Hagers Grove Road Southeast / 800-825-9605 / 207 spaces

RESTAURANTS
Alessandro's, 325 High Street Southeast / 503-370-9951 / Fine dining

The Arbor Cafe, 380 High Street Northeast / 503-588-2353

La Estrellita, 1111 Edgewater Northwest / 503-362-0522 / Mexican cuisine

Mekong Restaurant, 210 Liberty Street Southeast #150 / 503-364-4833

La Margarita Restaurant and Grill, 545 Ferry Street / 503-362-8861 / Open for lunch and dinner / Mexican cuisine

Jonathan's Restaurant and Oyster Bar, 445 State Street / 503-362-7219

Inn at Orchard Heights, 695 Orchard Heights Road Northwest / 503-378-1780 / Fine din

Kyoto Japanese Restaurant, 2653 Commercial Street Southeast / 503-362-1100

Ma's Oriental Cuisine, 3305 Lancaster Drive Northeast / 503-581-3017

McGrath's Fish House, 350 Chemeketa Northeast / 503-362-0736

Nona Roselli's, 1311 Edgewater Street Northwest / 503-391-1010

Rock-N-Roger's Diner, 1405 Broadway Northeast / 503-364-5734
Boon's Treasury, 888 Liberty Street Northeast / 503-399-9062 / Brewpub with good food
Thompson Brewery and Public House, 3575 Liberty Road South / 503-363-7286
White's Restaurant, 1138 Commercial Street Southeast / 503-363-0297 / Hearty breakfasts
Ixtapa Mexican Restaurant, 111 West Locust (Stayton) / 503-769-6524
Giovanni Mountain Pizza, 146 Northwest Santiam Boulevard (Mill City) / 503-897-2614

VETERINARY CLINICS
Oak Hill Veterinary Clinic, 1212 Wallace Road Northwest / 503-581-1438
South Salem Animal Clinic, 3230 Triangle Drive Southeast / 503-581-1438
Associates Bird and Animal Hospital, 2700 Market Street Northeast / 503-581-2408 / Mon–Fri 7AM–8PM / Sat 10AM–3PM
Companion Pet Clinic, 4580 Commercial Southeast / 503-399-8300 / Mon–Sat 8AM–6PM
Companion Pet Clinic, 3068 Lancaster Drive, Northeast / 503-588-1603 / Mon–Sat 8AM–6PM
Companion Pet Clinic, 4975 River Road North, Keizer / 503-393-7462 / Mon–Sat 8AM–6PM

DOG BOARDING
Animal Inn, 3780 Boone Road Southeast / 503-363-0672
Pet Village Ltd., 3185 Turner Road Southeast / 503-363-3647
South Salem Animal Clinic, 3230 Triangle Drive Southeast / 503-581-1438

AUTO REPAIR
AJ's Auto Repair, 1858 13th Street Southeast / 503-581-7737
Elliott Auto Service, 4516 Sunny Side Road Southeast / 503-362-7634
Japanese Connection, 2515 Commercial Street Northeast / 503-581-4604
Keizer Automotive, 6558 Wheatland Road North / 503-390-2850
Madrona Auto Repair, 3498 Pringle Road Southeast / 503-365-7330

AUTO RENTAL
Budget Rent-a-Car, 3065 Ryan Drive Southeast / 503-362-0041
Enterprise Rent-a-Car, 80812 Street Southeast / 503-364-1911

SPORTING GOODS
Anderson's Sporting Goods, 241 Liberty Street Northeast / 503-364-4400
GI Joe's, Inc., 275 Lancaster Drive Northeast / 503-364-3365
Good Guys Guns, 3284 Lancaster Drive Northeast / 503-362-2226
Ole's Gun Shop, 1198 Walker Road Northeast / 503-585-3889
Rite Aid, 823 Lancaster Drive Northeast / 503-585-4800
Shooters Mercantile, 4700 Silverton Road Northeast / 503-361-2314
Bi-Mart, 2155 Lancaster Drive Northeast / 503-588-3211

Willamette Valley Canada geese.

MEDICAL
Salem Memorial Hospital, 665 Winter Street Southeast / 503-370-5200

AIR SERVICE
Portland International Airport, one hour north of Salem

FOR MORE INFORMATION
Salem Area Chamber of Commerce
1110 Commercial Street Southeast
Salem, OR 97301-1020
503-581-1466
email: info@salemchamber.org

Corvallis
Benton and Linn Counties

County Population:
  Benton–76,000
  Linn–100,000
County Area:
  Benton–679 sq. mi.
  Linn–2,297 sq. mi.
	Corvallis Population–49,630
	County Acres in CRP:
	  Benton–56
	  Linn–78
	October Temperature–53°

Oregon's grass seed industry is very much in evidence in many parts of Benton and Linn Counties, which occupy opposite sides of the Willamette Valley between Salem and Eugene. Huge, barren fields offering little in the way of upland bird cover demonstrate perfectly one of the reasons western Oregon's pheasant populations have fallen on hard times. Nonetheless, it is these same grass seed-producing fields that now attract so many Canada geese that the birds have become a financial liability to the farmers. Some 200,000 geese winter in the valley and recently expanded goose hunting opportunities in western Oregon are aimed largely at providing a solution to exploding bird populations.

Along the fringes of the valley, including parts of these two counties, hunters can still find pheasant along with the more numerous valley quail. Blue grouse occupy the timbered tracts of the east side of the Coast Range and Cascades, while ruffed grouse abound where appropriate mixed growth riparian habitat exists. Mountain quail thrive on steep, brushy forest edges in the mountainous regions of both counties.

Corvallis, the seat of Benton County, is the largest city between the two counties and is also home to Oregon State University. Interstate 5 runs north-south along the east side of the Willamette River; SR 99W does the same on the river's west side. US 20 departs Corvallis to the west and ends in Newport. Its eastward extension crosses the Willamette at Albany, the Linn County seat, and ventures into and across the Cascade Mountains, first visiting the timber towns of Lebanon and Sweet Home. East of Sweet Home, the highway soon enters the Willamette National Forest, where excellent public access and lots of prime habitat awaits grouse and quail fanatics.

UPLAND BIRDS
Blue Grouse, Ruffed Grouse, Valley Quail, Mountain Quail, Ring-necked Pheasant, Mourning Dove, Band-tailed Pigeon, Common Snipe

WATERFOWL
Ducks and Canada Geese

ACCOMMODATIONS

Corvallis Budget Inn, 1480 Southwest 3rd / 541-752-8756 / 24 units / Dogs allowed / $–$$

Econo-Lodge, 345 Northwest 2nd / 541-752-9601 or 800-553-2666 / 61 units / Dogs allowed / $$

Jason Inn, 800 Northwest 9th / 541-753-7326 or 800-346-3291 / 51 units / Dogs allowed / $$

Motel Orleans, 935 Northwest Garfield / 541-758-9125 or 800-626-1900 / 61 units / Dogs allowed / $$

Shanico Inn, 1113 Northwest 9th / 541-754-7474 or 800-432-1233 / 76 units / Dogs allowed / $$

Super 8 Motel, 407 Northwest 2nd / 541-758-8088 or 800-800-8000 / 101 units / Dogs allowed / $$$

Townhouse Motor Inn, 350 Southwest 4th / 541-753-4496 or 800-898-4496 / 99 units / Dogs allowed / $$

CAMPGROUNDS AND RV PARKS

Chapman House Bed and Breakfast, 6120 Southwest Country Club Drive / 541-758-3323 / Full hookups

KOA Campground, 337750 Will Road (Albany) / 541-967-8521 / Full hookups

Corvallis Mobile Home Park, 200 Northwest 53rd / 541-752-2334 / Full hookups

Willamette Park, Goodnight Road / 541-757-6918

RESTAURANTS

Michael's Landing, 603 Northwest 2nd / 541-754-6141 / Mon–Sat 1130AM–9PM

The Gables, 1121 Northwest 9th / 541-752-3364 / Open 5PM daily

Mazzi's, 1597 Northwest 9th / 541-757-8225 / Open for lunch and dinner / Italian

The Pavilion, 777 Northwest 9th / 541-752-5828 / Open 7 days, lunch and dinner / European cuisine

El Tapatio, 1845 Northwest Circle Boulevard / 541-758-1735 / Mexican

Burton's Restaurant, 119 Southwest 3rd / 541-753-1248 / Open seven days, 6AM–10PM

Playa Azul, 225 Southwest 4th / 541-754-5658 / Mexican

Shari's, 1117 Northwest 9th / 541-754-8240 / Open 24 hours

VETERINARY CLINICS

Town and Country Animal Clinic, 2621 Northwest 9th / 541-752-9914 / Mon–Fri 8AM–6PM; Sat 8AM–12PM / 24-hour emergency service

Corvallis Veterinary Hospital, 1543 Northwest 9th / 541-752-5595 / Mon–Fri 8AM–6PM; Sat 9AM–12 NOON

West Hills Animal Hospital, 430 Southwest 53rd / 541-758-4509 / Mon–Fri 8AM–6PM; Sat 9AM–12PM

Willamette Veterinary Clinic, 650 Southwest 3rd / 541-753-2223 / Mon–Fri 8:30AM–6:30PM; Sat 8:30AM–noon / 24-hour emergency service

DOG BOARDING
Corvallis Kennels, 720 Southwest Wake Robin Avenue / 541-757-9089
Curry's South Valley Boarding Kennels, 31533 Fern Road / 541-929-5476
Hedgerow Kennels, 32234 Country Road (Tangent) / 541-967-8546

AUTO REPAIR
B and R Auto Body and Paint Shop, 3065 Southeast 3rd / 541-757-7268
Main Auto Body, 210 Northwest 2nd / 541-754-1177
Clayton's Auto Repair Service, 787 Northeast Circle Boulevard / 541-752-2263
South Side Auto, Truck and RV Repair, 1750 Southwest Allen / (501) 754-9390

AUTO RENTAL
Enterprise Rent-a-Car, 400 Northwest Walnut #200 / 541-758-0000
Malcolm's Auto Electric, 442 Southwest 2nd / 541-757-7511

24-HOUR GAS STATIONS
Truax Arco, 45 Northwest 3rd / 541-752-2842

SPORTING GOODS
Anderson's Sporting Goods, 137 Southeast 3rd / 541-757-1666
Bi-Mart, 2045 North 9th and Circle Drive / 541-752-7158
          1555 Southwest 53rd Street / 541-758-2256

AIR SERVICE
Corvallis Airport (no commercial service) / Call Avia Aviation: 541-757-2842
Eugene Airport (served by United and Alaska) / 800-241-6522

24-HOUR ATM MACHINES
Bank of America, 324 Southwest 3rd
First Security Bank, 200 Southwest 4th
Citizens Bank, 275 Southwest 3rd

MEDICAL
Good Samaritan Hospital, 3600 Northwest Samaritan Drive / 541-757-5111
Samaritan Family Medicine, 3615 Northwest Samaritan, #201 / 541-757-5142

SHOTGUN RANGES
Muddy Creek Sporting Clays, 9499 Buchanan Road / 541-753-9679

FOR MORE INFORMATION
Corvallis Convention and Visitors Bureau
420 Northwest 2nd
Corvallis, OR 97330
541-757-1544
email:ccvb@visitcorvallis.com

Eugene and Springfield
Lane County

County Population–305,800	Eugene Population–133,460
County Area–4,620 sq. mi.	Springfield Population–51,700
County Acres in CRP–51	October Temperature–53°

Sprawling Lane County reaches from the crest of the Cascade Mountains east of Eugene to the Pacific beaches between Yachats and Florence. Western Oregon's second-largest county, Lane covers some 4,620 square miles. Much of the county is adorned in coniferous forest, but the Willamette and McKenzie Rivers cut a wide valley through the county's heart near Springfield and Eugene. To the west, the Siuslaw River drains a sizable portion of the Coast Range before surrendering its waters to the Pacific at Florence (pop. 6,400). The city of Eugene—Oregon's second largest town—serves as home to the University of Oregon, which provides the community with a distinct college town flavor.

Dave McNeese with Willamette River mallards.

The huge expanse of diverse habitats that comprises Lane County allows for many fine opportunities for the wingshooter. Waterfowl abounds along the Willamette River and its floodplain, including Fern Ridge Reservoir just west of Eugene. Pheasant and valley quail inhabit the valley floor and its attendant foothills, although neither species exists in high densities. The hills and mountains on both sides of the county offer countless acres of prime grouse and mountain quail habitat. All three forest species—blue grouse, ruffed grouse, and mountain quail—thrive in high densities throughout the mountainous regions of the Coast and Cascade Ranges. What's more, the Cascade Range is dominated by public lands administered by the Willamette National Forest. Myriad logging roads provide ready access.

Interstate 5 cuts through the heart of the Willamette Valley in a north-south direction. From Eugene, two major highways depart I-5 and head east through the Cascades to central Oregon. SR 126 passes through Springfield and then follows the McKenzie River through the mountains, eventually joining US 20 west of the town of Sisters, some 15 miles east of the Cascade crest. SR 58 heads southeast out of Eugene, crossing the Cascades after passing through the logging community of Oakridge (pop. 3,200). On the west side of Eugene, SR 126 extends over the Coast Range to Florence.

Oregon's second-largest airport (Eugene Municipal Airport) provides service to Lane County, with direct flights to and from Seattle, San Francisco, Denver, and Portland. United and Horizon serve the airport. Lane County boasts more than 300,000 people, almost half of that total in Eugene, a town replete with more good restaurants than can be listed here.

UPLAND BIRDS
Blue Grouse, Ruffed Grouse, Valley Quail, Mountain Quail, Ring-necked Pheasant, Mourning Dove, Band-tailed Pigeon, and Common Snipe

WATERFOWL
Ducks, Canada Geese, Black Brant

ACCOMMODATIONS
Eugene
Best Western Greentree Inn, 1759 Franklin Boulevard / 541-485-2727 or 800-528-1234 / 65 units / Dogs allowed / $$–$$$
Classic Residents Inn, 1140 West 6th Avenue / 541-343-0730 / 34 units / Dogs allowed / $–$$
Country Squire Inn, 33100 Van Duyn Road / 541-484-2000 / 105 units / Dogs allowed / $–$$$
Courtesy Inn, 345 West 6th Avenue / 541-345-3391 / 34 units / Dogs allowed / $–$$
Red Lion Inn, 205 Coburg Road / 541-342-5201 or 800-Red-Lion / 137 units / Dogs allowed / $$–$$$

Sixty Six Motel, 755 East Broadway / 541-342-5041 / 626 units / Dogs allowed / $–$$

Travelodge, 1859 Franklin Boulevard / 541-342-6383 / 60 units / Dogs allowed / $$–$$$

Springfield

Doubletree Hotel, 3280 Gateway / 541-1726-8181 / 234 units / Dogs allowed / $$$

Roadway Inn, 3480 Hutton Street / 541-746-8471 / 58 units / Dogs allowed / $$–$$$

Shilo Inn, 3350 Gateway / 541-747-0332 or 800-222-2244 / 142 units / Dogs allowed / $$–$$$

Village Inn Motel, 1875 Mohawk Boulevard / 541-747-4546 or 800-327-6871 / 70 units / Dogs allowed / $$–$$$

CAMPGROUNDS AND RV PARKS

Eugene

Shamrock Mobil and RV Park, 4531 Franklin Boulevard / 541-747-7473 / 30 full hookups, 8 partial hookups

Coburg Hills RV Park, 33022 Van Duyn Road / 541-686-3152 / 131 full hookups

Eugene Mobil Village, 4750 Franklin Boulevard / 541-747-2257 / 20 full hookups / No pets

Fern Ridge Shores, 29652 Jeans Road, Veneta / 541-935-2335 / 61 full hookups / Located on Fern Ridge Reservoir

Richardson County Park, Richardson Park Road / 541-682-6940 / 50 hookups / Located on Fern Ridge Reservoir / Open through mid-October

RESTAURANTS

Eugene

Ambrosia Restaurant, 174 East Broadway / 541-342-4141 / 11:30AM–9:30PM / Northern Italian cuisine.

The Big River Grill, inside the Eugene Hilton, 66 East 6th Avenue / 541-342-6658 / Mon–Sun 6:30AM–10PM / Pacific Northwest cuisine

Cafe Navarro, 454 Willamette Street / 541-344-0943 / Open for breakfast, lunch, dinner; closed Monday / Latin and Caribbean cuisine

El Torito, 1003 Valley River Way / 541-683-7294 / Mon–Thur 11AM–MIDNIGHT; Fri–Sat 11AM–1AM; Sun 10AM–11PM / Mexican cuisine

Fields Restaurant and Brew Pub, 1290 Oak Street / 541-341-6599 / Open for lunch and dinner / Microbrews and Northwest pub fare

Glenwood Restaurant, 2588 Willamette Street / 541-687-8201 1340 Alder Street / 541-687-0355 / Mon–Fri. 6:30AM–10PM; Sat–Sun 7AM–10PM / Highly regarded, award-winning local favorite

Mazzi's Restaurant, 3377 East Amazon / 541-687-2252 / Italian Sicilian cuisine

McGrath's Fish House, 1036 Valley River Way / 541-342-6404 / Sun–Thur / 11AM–10PM; Fri–Sat 11AM–11PM; Sun 10AM–2PM / Eugene's largest selection of fresh seafood

Oregon Electric Station, 27 East 5th Avenue / 541-485-4444 / Open for lunch and dinner / One of Eugene's perennial favorite fine dining establishments

Steelhead Brewing Co., 199 East 5th Avenue / 541-686-2739 / Open daily 11:30AM–MIDNIGHT / Microbrew and Northwest pub fare

Track Town Pizza, 1809 Franklin Boulevard / 541-484-2799 / 11AM–MIDNIGHT / Eugene's favorite campus-area pizza

West Brothers Barbecue, 844 Olive Street / 541-345-8489 / Open for lunch and dinner / One of Eugene's most eclectic and creative menus; microbrewery

Lyons Restaurant, 1933 Franklin Boulevard / 541-484-4333 / Open 24 hours

VETERINARY CLINICS

Eugene

Westmoreland Animal Hospital, 1748 West 18th / 541-485-4595 / 24-hour emergency service available

South Hills Veterinary Clinic, 4175 East Amazon Drive / 541-485-5666

West Eugene Animal Hospital, 1175 City View / 541-342-5858

Springfield

Emergency Veterinary Hospital, 103 Q Street / 541-746-0112 / Open week-nights 6PM–8AM; open 24 hours weekends and holidays

McKenzie Animal Clinic, 5303 Main Street / 541-747-3859

DOG BOARDING

Eugene

Willamette Valley Dog and Cat Motel, 28438 Bodenhamer Road / 541-688-0978 / 5 minutes from airport off Greenhill Road

Browning's Dog Ranch, 28794 Hillaire / 541-688-8276

Claymore Waggin' Inn, 90558 Alvadore Road / 541-688-3260 / 5 minutes west of Eugene airport

Bondale Kennels, 29083 Airport Road / 541-689-0367

Utopia Retriever Kennel, 24019 Hwy 99W (Junction City) / 541-847-5190

Springfield

Country Inn, 41557 McKenzie Hwy, 15 minutes east of Springfield / 541-896-3435

GUN DOG TRAINERS

Eugene

Utopia Retriever Kennel, 24019 Hwy 99W (Junction City) / 541-847-5190

Hidden Hill Kennels, 21624 Glaze Road / 541-935-2014

AUTO REPAIR

Eugene

Action Automotive, 720 Taylor / 541-686-0191

Firestone Mastercare Car Service, 185 East 11th Street / 541-345-1593

Allen Automotive, 274 Coburg Road / 541-343-5022
East Amazon Auto Repair, 3475 East Amazon Drive / 541-485-2819
Schweitzer's Automotive, 1120 Arthur Street / 541-342-1664
Ford Authorized Service (Kendall Ford), 344 Goodpasture Island Road /
541-485-3686
Dodge Authorized Service, Emerald Chrysler-Plymouth, 383 Goodpasture Island
Road / 541-342-6600
Chevrolet Authorized Service (Romania Chevrolet), 2020 Franklin Boulevard /
541-342-1121
Honda Authorized Service (Kendall Honda), 20 Coburg Road / 541-485-6111
Isuzu Authorized Service (Dunham Isuzu), 345 Goodpasture Island Road / 541-
345-1511
Jeep-Eagle Authorized Service (Emerald Chrysler Plymouth), 383 Goodpasture
Island Road / 541-1342-6600
Hutchins Eugene Nissan, 2060 Centennial Boulevard / 541-686-2211
Toyota Authorized Service (Romania Toyota), 388 Goodpasture Island Road /
541-344-5566
Subaru Authorized Service (Romania Subaru), 388 Goodpasture Island Road /
541-344-5566

Auto Rental
Eugene
Avis Rent-A-Car, Eugene Municipal Airport / 541-688-9053 or 800-831-2847
Budget Car and Truck Rental, Eugene Municipal Airport / 541-688-1229
Enterprise Rent-A-Car, 110 West 6th / 541-683-0874
Hertz Rent-A-Car, Eugene Municipal Airport / 541-688-9333
Premier Car Rental, 10½ Coburg Road / 541-687-1970

Sporting Goods
Eugene
Anderson's Sporting Goods, 199 West 8th / 541-484-7344
G.I. Joe's, 1030 Green Acres Road / 541-343-1668
Rite Aid, 1560 Coburg Road / 541-484-1464
1970 Echo Hollow Road / 541-461-0700
57 West 29th Avenue / 541-342-5571
Baron's Den, 86321 College View Road / 541-744-6229
S-M Gun Shop, 1375 River Road / 541-688-8700
Bi-Mart, 2030 River Road / 541-687-7618
1680 West 18th / 541-687-76022510 Willakenzie Road / 541-687-7610
Springfield
Rite Aid, 2130 Marcola Road / 541-747-3361
The Gun Works, 247 South 2nd / 541-741-4118
Bi-Mart, 1521 Mohawk Boulevard / 541-687-7628

MEDICAL
Eugene
  Sacred Heart Medical Center, 1255 Hilyard Street / 541-686-7000
Springfield
  McKenzie-Willamette Hospital, 1460 G Street / 541-726-4400

AIR SERVICE
  Eugene Airport, Airport Road northwest of Eugene / 541-687-5430
  Nonstop flights to: Seattle, Denver, San Francisco, Portland
  Serviced By: United Airlines (800-241-6522), Horizon Airlines (800-547-9308)

FOR MORE INFORMATION
  Eugene Area Chamber of Commerce
  1401 Willamette Street
  P.O. Box 1107
  Eugene, OR 97440-1107
  541-484-1314

Lincoln City and Newport
Lincoln County

County Population–42,200	Lincoln City Population–6,855
County Area–992 sq. mi.	Newport Population–10,240
County Acres in CRP–0	October Temperature–53°

Lincoln County stretches from the mouth of the Salmon River near massive Cascade Head south to Cape Perpetua near the community of Yachats. In addition to Lincoln City and Yachats, Lincoln County includes the important coast towns of Newport and Waldport. Newport, the county seat, ranks as the third largest coastal community. Lincoln County, like other coast counties, relies heavily on tourism as a chief industry, though the more traditional industries—timber and fishing—remain dominant sources of employment and revenue.

Lincoln County offers much to the bird hunting enthusiast. Duck hunting opportunities abound in the county's major estuaries, especially Siletz Bay just south of Lincoln City where expansive tidal flats and marshes attract large flights of wigeon, pintail, and mallard along with many other species. Likewise, various reaches of Alsea Bay (Waldport), Yaquina Bay (Newport), and the Salmon River delta provide similar sport for both dabblers and divers. Black brant winter in the area, mostly in Yaquina Bay, and common snipe abound by mid-autumn.

Upland birds thrive in the wooded slopes, from immediately east of the beach environment to the crest of the Coast Range, from which the county's major rivers draw their respective headwaters. Included among these important waterways are the lengthy Siletz and Alsea Rivers, the Salmon River, and the Yaquina River. Extensive riparian habitat, complete with dense stands of red alder and maple, provide lots of cover for ruffed grouse. Blue grouse occupy the high ridges, and mountain quail abound on steep, brushy slopes near forest edges. Band-tailed pigeons nest here, and local populations are bolstered in the fall by the arrival of migrants.

Highway 101 forms the north-south artery through Lincoln County. Newport is about one hour west of Corvallis via US 20. State Route 22 connects Lincoln City and Salem, while SR 34 leads from Corvallis to Waldport. While access to the estuaries is excellent, especially for boaters, much of the Coast Range is owned by private timber companies. Be wary of gate closures, and if you are unsure of the open or closed status of any forest roads, check with the nearest ranger district (Siuslaw National Forest) or consult the timber company that owns the property.

Owing largely to their status as tourist destinations, the towns of Lincoln County and Newport offer many fine eating establishments and countless upscale accommodations. Lodging prices often drop during the winter season, so budget-minded hunters can find motel rooms for around $30 per night in many locations. Also, several state parks in the county offer camping and RV space. The largest of these is at Beverly Beach north of Newport.

UPLAND BIRDS
Blue Grouse, Ruffed Grouse, Mountain Quail, Mourning Dove, Band-tailed Pigeon, Common Snipe

WATERFOWL
Ducks, Canada Geese, Black Brant

ACCOMMODATIONS
Lincoln City
Beachfront Garden Inn, 3313 Northwest Inlet Avenue / 503-994-2324 / Dogs allowed / $$
Coho Inn, 1635 Northwest Harbor / 503-994-3684 / Dogs allowed / $$–$$$
Rodeway Inn, 861 Southwest 50th / 503-996-3996 or 1-800-843-4940 / Dogs allowed / $–$$$
Sea Echo Motel, 3510 Northeast Highway 101 / 503-994-2575 / Dogs allowed / $$
Shilo Inn, 1501 Northwest 40th Street / 503-994-3655 / Dogs allowed / $$–$$$

Newport
Agate Beach Motel, 175 Gilbert Way / 541-265-8746 or 800-755-5674 / Dogs allowed / $$$
Newport City Center Motel, 538 Southwest Coast Hwy / 541-265-7381 / Dogs allowed / $$
Driftwood Village Motel, 7947 North Coast Hwy / 541-265-5738 / Dogs allowed / $$
Holiday Inn, 3019 North Coast Highway / 541-265-9411 or 800-547-3310 / Dogs allowed / $$–$$$
Newport Motor Inn, 1311 North Coast Hwy / 541-265-8516 / Dogs allowed / $–$$
Penny Saver Motel, 710 North Coast Hwy / 541-265-6631 or 800-477-3669 / Dogs allowed / $
Shilo Inn, 536 Southwest Elizabeth / 541-265-7701 or 800-222-2244 / Dogs allowed / $$$
Summer Wind Motel, 728 North Coast Hwy / 541-265-8076 / Dogs allowed / $
Troller's Lodge, 355 South West Coast Hwy / 541-765-2287 / Dogs allowed / $
Whaler, 155 Southwest Elizabeth / 541-265-9261 / Dogs allowed / $$

CAMPGROUNDS AND RV PARKS
Lincoln City
Devils Lake RV Park, 4041 Northeast West Devils Lake Road / 503-994-3400
Siletz Valley RV Park, 162 Gaither (Siletz) / 503-444-2508 / 11 full hookups
Tree 'N' Sea Trailer Park, 1015 Southwest 50th Street / 503-996-3801

Newport
Agate Beach RV Park, 6138 North Coast Hwy / 541-265-7670 / 32 spaces, full hookups / Pets allowed

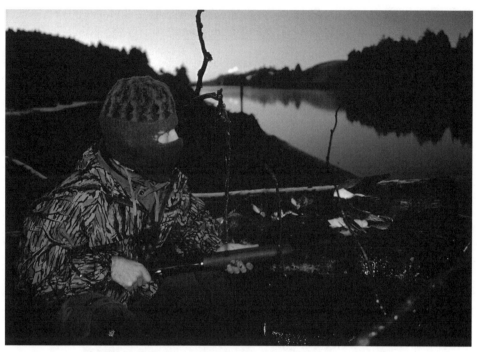

Natural blind material abounds on Oregon's estuaries.

Beverly Beach State Park, 198 Northeast 123rd Street / 1-800-551-6949 / 52 full hookups, 75 partials, 152 tent sites

Pacific Shores RV Resort, 6225 North Coast Hwy / 1-800-333-1583 / 287 spaces

South Beach State Park, 5580 South Coast Hwy / 1-800-551-6949 / 254 spaces

RESTAURANTS

Lincoln City

Bay House Restaurant, 5911 Southwest Hwy 101 / 503-996-3222 / Fresh Northwest cuisine

Chase the Wave Cafe, 2156 Northeast Hwy 101 / 503-994-7323

Dory Cove, 5819 Logan Road., Roads End (north end of Lincoln City) / 503-994-5180

Kernville Steak and Seafood House, 186 Siletz Hwy / 503-994-6200 / Open 7 nights from 4PM / Overlooking the Siletz River

Hobie's Adobe, 2733 Northwest Hwy 101 / 503-994-4419 / Open daily for lunch and dinner / Mexican and Pacific Rim cuisine

Kyllo's Seafood and Grill, 1110 Northwest First Ct / 503-994-3179

Lighthouse Brew Pub, 4157 North Hwy 101 / 503-994-7238

Mazatlan Mexican Restaurant, 3001 Northwest Hwy 101 / 503-996-6090
Siletz Public House and Brewery, 267 Gaither (Siletz) / 503-444-7012
Newport
  Apple Peddler Restaurant, 705 Southwest Coast Hwy / 541-265-5165
  Chalet Restaurant, 2026 North Coast Hwy / 541-265-6900
  Galley Ho, 1255 North Coast Hwy / 541-265-5104
  Mazatlan Mexican Restaurant, 404 Southwest Coast Hwy / 541-265-8595
  Mo's Restaurant, 622 Southwest Bay Boulevard / 541-265-7512 / Famous clam
    chowder
  McIvar's Landing, 1226 North Coast Hwy / 541-265-9233

VETERINARY CLINICS
Lincoln City
  Lincoln City Animal Clinic, 4090 Northeast Hwy 101 / 541-994-8181
Newport
  Grove Veterinary Clinic, 448 East Olive / 541-265-2381 / 9AM–11AM and 1PM–
    5PM weekdays
  Animal Medical Care of Newport, 159 Northeast 10th / 541-265-6671

DOG BOARDING
Lincoln City
  Rose Lodge Boarding Kennels, 146 North Holiday Lane, Rose Lodge (east of
    Lincoln City) / 503-994-8595
Newport
  Noah's Ark Kennel, 8790 Northwest Kinglet, Seal Rock / 541-563-5866

AUTO REPAIR
Lincoln City
  Car Care Specialists, 2185 Northwest Hwy 101 / 503-996-6099
  Glenndale Auto Repair, 3232 Northeast Hwy 101 / 503-996-3131
  Joe's Professional Truck and Auto Repair, 2654-A Southeast Hwy 101 /
    503-994-5331
  Nelscott Garage, 3330 Northeast Hwy 101 / 503-996-2222
  Shaffer's Automotive and Towing, 906 Southeast Hwy 101 / 503-994-5545
Newport
  ABC Auto Plus, 846 Southwest Coast Hwy / 541-265-6965
  Auto Doctors, Highway 101 and 32nd / 541-265-6769
  McDowell's Auto Clinic, 113 East Olive / 541-265-2637
  Pacific Car Repair, 831 Northeast 3rd / 541-265-8929

AUTO RENTAL
Lincoln City
  Burton's Auto Rentals, 1220 Northeast Hwy 101 / 503-994-2211
  Robben Rent-A-Car, 3244 Northeast Hwy 101 / 503-994-2452
  Gesik's Auto Rental, 1949 Northeast Hwy 101 / 503-994-5500
Newport
  Surf Side Motors, 27 South Coast Hwy / 541-265-6686

SPORTING GOODS
Lincoln City
  Rite Aid, 4041 Northwest Logan Road / 503-994-9478
  Bi-Mart, 4157 North Hwy 101 / 541-994-3319
Newport
  Bittler Bros. Sports Center, 355 Southwest Coast Hwy / 541-265-7192 / Open 7
    days
  Rite Aid, 2336 North Coast Hwy / 541-265-8844

MEDICAL
Lincoln City
  North Lincoln Hospital, 3043 Northeast 28th / 541-994-3661
Newport
  Pacific Communities Hospital, 930 Southwest Abbey / 541-265-2244

TAXIDERMISTS
Lincoln City
  Memories Taxidermy Studio, 1990 Northeast Reef / 541-996-3621
Newport
  Bernard's Taxidermy, Highway 20, Chitwood / 541-875-2222

AIR SERVICE
Lincoln City and Newport
  Newport Airport, off Hwy 101 south of town / 503-867-7767 or 867-3655

FOR MORE INFORMATION
  Lincoln City Chamber of Commerce
  4039 Northwest Logan Road
  Lincoln City OR 97367
  503-994-3070

  Greater Newport Chamber of Commerce
  555 Southwest Coast Highway
  Newport, OR 97365
  503-265-8801 or 800-262-7844

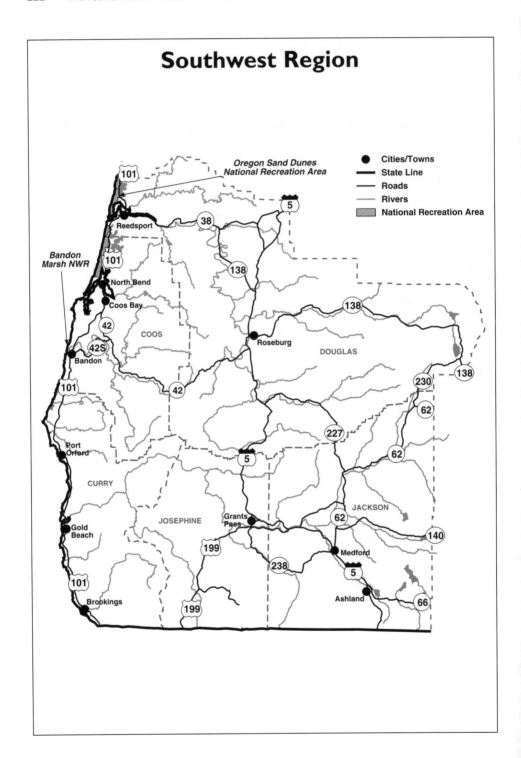

Southwest Region

Southwest Region

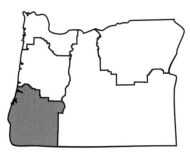

Oregon's Southwest Region earns bragging rights for the state's highest densities of both wild turkey and mountain quail, both of which thrive in many locations around this five-county region. Oregon's special fall turkey hunt occurs in Douglas and Jackson Counties. Blue grouse and ruffed grouse hunting is equally productive, and the southwest Oregon coast offers some fine estuary duck hunting along with opportunities for common snipe and band-tailed pigeon.

In the southwest, the Coast Range of northern and central Oregon yields to the Siskiyou Mountains. The Cascade Range dominates the eastern portion of Douglas and Jackson Counties. Counted among the region's treasures is stunning 9,182-foot Mt. Thielsen and nearby Diamond Lake. Two of Oregon's most important rivers—the Umpqua and the Rogue—drain a huge portion of the region. Both are steelhead streams of long-standing national repute, especially among fly anglers. This region includes several prominent Oregon cities: Roseburg, Coos Bay, Grants Pass, Medford, Ashland, and a host of smaller towns.

Traditionally, the entire region has been dominated by the timber industry, which remains the most important and powerful industry in each of the five counties. National forest lands predominate in the Cascade Range; parts of the Siskiyou and Coast Ranges include lands administered by Siskiyou, Rogue, and Siuslaw National Forests. However, the region's forested expanses also include huge private timber holdings where hunters may or may not be allowed access. When in doubt, check with the Forest Service or with the timber companies.

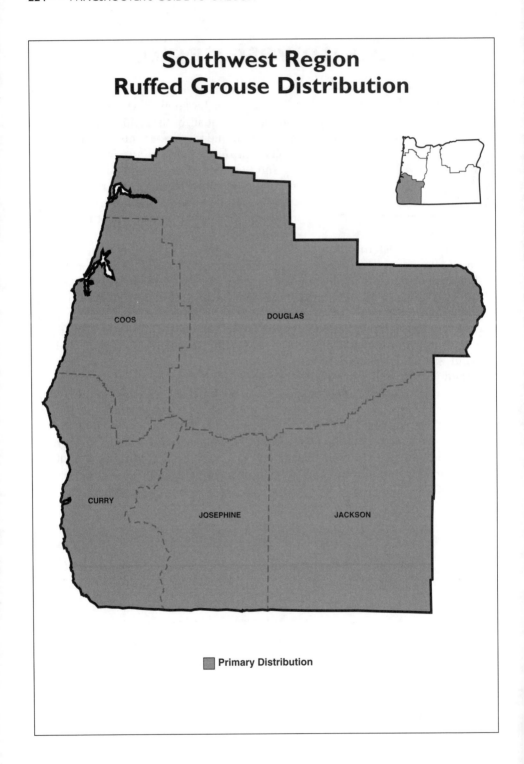

Southwest Region
Ruffed Grouse Distribution

COOS

DOUGLAS

CURRY

JOSEPHINE

JACKSON

■ Primary Distribution

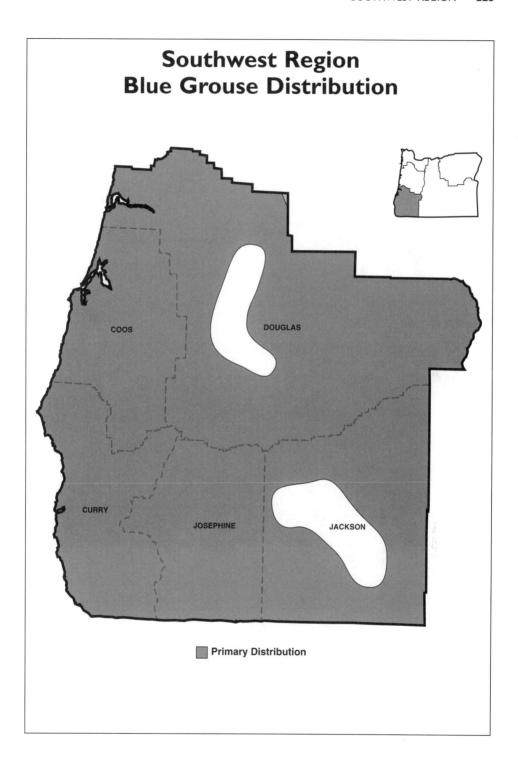

Southwest Region
Blue Grouse Distribution

COOS

DOUGLAS

CURRY

JOSEPHINE

JACKSON

Primary Distribution

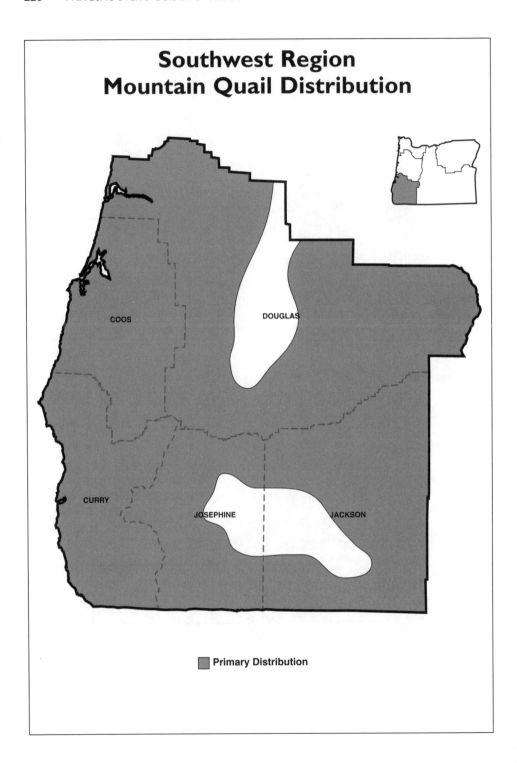

Southwest Region
Mountain Quail Distribution

Primary Distribution

Southwest Region
Valley Quail Distribution

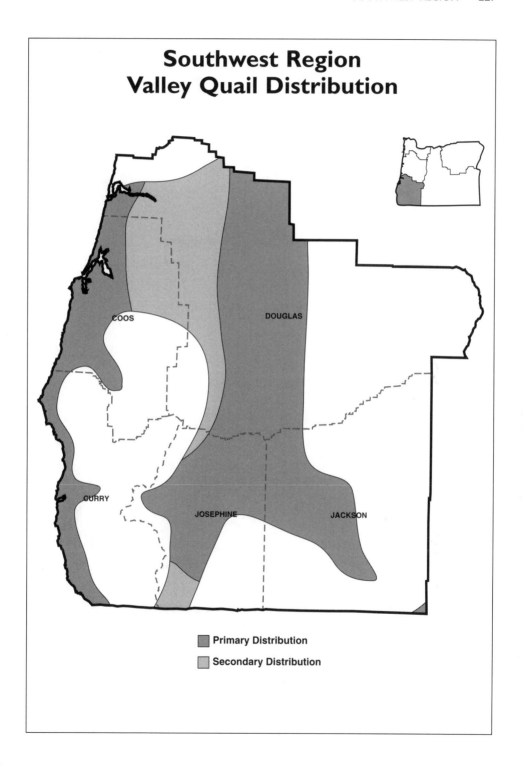

COOS

DOUGLAS

CURRY

JOSEPHINE

JACKSON

Primary Distribution
Secondary Distribution

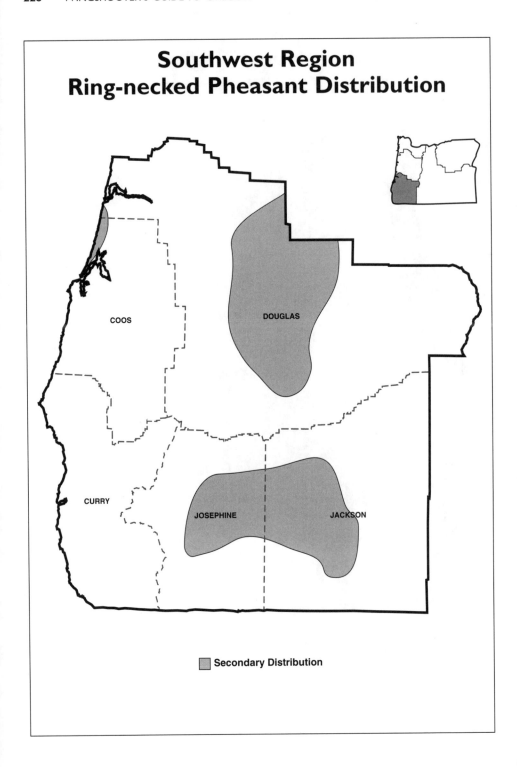

Southwest Region
Ring-necked Pheasant Distribution

COOS

DOUGLAS

CURRY

JOSEPHINE

JACKSON

Secondary Distribution

Southwest Region
Wild Turkey Distribution

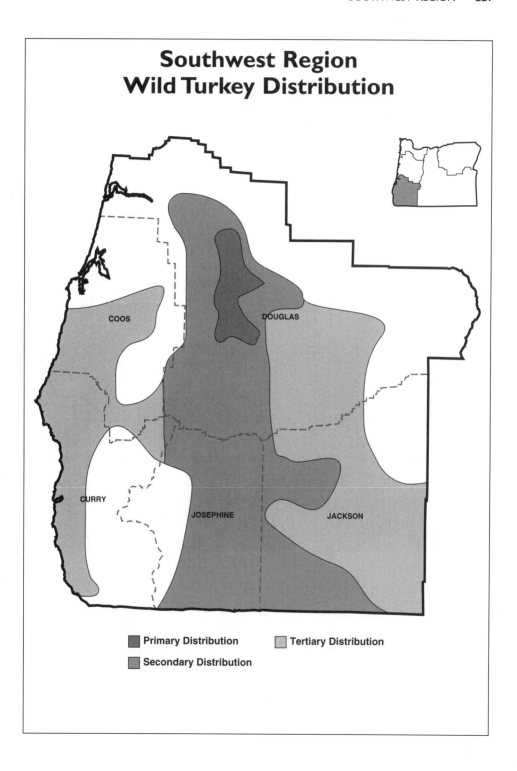

Primary Distribution

Secondary Distribution

Tertiary Distribution

COOS

DOUGLAS

CURRY

JOSEPHINE

JACKSON

Southwest Region
Common Snipe Distribution
(Migration Season)

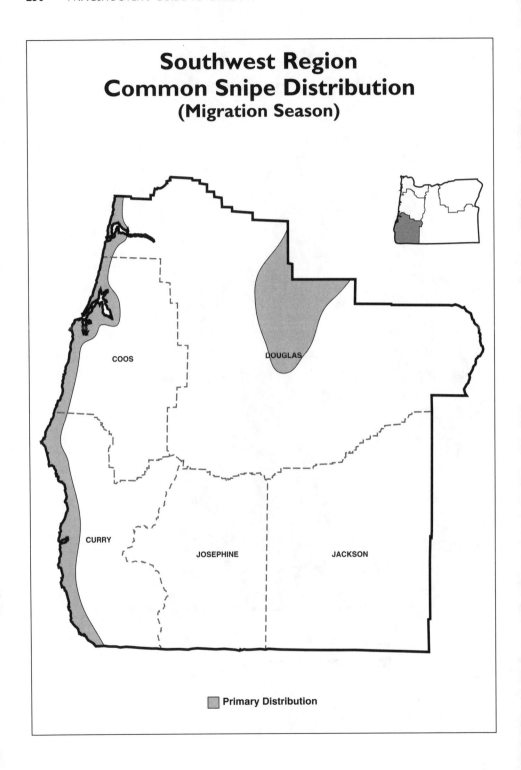

COOS

DOUGLAS

CURRY

JOSEPHINE

JACKSON

Primary Distribution

Roseburg and Reedsport
Douglas County

County Population–98,600	Roseburg Population–20,215
County Area–5,071 sq. mo.	Reedsport Population–4,860
County Acres in CRP–245	October Temperature–55°

Douglas County, western Oregon's largest county, offers a rich diversity of bird hunting opportunities owing largely to its modest population and to the fact that this sprawling expanse stretches from the coast to the crest of the Cascades. Throughout, Douglas County covers many different habitat types, which are occupied by numerous game birds. Blue grouse thrive in the Cascades and Coast Ranges, where steep, timbered ridges and lush berry patches offer ideal cover. Ruffed grouse flourish along the creeks and rivers. Mountain Quail inhabit the mountainous areas in surprising densities and are definitely underhunted.

Meanwhile, Douglas County offers the state's best opportunities for hunting Rio Grande turkeys, whose numbers are so high that ODFW now offers a second turkey season in the fall (October 15–November 15). In 1998, 750 fall turkey permits were issued for Douglas County and another 150 for Jackson County. During fall, either sex turkey may be taken, and hunters are allowed the use of dogs. Turkey habitat abounds because much of central Douglas County features extensive stands of oak mixed with a varied understory and at the edges with other hardwoods and conifers.

Waterfowl hunters will find plenty of action in Douglas County, especially at the Umpqua River estuary near Reedsport and at various lakes throughout the county, including the big, many-armed coastal waters such as Tahkenitch Lake and Siltcoos Lake.

Interstate 5 cuts north to south through the heart of Douglas County and through the hub city of Roseburg. Other I-5 towns include Sutherlin and Myrtle Creek. Reedsport straddles US 101 on the south side of the lower Umpqua River, while the little hamlet of Gardener occupies the north bank. Both towns offer boat ramps for duck hunters using the estuary. State Route 38 follows the Umpqua from Reedsport to I-5 at Sutherlin; SR 138 continues from Roseburg all the way to central Oregon, this time following the North Umpqua, a steelhead river of long standing repute with fly anglers.

UPLAND BIRDS
Blue Grouse, Ruffed Grouse, Mountain Quail, Valley Quail, Ring-necked Pheasant, Wild Turkey, Mourning Dove, Band-tailed Pigeon, and Common Snipe

WATERFOWL
Ducks, Canada Geese, Black Brant

ACCOMMODATIONS
Roseburg

Best Western Douglas Inn, 511 Southeast Stevens / 541-673-6625 or 800-528-1234 / 52 units / Dogs allowed / $$–$$$

Best Western Garden Villa Motel, 760 Northwest Garden Way / 541-672-1601 or 800-547-3446 / 122 units / Dogs allowed / $$$$

Budget 16, 1067 Northeast Stephens / 541-673-5556 / 48 units / Dogs allowed / $

Casa Loma,1107 Southeast Stephens / 541-673-5569 / 18 units / Dogs allowed / $–$$

City Center Motel, 1321 Southeast Stephens / 9 units / Dogs allowed / $

Dunes Motel, 610 West Madrone / 46 units / Dogs allowed / $$–$$$

Holiday Motel, 444 Southeast Oak / 541-672-4457 / 40 units / Dogs allowed / $

National 9 Inn, 1627 Southeast Stephens / 541-672-3354 / 12 units / Dogs allowed / $

Rose City Motel, 1142 Northeast Stephens / 541-673-8209 / 12 units / Dogs allowed / $$

Vista Motel, 1183 Northeast Stephens / 541-673-2736 / 15 units / Dogs allowed / $

Reedsport

Economy Inn, 1593 Hwy 101 / 541-271-3671 / Dogs allowed / $–$$

Salbasgeon Inn of the Umpqua, 45209 Hwy 38 / 541-271-2025 / Dogs allowed / $$–$$$

Best Budget Inn, 1894 Winchester Avenue / 541-271-3686 / No Pets

Fir Grove Motel, 2178 Winchester Avenue / 541-271-4848

Salty Seagull, 1806 Winchester Avenue / 541-271-3729

CAMPGROUNDS AND RV PARKS
Roseburg

Amacher County Park, Exit 129 off I-5 / 541-672-4901 / 20 full hookups, 10 tent sites

Douglas County Fairgrounds RV Park, 2110 Frear Street / 541-440-4505 / 50 hookups

Susan Creek Park (BLM), Hwy 138, 30 miles east of Roseburg / 541-440-4930 / 31 sites

Reedsport

Coho RV Park and Marina, 1580 Winchester Avenue / 541-271-5411

Discovery Point Resort and RV Park, Salmon Drive in Winchester Bay / 541-271-3443

RESTAURANTS
Roseburg

Apple Peddler, 1350-1 Northeast Stephens / 541-673-0503 / Open 24 hours

Denny's Restaurant, 350 West Harvard / 541-672-3134 / Open 24 hours

International House of Pancakes, 1370 Northwest Garden Valley / 541-672-6709

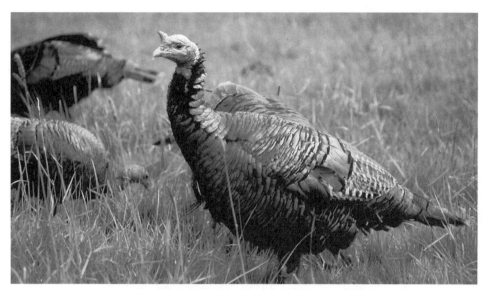

Rio Grande turkeys thrive in southwest Oregon.

Sandpiper Restaurant, 1450 Northwest Mulholland / 541-673-0021
Sizzler, 1156 Northwest Garden Valley / 541-672-5443
Umpqua Brewing Company, 328 Southeast Jackson / 541-672-0452
Asia Garden Restaurant, 2405 Northeast Diamond Lake / 541-673-1342
Los Dos Amigos, 537 Southeast Jackson / 541-673-1351
Reedsport
Harbor Light Family Restaurant, 390 Hwy 101 / (541)271-3848
Unger's Landing, 345 Riverfront Way / 541-271-3328
Windjammer Restaurant, 1281 Highway 101 / 541-271-5415

VETERINARY CLINICS
Roseburg
Animal Medical Clinic, 575 Northeast Stephens / 541-673-3062
Bailey Veterinary Clinic, 248 Northwest Garden Valley Boulevard / 541-673-4403 /
   Mon–Fri 8AM–5:30PM; Sat 9AM–12NOON and 1:30PM–4PM
Companion Animal Clinic, 736 West Military Road / 541-673-1345 / Mon–Fri
   8AM–5:30PM; Sat 8–NOON
Reedsport
Lower Umpqua Veterinary Clinic, 199 Port Dock Road / 541-271-4696
Osburn Veterinary Clinic, 130 East Railroad Avenue / 541-271-5824

DOG BOARDING
Roseburg
Lone Pine Kennel, 1417 Northeast Rifle Range Road / 541-673-8657

Reedsport
(See listings for Coos Bay-North Bend)

AUTO REPAIR
Roseburg
Allen Automotive, 1980 Northeast Stephens / 541-672-4213
Fray's Automotive, 1350 Southeast Short / 541-672-4072
Walker Brothers Auto Repair, 1225 Northeast Stephens / 541-672-1527
Koble's Auto Repair, 1320 Northeast Cedar / 541-672-0249
Chuck Swarm Auto Repair, 3986 Old Hwy 99 S / 541-679-4704
Reedsport
Kirk's General Repair, 563 Winchester Avenue / 541-271-0236
Migas Automotive, 1199 Highway 101 / 541-271-3530
Artoo Mechanical, 735 East Railroad Avenue / 541-271-2381

AUTO RENTAL
Roseburg
Certified Auto Rentals, 1410 Southeast Stephens / 541-672-8747
Enterprise Rent-A-Car / 541-440-3030 or 800-325-8007
Ford Authorized Rentals, 1650 Northeast Stephens / 541-673-4485

SPORTING GOODS
Roseburg
Gunner's Club, 1425 Southeast Stephens / 541-672-2761
Surplus Center, 515 Southeast Spruce / (501) 672-4312
Rite Aid, 1430 Northwest Garden Valley Boulevard / 541-673-4125
        464 Southeast Jackson / 541-672-3433
        1350 Northeast Stephens / 541-672-0127
Bi-Mart, 1381 Northwest Garden Valley Boulevard / 541-672-6771
Reedsport
Reedsport Outdoor Store, 2049 Winchester Avenue / 541-271-2311

MEDICAL
Reedsport
Lower Umpqua Hospital, 600 Ranch Road / 541-271-2171

MORE INFORMATION
Roseburg Area Chamber of Commerce
410 Southeast Spruce
P.O. Box 1026
Roseburg OR 97470
541-672-2648 or 800-444-9584

Reedsport-Winchester Bay Chamber
of Commerce
Intersection of Hwy 101 and Hwy 38
P.O. Box 11
Reedsport, OR 97467
541-271-3495
email: reewbycc@mail.coos.or.us

Grants Pass
Josephine County

County Population–72,000	Grants Pass Population–20,590
County Area–1,641 sq. mi.	October Temperature–56°
Count Acres in CRP–0	

At the heart of Josephine County is the mighty Rogue River, whose awesome whitewater reaches carve spectacular forested canyons through the rugged Siskiyou Mountains of southwestern Oregon. Long ago, the Rogue attracted national attention for its world-class steelhead angling. Among the river's most noted anglers and proponents was the fabled writer Zane Grey. At Grave Creek, in north central Josephine County, the Rogue River begins its lengthy and roadless wild and scenic section, which attracts hordes of thrill-seeking whitewater adventurers.

Josephine County, dominated by forested mountains, offers ample opportunity for mountain quail, blue grouse, and ruffed grouse. A few pheasant still survive in the valley around Grants Pass, but densities are quite low. Valley quail are available also, and wild turkey populations are strong. Duck hunting is limited mostly to the Rogue River itself and to a handful of ponds and lakes.

Grants Pass, the county seat, boasts about 20,000 residents and offers lots of good restaurants along with all other amenities. The community takes its name from General U.S. Grant. Interstate 5 takes you to Grants Pass, some 4 and a half hours south from Portland. US 199 swings southwest at Grants Pass and heads for the community of Cave Junction (pop. 1,300) in the Illinois River Valley. US 199 then continues south into the redwood country of northern California. Before exploring the mountains in search of quail and grouse, hunters in Josephine County should obtain a copy of the Siskiyou National Forest map or, better yet, of the individual ranger districts within the Oregon portion of the forest (see *National Forests*).

UPLAND BIRDS
Blue Grouse, Ruffed Grouse, Mountain Quail, Valley Quail, Ring-necked Pheasant, Wild Turkey, Mourning Dove, Band-tailed Pigeon, and Common Snipe

WATERFOWL
Ducks and Canada Geese

ACCOMMODATIONS
Best Western Grants Pass Inn, 111 Northeast Agness / 1-800-553-7666 / Dogs allowed / $$–$$$

Flamingo Inn, 728 Northwest 6th Street / 541-476-6601 / Dogs allowed / $–$$

Motel 6, 1800 Northeast 7th / 541-474-1331 / Dogs allowed / $–$$

Redwood Motel, 815 Northeast 6th Street / 541-476-0878 / Dogs allowed / $–$$

Riverside Inn, 971 Southeast 6th Street / 541-476-6873 / Dogs allowed / $$–$$$
Royal Vue Motel, 110 Northeast Morgan Lane / 541-479-5381 / Dogs allowed / $$
Shilo Inn, 1880 Northwest 6th Street / 1-800-222-2244 / Dogs allowed / $$
Super 8 Motel, 1949 Northeast 7th / 1-800-800-8000 / Dogs allowed / $$

CAMPGROUNDS AND RV PARKS
Bend of the River RV Park, 7501 Lower River Road / 541-479-2547
Grants Pass Over-Niters, 5941 Highland Avenue / 541-479-7289
Joe Creek Waterfalls RV Park, 699 Jump-off Joe Creek Road / 541-479-7974
River Park RV Resort, 2956 Rogue River Hwy / 541-479-0046

RESTAURANTS
Mexx's Mexican Restaurant and Cantina, 820 Northeast E Street / 541-474-6399 /
   Open seven days 11AM–MIDNIGHT; Thur–Sat until 2AM / Southwestern cuisine
The Brewery, 509 Southwest G Street / 541-479-9850 / Open for dinner Tues–Sun
Black Forest Family Restaurant, 820 Northeast E Street / 541-474-2353 / Open
   24 hours Fri–Sat; Sun–Thur 6AM–10PM
The Bistro, 1214 Northwest 6th / 541-479-3412
Denny's Restaurant, 115 Northeast Morgan Lane / 541-479-4544 / Open 24 hours
Duangratana, 1571 Northeast 6th / 541-479-1345 / Thai-Chinese cuisine
Elmer's Pancake and Steak House, 175 Northeast Agness / 541-474-0740
Hamilton River House, 1936 Rogue River Hwy / 541-479-3938 / Fine dining
Matsukaze Japanese Restaurant, 1675 Northeast 7th / 541-479-2961
Morrison's Rogue River Lodge, 8500 Galice Road, Merlin / 541-476-3825
Shari's, 190 Northeast Agness / 541-474-6699 / Open 24 hours
Wild River Brewing and Pizza Co., 595 Northeast E Street / 541-471-7487 /
   Microbrews and pub food

VETERINARY CLINICS
Grants Pass Veterinary Clinic, 535 Southwest Lincoln Road / 541-and 476-3163 /
   Mon–Fri 8AM–5:30PM; Saturdays by appointment / 24-hour emergency service
Animal Medical Clinic, 1777 Williams Hwy / 541-476-8546
Cedar View Veterinary Hospital, 458 Redwood Hwy / 541-472-1736
Crossroads Animal Hospital, 421 Caves Hwy, Cave Junction / 541-592-3222
Jacksonville Veterinary Hospital, 937 North 5th Street, Jacksonville / 541-899-1081
Oregon Veterinary Services, 100 Pleasant Valley Road, Merlin / 541-479-6802

DOG BOARDING
SORE, 6083 Holland Loop Road, Cave Junction / 541-592-6150

AUTO REPAIR
Grants Pass Auto Care Center, 1693 Lynda Lane / 541-479-2024
Star Import Service, 414 Northeast F Street / 541-476-9646 or 800-476-9646
The Tool Box, 1661 Northeast 6th / 541-476-6964

Auto Rental
Enterprise Rent-A-Car, 1325 Northeast 7th / 541-471-7800
Budget Car and Truck Rental, 825 Northeast F Street / 541-471-6311

Sporting Goods
Bradbury's Gun-N-Tackle, 1809 Rogue River Hwy / 541-479-1531
Fox Firearms, 520 Northeast F Street / 541-479-1163
Lock Stock and Barrel, 115 Southwest H Street / 541-474-0775
Rite Aid, 1642 Williams Hwy / 541-479-2023
        915 Northeast D Street / 541-479-2656
Bi-Mart, 230 Southwest Redwood Hwy / 541-479-8365

Medical
Three Rivers Community Hospital and Health Center, 1505 Northwest
    Washington Boulevard / 541-479-7531

Air Service

For More Information
Grants Pass/Josephine County Chamber of Commerce
1995 Northwest Vine Street
P.O. Box 970
Grants Pass, OR 97528
541-476-7717 or 800-547-5927
email: gpcoc@chatlink.com

Medford and Ashland
Jackson County

County Population–168,000	Medford Population–58,895
County Area–2,801 sq. mi.	Ashland Population–19,220
County Acres in CRP–0	October Temperature–53°

Second best of Oregon's turkey-hunting counties, much of Jackson County is characterized by extensive oak woodlots, in many places mixed with cedar, pine, and fir. This ideal turkey habitat is further enhanced by a mild, rather dry climate throughout much of the county. In fact, Medford, the county seat, receives little more than half of the annual precipitation that rains down on Grants Pass, the county seat of neighboring Josephine County. Oregon's sixth largest city, Medford also ranks as one of the state's warmest communities during the summer. Daytime highs during July and August frequently climb over 100 degrees. Nearby Ashland is regionally renowned for its annual Shakespeare Festival.

Like all of southwestern Oregon, Jackson County boasts some of the best mountain quail hunting found on the West Coast. The birds abound in the Siskiyou Mountains, especially along the western edge of Jackson County where mile upon mile of forest road provides ready access to the steep, brushy forest edges preferred by these handsome quail. Blue grouse and ruffed grouse are fairly common as well. Jackson County's east edge runs along the crest of the Cascade Mountains, from the California border through the expansive Brown Mountain Lava Fields, across 9,945-foot Mt. McLoughlin and up along the western border of Crater Lake National Park. All of this country—and, indeed, virtually all of Jackson County—falls within the Rogue River watershed, one of Oregon's most voluminous

Interstate 5 cuts diagonally across the southwest corner of Jackson County and through Medford and Ashland. US 66 connects Ashland to Klamath Falls, and SR 62 climbs along beside the upper Rogue River all the way to Diamond Lake, the river's source. SR 140 departs Eagle Point, north of Medford, traverses the Cascades just south of Mt. McLoughlin, and arrives at Upper Klamath Lake's west shore.

UPLAND BIRDS
Blue Grouse, Ruffed Grouse, Mountain Quail, Valley Quail, Ring-necked Pheasant, Wild Turkey, Mourning Dove, Band-tailed Pigeon, and Common Snipe

WATERFOWL
Ducks and Canada Geese

ACCOMMODATIONS
Medford
Best Western Pony Soldier Inn, 2340 Crater Lake Hwy / 800-528-1234 / Dogs allowed / $$–$$$
Cedar Lodge Motor Inn, 518 North Riverside / 541-773-7361 / Dogs allowed / $–$$
Holiday Inn Medford, 2300 Crater Lake Hwy / 800-465-4329 / Dogs allowed / $$
Horizon Motor Inn, 1150 East Barnett Road / 800-452-2255 / Dogs allowed / $$
Motel 6, 2400 Biddle Road / 541-779-0550 / Dogs allowed / $–$$
950 Alba Drive / 541-773-4290 / Dogs allowed / $
Red Lion Inn, 200 North Riverside / 1-800-547-8010 / Dogs allowed / $$$
Shilo Inn, 2111 Biddle Road / 1-800-222-2244 / Dogs allowed / $$–$$$
Windmill Inn of Medford, 1950 Biddle Road / 1-800-547-4747 / Dogs allowed / $$–$$$
Ashland
Ashland Super 8 Motel, 2350 Ashland Street / 541-42-8887 or 800-800-8000 / 67 units / Dogs allowed / $$
Flagship Quality Inn, 2520 Ashland Street / 541-488-2330 or 800-334-2330 / 60 units / Dogs allowed / $$–$$$
Knights Inn, 2359 Ashland Street / 541-482-5111 or 800-547-4566 / 40 units / Dogs allowed / $–$$
Windmill Inn, 2525 Ashland Street / 541-482-8310 or 800-547-4747 / 230 units / Dogs allowed / $$–$$$
Ashland Valley Inn, 1193 Siskiyou Boulevard / 541-482-2641 / Dogs allowed / $–$$
Super 8 Motel, 2350 Ashland Street / 1-800-800-8000 / Dogs allowed / $–$$
Best Western Heritage Inn, 132 Main Street / 1-800-528-1234 / Dogs allowed / $$–$$$

CAMPGROUNDS AND RV PARKS
Medford
Pear Tree RV Park, I-5 Exit 24 / 541-535-4445
Rogue Valley Mobile Village, 3761 South Pacific Hwy / 541-535-1468
Bel Air RV and Mobile Park, 3653 South Pacific Hwy / 541-535-2259
Ashland
Glenyan KOA, 5310 Hwy 66 / 541-482-4138
Ashland Regency Inn and RV Park, 50 Lowe Road / 541-482-4700 or 800-482-4701

RESTAURANTS
Medford
Kim's Fine Foods, 2321 South Pacific Hwy / 541-773-3653 / Chinese cuisine
Ali's Thai Kitchen, 2392 North Pacific Hwy / 541-770-3104
Apple Annie's Family Restaurant, 510 North Riverside / 541-858-5455
Applebee's Grill and Bar, 1388 Biddle Road / 541-770-1188

Azteca Mexican Restaurant, 1253 North Riverside / 541-776-2808
The Branding Iron, 1701 North Riverside / 541-779-2300
Coyote Grill, 2300 Crater Lake Hwy / 541-779-3141
Denny's Restaurant, 2320 Crater Lake Hwy / 541-773-3320 / Open 24 hours
India Palace, 820 Crater Lake Avenue, Ste 107 / 541-776-3508
La Comida Mexican Restaurant, 1703 East McAndrews Road / 541-773-6141
McGrath's Fish House, 68 East Stewart Avenue / 541-732-1732 / Fresh seafood
Osprey Ale Brew Pub, 404 East Main Street / 541-734-4808 / Microbrewery
Shari's, 71 Stewart Avenue / 541-857-8969 / Open 24 hours
Shoji's, 2640 East Barnett Road / 541-779-6860 / Fine Japanese cuisine
Stuft Pizza, 2425 Crater Lake Hwy / 541-770-1295 / Gourmet pizza

Ashland
Azteca Restaurant, 2345 Ashland Street / 541-488-2610
Black Sheep, 51 North Main / 541-482-6414 / European cuisine
Chateaulin Restaurant, 50 East Main / 541-482-2264 / French cuisine
Gen Kai Restaurant, 180 Lithia Way / 541-482-9632 / Japanese cuisine
Omar's Fresh Seafood and Steak, 1380 Siskiyou Boulevard / 541-482-1281
Primavera, 1st and Hargadine / 541-488-1994 / Continental
Siskiyou Micro Pub, 31B Water Street / 541-482-7718 / Microbrewery
Standing Stone Brewing Co., 101 Oak Street / 541-482-2448 / Microbrewery

VETERINARY CLINICS

Medford
Crater Animal Clinic, 805 East Vilas / 541-779-0951
Jackson Animal Hospital, 902 East Jackson / And 541-779-4893
Lakeway Veterinary Hospital, 2540 Crater Lake Hwy / 541-779-7731
Medford Animal Hospital, 619 Market Street / 541-772-2222
Mountain View Veterinary Clinic, 15050 Hwy 62, Eagle Point / 541-826-3355

Ashland
Ashland Veterinary Hospital, 1645 Ashland Street / 541-482-1386
Animal Medical Hospital, 1525 Hwy 99 North / 541-482-2786

DOG BOARDING

Medford
Your Precious Pets, Inc., 501 North Fir Street / 541-779-7770
Roblen Kennels, 4925 Tioga Way, Central Point / 541-664-6744
Canine Country Club, 476 Galls Creek Road, Gold Hill / 541-855-7492

Ashland
Animal Medical Hospital, 1525 Hwy 99 North / 541-482-2786
North Pole Kennels, 2868 North Valley View Way / 541-482-7015

AUTO REPAIR

Medford
Baird's Auto Repair, 409 Earhart Street / 541-772-7311
Lithia, 360 East Jackson / 541-776-6365

Blue grouse.

Keith Schulz Garage, 400 East McAndrews Road / 541-772-4756
Chevrolet Authorized Service, Airport Chevrolet, Inc. 3001 Biddle Road /
  541-770-1300
Ford Authorized Service, Crater Lake Ford, 2611 Biddle Road / 541-770-3642
Isuzu Authorized Service, Lithia Isuzu, 700 North Central Avenue / 541-770-3695
Toyota Authorized Service, Lithia Toyota, 360 East Jackson / 541-776-6400
Medford Nissan, 600 North Central Avenue / 541-773-3655
Ashland
Ashland 76, Hwy 66 and I-5, Exit 14 / 541-482-1464 / Open 24 hours
Fleck's Auto Service, 2445 Siskiyou Boulevard / 541-482-4384
Joss' Richard Siskiyou Service Center, 7583 Hwy 66 / 541-482-8493
Valley View Auto Repair, I-5 and Valley View Road / 541-482-5133

Auto Rental
Medford
Enterprise Rent-A-Car, 1046 Court / 541-772-1200
Lithia's Discount Rent-A-Car, 326 North Bartlett / 541-770-7164
Avis Rent-A-Car, Rogue Valley International Airport / 541-773-3003 or
800-831-2847
Hertz Rent-A-Car, Medford-Jackson County Airport / 541-773-4293 or
800-654-3131

Sporting Goods
Medford
G. I. Joe's, Inc., 2370 Poplar Drive / 541-772-9956
Good Guys Guns, 259 East Barnett / 541-858-0335
Wyatt's Outdoor, 4856 Pioneer Road / 541-776-8417
Rite Aid, 981 Medford Center / 541-773-7474
Bi-Mart, 2687 Jacksonville Hwy / 541-779-8010
990 Biddle Road / 541-772-3466
Ashland
Rite Aid, 2341 Ashland Street / 541-482-7406
Bi-Mart, 2280 Ashland Street / 541-482-8510

Medical
Medford
Providence Medford Medical Center, 1111 Crater Lake Avenue / 541-773-6611
Rogue Valley Medical Center, 2825 Barnett Road / 541-773-4900
Ashland
Ashland Community Hospital, 280 Maple Street / 541-482-2441

Air Service
Medford
Rogue Valley Airport, 3650 Biddle Road, Medford / 541-776-7222
Ashland
Ashland Municipal Airport (Skinner Aviation), 403 Dead Indian Memorial Road /
541-482-7675

For More Information
Medford/Jackson County Chamber of Commerce
101 East 8th Street
Medford, OR 97501
541-779-4847
email: business@medfordchamber.com

Ashland Chamber of Commerce
P.O. Box 1360
110 East Main Street
541-482-3486

Coos Bay/North Bend and Bandon
Coos County

County Population–61,700	Coos Bay/North Bend Population–24,425
County Area–1,629 sq. mi.	Bandon Population–2,820
County Acres in CRP–0	October Temperature–55°

Coos County, on the southern Oregon coast, may well offer the state's most unheralded wingshooting. Mountain quail abound in this part of Oregon, but relatively few people pursue them. Ruffed grouse and blue grouse occupy the same forested mountains throughout the county, and waterfowl prospects are among the best on the Oregon coast, especially for those who explore by boat the far reaches of sprawling Coos Bay. Likewise, the lower Coquille River—including Bandon Marsh National Wildlife Refuge—offers productive hunting for a variety of duck species.

Coos Bay is the largest town on the Oregon Coast, and as one might expect, its traditional industries are timber and fishing. Considered the best natural harbor between Puget Sound and San Francisco, Coos Bay ranks as the world's largest forest products shipping port. More recently, tourism and related activities have become a thriving and critical industry all along the southern Oregon coast. The little town of Bandon is perfectly located for waterfowlers who hunt the national refuge, whose south border abuts this town. Inland from Bandon are the small towns of Coquille, which is actually the county seat, and Myrtle Point. US 101 runs the length of the county.

UPLAND BIRDS
Blue Grouse, Ruffed Grouse, Mountain Quail, Valley Quail, Ring-necked Pheasant, Wild Turkey, Mourning Dove, Band-tailed Pigeon, and Common Snipe

WATERFOWL
Ducks, Canada Geese, Black Brant

ACCOMMODATIONS
Coos Bay/North Bend

Best Western Holiday Motel, 411 North Bay Shore Drive / 541-269-5111 / 77 units / Dogs allowed / $$–$$$

Edgewater Inn, 275 East Johnson Avenue / 541-267-0423 or 800-233-0423 / 82 units / Dogs allowed / $$–$$$

Lazy J Motel, 1143 Hills Street / 541-269-9666 / 11 units / Dogs allowed / $–$$

Motel 6, 1445 Bay Shore Drive / 541-267-7171 / 94 units / Dogs allowed / $–$$

Parkside Inn, 1480 Sherman / 541-756-4124 / Sixteen units / Dogs allowed / $–$$

Plainview Motel, 2760 Cape Arago Hwy / 541-8088-5166 / Ten units / Dogs allowed / $-$$

Pony Village Motor Lodge, Virginia Avenue / 541-756-3191 / 119 units / Dogs allowed / $$

Red Line Inn, 1313 North Bay Shore Drive / 541-267-4141 or 800-733-5466 / 143 units / Dogs allowed / $$-$$$

Sea Psalm Motel, 1250 Cape Arago Hwy / 541-888-9053 / 8 units / Dogs allowed / $-$$

Timber Lodge Motel, 1001 North Bay Shore Drive / 541-267-7066 or 800-782-7592 / 53 units / Dogs allowed / $-$$

Bandon

Best Western Inn at Face Rock, 3225 Beach Loop Road / 541-347-9441 or 800-638-3092 / $$-$$$

Caprice Motel, Hwy 101 South / 541-347-4494 / Small dogs allowed / $-$$

Sunset Motel, 1755 Beach Loop Drive / 541-347-2453 or 800-842-2407 / $$-$$$

Harbor View Motel of Bandon, Hwy 101 / 541-347-4417 or 800-526-0209 / $$$

Bandon Wayside Motel, Hwy 42 South / 541-347-3421 / $$

CAMPGROUNDS AND RV PARKS

Coos Bay/North Bend

Charleston Marina RV Park, 7984 King Fisher Drive / 541-888-9512 / 110 sites

Lucky Loggers RV Park, 250 East Johnson Avenue / 541-267-6003 / 78 sites

Oregon Dunes KOA, 4135 Coast Hwy / 541-756-4851 / 75 sites

Oceanside RV Park, 9838 Cape Arago Hwy / 541-888-2598 / 20 sites

Seeport RV Park, Boat Basin Drive / 541-888-3122 / 26 sites

Sunset Bay State Park / 63 sites / 1-800-452-5687

Bandon

Bluejay Campground and RV Park, 885C Beach Loop Road / 541-347-7904

RESTAURANTS

Coos Bay/North Bend

Autumn House Restaurant, 155 South Empire Boulevard / 541-8088-6317 / Open 7AM–8PM

Bank Brewing Co., 201 Central Avenue / 541-267-0963 / Open 11AM–10PM; Fri–Sat until MIDNIGHT; Sun NOON–8PM / The south coast's only brewpub

Benetti's Italian Restaurant, 260 South Broadway / 541-267-6066 / Open 5PM–10PM

Blue Heron Bistro, 100 Commercial / 541-267-3933 / Daily 11AM–9PM / European specialties

Cedar Grill, 274 South Broadway / 541-267-7100 / Lunch 11AM–2:30PM; Dinner 5PM–9PM

Fishermen's Grotto, Pony Village Mall / 541-756-0341 / Mon–Sat 10AM–8PM; Sun 10AM–6PM

Gregson's, 1890 Virginia Avenue / 541-756-6275 / Wed–Sat 5PM–9PM

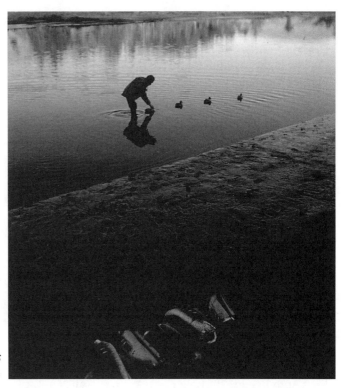

*Setting out decoys
near Coos Bay.*

Los Dos Amigos, 1611 Virginia Avenue / 541-756-4799 / Open 11AM–10PM
The Pancake Mill, 2390 Hwy 101 / 541-756-2751 / Daily 6AM–3PM
Ming Palace, corner of Newmark and Hwy 101 / 541-756-2537 / Open daily
  NOON–9PM
Bandon
Bandon Boatworks Restaurant, South Jetty Road / 541-347-2111
Caffe Santoro, 1212 Alabama / 541-347-2128
Chicago Street Grill, 130 Chicago Avenue / 541-347-6022
Christophe at Face Rock, 3225 Beach Loop Drive / 541-347-3261
Harp's Restaurant, 480 1st Street, Southwest / 541-347-9057 / Fine dining; fresh
  seafood, pasta, steaks
House of Stewart, Hwy 101 South and Seabird Avenue / 541-347-2373
La Fiesta Mexican Restaurant, 396 Southeast 1st, Ste. 11 / 541-347-2450
Shin's Asian Cuisine, 150 North Avenue Southeast / 541-347-2264 / Japanese,
  Chinese, Korean cuisine
Wheelhouse Restaurant and Crowsnest Lounge, 125 Chicago Avenue /
  541-347-9331

VETERINARY CLINICS

Coos Bay/North Bend
  Hanson Animal Hospital, 45 East Lockhart / 541-269-2415
  Harbor Lights Animal Hospital, 1710 Virginia Avenue / 541-756-5156
  Morgan Veterinary Clinic, 230 Market / 541-269-5846
Bandon
  Bandon Veterinary Hospital, June Avenue and Hwy 101 / 541-347-9471

DOG BOARDING

Coos Bay/North Bend
  Birdwell Kennels, 4460 Shinglehse Slg. Road / 541-267-3586
  Harbor Lights Animal Hospital, 1710 Virginia Avenue / 541-756-5156
  Wildwood Kennels, 12120 Wildwood Drive / 541-759-3640
Bandon
  Riverview Kennels, 2078 North Bank Road / 541-347-4689 / Mon–Fri
    8:30AM–5:30PM, Sun 8:30AM–5PM

AUTO REPAIR

Coos Bay/North Bend
  Action Automotive, 175 Elrod / 541-267-2211
  Automotive Electric, 333 Newport Street / 541-267-2127
  Tower Ford, 505 South Broadway / 541-267-2118
  Express Auto Service, 1560 Ocean Boulevard / 541-8088-6449
  Greg's Garage, 2895 Ocean Boulevard / 541-267-2155
  Jim's Auto Repair, 1901 Hwy 101 South / 541-269-5745
Bandon
  B and C Auto Repair, 885 Oregon Avenue / 541-347-2621
  Bandon Automotive Specialties, 385 Grand Avenue / 541-347-3322
  Larry Johnson's Automotive, 125 North Avenue / 541-347-2749

AUTO RENTAL

Coos Bay/North Bend
  Good Sense Auto Rental, 465 North Broadway / 541-267-3300
  Verger Rent-A-Car, 1400 Ocean Boulevard / 541-888-5594
  Enterprise Rent-A-Car, 1595B Newmark / 541-756-7700

SPORTING GOODS

Coos Bay/North Bend
  Coos River Outfitters, 818 South Broadway / 541-269-1075
  Bore Site Gun Shop, 2690 Colorado Street / 541-756-7909
  The Outdoor Store, corner of Hwy 101 and North Ingesoll / 541-269-2433
  Rite Aid, 187 South 2nd Street / 541-267-3952
  Fred Meyer, 1020 South 1st Avenue / 541-269-4000
  Bi-Mart, 2131 Newmark / 541-756-7526
Bandon
  Gary's Gun Shop, 52 Brown Road / 541-347-4238

AIR SERVICE
Coos Bay/North Bend/Bandon
  North Bend Municipal Airport (Horizon Air) / 541-756-2170 or 800-547-9308

MEDICAL
Coos Bay/North Bend
  Bay Area Hospital, 1775 Thompson Road / 541-269-8482
  NBMC Medical Centers, 1900 Woodland Drive / 541-267-5151 or 800-234-1231
Bandon
  Southern Coos General Hospital, 640 West 4th / 541-347-2426

TAXIDERMISTS
Coos Bay/North Bend
  Fish and Feather Taxidermy, 266 Norman Avenue / 541-888-2524
  J. Hertz, 887 4th Street / 541-267-8342
  Timberline Taxidermy, Hwy 42, Coquille / 541-396-2025

FOR MORE INFORMATION
Bay Area Chamber of Commerce
P.O. Box 210
Coos Bay OR 97420
541-269-0215 or 800-824-8486
email: bacc@ucinet.com

Bandon Chamber of Commerce
300 Southeast Second Street
P.O. Box 1515
Bandon, OR 97411
541-347-9616

Port Orford, Gold Beach, and Brookings
Curry County

County Population–22,000	Port Orford Population–1,055
County Area–1,648 sq. mi.	Gold Beach Population–2,150
County Acres in CRP–0	Brookings Population–5,510
October Temperature–55°	

The southernmost reaches of the Oregon coast fall within Curry County, through which flows the Lower Rogue River on the final leg of its glorious path to the Pacific. To the south lies the drainage of the Chetco River. The south coast and Curry County, in particular, offer some unheralded and productive hunting for mountain quail along with good prospects for blue and ruffed grouse. What's more, south coast Septembers are typically warm, dry, and pleasant, creating perfect conditions for traipsing around the mountains on old logging roads in pursuit of upland birds.

Public access abounds in Curry County's uplands, which are dominated by lands administered by the Siskiyou National Forest. Waterfowling options are somewhat limited, but good duck hunting awaits those who explore the Lower Rogue. The county seat, Gold Beach, looks out over the mouth of the mighty Rogue River. Port Orford is a quiet little town come autumn, and it rests above a large, scenic cove whose calm waters result from its being sheltered from the Pacific by Cape Blanco to the immediate north. Rapidly growing Brookings, just north of the California border, offers all necessary amenities.

UPLAND BIRDS
Blue Grouse, Ruffed Grouse, Mountain Quail, Valley Quail, Wild Turkey, Mourning Dove, Band-tailed Pigeon, Common Snipe

WATERFOWL
Ducks, Canada Geese, Black Brant

ACCOMMODATIONS
Port Orford
   Cast Away by the Sea, 545 5th Street / 541-332-4502 / 13 units / Dogs allowed / $$
   Shoreline Motel, Highway 101 South And Battle Rock Park / 541-332-2903 / 13 units / Dogs allowed / $–$$
   Holly House Inn, 600 Jackson / 541-332-7100 / Dogs with deposit / $$
   Battle Rock Motel, Battle Rock Park / 541-332-7331 / No pets / $–$$
Gold Beach
   Best Western Inn of the Beachcomber, 29266 Ellensburg / 541-247-6691 / Dogs allowed / $$–$$$

Drift Inn Motel, 94250 Port Drive / 541-247-4547 / Dogs allowed / $$
Inn at Gold Beach, 29171 Ellensburg Avenue / 541-247-6606 or 800-503-0833 /
 Dogs allowed / $–$$
Motel 6, 94433 Jerry's Flat Road / 541-247-4533 / Dogs allowed / $–$$
Western Village Motel, 29399 Ellensburg Avenue / 541-247-6611 / Dogs allowed /
 $–$$
Brookings
Best Western Beach Front Inn, Boat Basin Road / 541-469-7779 or 800-468-4081 /
 70 units / Dogs allowed / $$$
Bonn Motel, 1216 Chetco Avenue / 541-469-2161 / 37 units / Dogs allowed /
 $$
Harbor Inn, 15991 Hwy 101 S / 541-469-3194 or 800-469-8444 / 30 units /
 Dogs allowed / $$
Pacific Sunset Inn, 1144 Chetco Avenue / 541-469-2141 or 800-469-2141 /
 40 units / Dogs allowed / $$
Westward Motel, 1026 Chetco Avenue / 541-469-7471 or 888-521-6020 /
 32 units / Dogs allowed / $$

CAMPGROUNDS AND RV PARKS
Port Orford
Agate Beach RV Park, 1155 9th Street / 541-332-3031
Arizona Beach RV and Motel, 36939 Hwy 101 South / 541-332-6491 / 70 RV
 sites/17 tent sites
Bandon-Port Orford KOA, 46612 Hwy 101, Langlois / 541-348-2358
Elk River Campground, 93363 Elk River Road / 501-332-2255 / 50 RV sites/20
 tent sites
Port Orford RV Village, 2855 Port Orford Loop / 541-332-1041 / 50 RV sites
Cape Blanco State Park, 9 miles north of Port Orford on Highway 101 /
 501-332-6774
Brookings
River's Edge RV Park, 98203 South Bank Road / 541-469-3356 / Full
 hookups/tent sites
Chetco RV Park, 16117 Hwy 101 / 541-469-9089
Riverside RV Park, 97666 North Bank Road / 541-469-4799 / Full hookups/tent
 sites
Beach Front RV, Boat Basin Road / 541-469-5867 or 800-441-0856 / Full
 hookups/tent sites

RESTAURANTS
Port Orford
Bartlett's Cafe, 831 Oregon Street / 541-332-4175 / Open 5AM–8PM
Paradise Cafe, 1825 Oregon Street / 501-332-8104 / Open 6AM–3PM and 5PM–7PM
Ricardo's Cafe Mexicana, 812 Oregon Street / 501-332-7101 / Tues–Sat
 11:30AM–8PM

Wheelhouse Restaurant, Highway 101, Battle Rock Park / 541-332-1605 / Daily 7AM–9PM

Spaghetti West, 236 6th Street / 541-332-9378 / Open 11AM–3PM and 5PM–9PM

Grumpy's, 19063 Hwy 101 / 541-332-7575 / Closed Monday

Crazy Norwegian's, Hwy 101 / 541-332-8601

Sisters Natural Grocery and Cafe, 832 Oregon Street / 541-332-3640

Gold Beach

Chowderhead Restaurant, 29430 Ellensburg Avenue / 541-247-0588 / Specializing in fresh seafood

Crow's Nest Restaurant and Lounge, 29850 Ellensburg Avenue / 541-247-6837

El Dorado Mexican Restaurant, 29419 Ellensburg Avenue / 541-247-3441

Grant's Pancake and Omelette House, 94682 Jerry's Flat Road / 541-247-7208

Paul Bunyan Burgers, 380 North Ellensburg / 541-247-6424

Port Hole Café, 29975 Harbor Way / 541-247-7411 / Open 7 days 11AM–8PM

Rigorsnort's Restaurant, 29745 Ellensburg / 541-247-4089 / Family dining

Brookings

City Grill, 703 Chetco Avenue / 541-412-0375 / Open 7AM–9PM

Flying Gull Restaurant, 1153 Chetco Avenue / 541-469-5700 / Open daily 6AM–10PM

Lee's Dragon Gate, 777 Cottage Avenue / 541-469-3988 / Sun–Fri 11AM–9PM; Sat 8AM–9:30PM

Los Amigos Mexican Restaurant, 541 Chetco Avenue / 541-469-4102 / Mon–Sat 11AM–8PM; Sun 11AM–4PM

O'Holleran's, 1210 Chetco Avenue / 541-469-9907 / Daily 5PM–10PM

Pacific Blue Seafood in Grill, 16011 Boat Basin Road / 541-469-6006 / Sun–Thur 7:30AM–9PM, until 10PM Fri–Sat

Wild River Pizza Company, 16279 Hwy 101 South / 541-469-7454

VETERINARY CLINICS

Port Orford

Home and Farm Veterinary Service, 94049 Elk River Road / 541-33-2039

Gold Beach

Gold Beach Veterinary Hospital, 94211 3rd Street / 541-247-2513 / Mon–Fri 8AM–5PM / Emergency service available

Brookings

Brookings-Harbor Veterinary Hospital, 15630 Hwy 101 541-469-7788 / 8AM–5:30PM

DOG BOARDING

Port Orford

Riverview Kennels, 2078 North Bank Road, Bandon (45 minutes north) / 541-347-4689

Rowdy Creek Pet Motel, 10100 Hwy 101 N, Smith River, California (one hour south) / (707) 487-9645

Author with a handful of snipe from an Oregon estuary.

Gold Beach
Riverview Kennels, 2078 North Bank Road, Bandon (one hour north) / 541-347-4689
Rowdy Creek Pet Motel, 10100 Hwy 101 N, Smith River, California (one hour south) / 707-487-9645
Brookings
Riverview Kennels, 2078 North Bank Road, Bandon / 541-347-4689
Rowdy Creek Pet Motel, 10100 Hwy 101 North, Smith River, California / 707-487-9645

SPORTING GOODS
Gold Beach
  Coast-to-Coast Hardware, 29733 Ellensburg Avenue / 541-247-6822
  Rogue Outdoor Store, 29865 Ellensburg Avenue / 541-247-7142
Brookings
  Loring's Lighthouse Sporting Goods, 554 Chetco Avenue / 541-469-2148

AUTO REPAIR
Port Orford
  Joe's Auto Care, 1738 Oregon Street / 541-332-7141
  Kar Kare Parts, 1717 North Oregon / 541-332-6540
  Hogard's Garage, 14th and Hwy 101 / 541-332-7645 / 24-hour towing available
  Battle Rock Garage, Hwy 101 / 541-332-2131
Gold Beach
  Al's Mobile Repair, 29520 Broadway / 541-247-2040
  Central Curry Truck and Auto, 28746 Hunter Creek Loop / 541-247-2306
  Ev's Hi-Tech Auto and Towing, 29719 Ellensburg Avenue / 541-247-7525
  Gary's Auto and Electric, 235 South Ellensburg / 541) 247-6497
Brookings
  Bob and Don's Auto Shop, 99156 Winchuck River Road / 541-469-9544
  Randy Mark's Auto Repair, 531 Spruce / 541-469-3932
  Ron's Automotive, 924 Chetco Avenue / 541-469-6213

AUTO RENTAL
Brookings
  Carpenter Auto Center, 934 Chetco Avenue / 541-469-6511
  Coast Auto Center, 530 Chetco Avenue / 541-469-5321

MEDICAL
Port Orford
  Curry Family Medical, 525 Madrona / 541-332-3861 or 800-445-8085
  Curry General Hospital, 94220 4th Street, Gold Beach / 541-247-6621
  Southern Coos General Hospital, 640 West 4th, Bandon / 541-347-2426
Gold Beach
  Curry General Hospital, 94220 4th Street / 541-247-6621

AIR SERVICE
Port Orford
  Coos Bay-North Bend Airport, Horizon Air / 800-547-9308
Gold Beach
  North Bend Municipal Airport (Horizon Air) / 541-756-2170 or 800-547-9308

ATM MACHINES
Port Orford
  Chetco Federal Credit Union, 1000 Oregon Street
  Klamath First Federal, 716 North Highway 101

Buck's Sentry Market
Gold Beach
Chetco Federal Credit Union, 29620 Ellensburg Avenue
Klamath First Federal, 29804 Ellensburg Avenue
Western Bank, 29555 Ellensburg Avenue

FOR MORE INFORMATION
Port Orford Visitor Center/Chamber of Commerce
P.O. Box 637
Port Orford, OR 97465
email:pochamb@harborside.com

Gold Beach Chamber of Commerce
29279 Ellensburg Avenue
Gold Beach, OR 97444
541-247-7526 or 800-525-2334
email: goldbeach@harborside.com

Brookings Chamber of Commerce
P.O. Box 940
Brookings, OR 97415
541-469-3181
email: Chamber@wave.net

The Last Christmas Bird Count

The National Audubon Society undertakes a nationwide bird census every year at Christmas, and soon after we met and started hunting together, Timmy and I decided to participate. After all, we were both members of the local Audubon chapter. The whole thing began innocently enough. We arrived at the check-in station before sunup on a crisp December morning that promised scattered clouds and perhaps a sprinkle of light rain.

First on the agenda that morning was the assigning of count areas to parties of participants ranging in number from two to six individuals. Timmy and I made up one such party and were thrilled to draw the river unit north of town, which would no doubt provide the greatest diversity of different bird species. With duck hunting in mind for the following day, we had filled the trunk with all the required paraphernalia. A few minutes later, driving up the highway in the dawning light, we realized that our duck hunting might very well begin that afternoon, for we could first count the birds and then return later to shoot a few ducks. Naturally, we would adjust our final tallies for said duck species, subtracting those we bagged.

Now that may not sound like the kind of bird census the Audubon Society had in mind, but we kept reminding ourselves that we would first sneak quietly around the unit and record our sightings and only then return for some jump-shooting along the river. Besides—as we reminded ourselves with increasing frequency—John James Audubon and his crew of "collectors" were among the great all-time slaughterers of North American fowl.

The morning bird count went off without a hitch, which was always typical of any kind of bird-watching activity involving Timmy: You could blindfold him, plug one ear, and drop him anywhere in the continental U.S., and he could still tell the difference between any two look-alike tweety bird species long after I'd given up any hope. He knew his birds and had earned something of a "young gun" reputation among the local Auduboners, who likely regarded me as little more than Timmy's sidekick, which I suppose was reasonably accurate.

In stark contrast to the other local Audubon members, Timmy's love for watching and identifying birds had precious little impact on his desire to hunt and kill said birds when they fell under the category of either upland game or waterfowl.

In any event, by about 2PM, we returned to the vehicle with our tally sheets, which indeed boasted an impressive list of species. Having finished our volunteer work, we traded binoculars for shotguns and waders. We then returned to the riverbank, where tall cottonwoods and delicate willows were now being whipped about by an increasingly persistent wind. Heavy, black storm clouds closed in above, assembling all the elements required for some evening pass shooting. By sundown, we had killed a bag limit between us and decided we should return to the census check-in location and turn in our tally sheets.

Darkness had arrived in earnest when we pulled into the driveway where other Auduboners were gathered exchanging news over interesting sightings. We delivered our census sheets to the lady in charge, who scanned the list, sometimes pausing for a "Hmm" or an "Oh, interesting."

Then she got to our waterfowl list, which recorded significant numbers of Canada geese, mallards, pintails, wigeon, green-winged teal, buffleheads, common merganser, and wood ducks. Also listed were the odds and ends we had seen: a few shovelers, two redheads, six hooded mergansers, 15 ring-necked ducks and one greater scaup. At this last sighting, she looked up, commenting, "That's the only greater we've got—are you sure it wasn't a lesser?"

In his typically quiet demeanor, Timmy responded that he was sure it was a greater scaup. She should have just let it go at that. Timmy knows his birds and I'd had a long day. But she pushed the issue, saying to Timmy, "We get lots of lesser scaups and ringnecks, are you certain it wasn't a lesser?"

That's about the time I decided to defend Timmy's prowess as a bird watcher. That's also about the time I wore out my welcome—and Timmy's—with the local Audubon chapter, for the next and only words I had to say on the subject went something along these lines: "Look, if you want positive identification, I'll go out to the truck and get the damn duck, but you'll have to excuse the blood."

Northern pintail.

Oregon's Cooperative Access Program

For several decades now, the state of Oregon has worked with landowners in the Columbia Basin to provide public hunting access to private lands. The fruition of the so-called Upland Cooperative Access Program (UCAP) can best be seen near the communities of Heppner and Lexington, where in two counties perhaps 50,000 acres of private lands are posted with signs reading "Welcome to Hunt" or "Hunting by Written Permission." All told, more than 100,000 acres were made available last year through the UCAP.

For their part, the landowners are paid a small sum (up to 50 cents per acre) or the equivalent value in habitat or other land improvements to provide suitable bird habitat and reasonable public access. These funds come from the state's upland bird stamp program. Oregon Department of Fish and Wildlife then assumes responsibility (along with its enforcement arm, the Oregon State Police) for enforcing trespass laws and road closures.

Most of the UCAP lands provide access to pheasant, valley quail, chukar, and Hungarian partridge habitat. In some places, grouse are available. Currently, the UCAP features acreage in four counties: 42,000 acres in Gilliam County, 25,000 acres in Sherman County, 27,000 acres in Morrow County, and 7,400 acres in Wasco County.

The future of this program is largely dependent on hunters themselves, who must remember at all times that they are guests on private lands and that access privileges for any and everyone can be revoked at any time. Hunters must abide by the established rules governing access, wherein, on UCAP lands, it is unlawful to do the following:

- Hunt or enter any posted area without a valid hunting entry by permission document unless the area is posted "Welcome to Hunt."

- Hunt or enter any upland area other than during the upland season for which it is designated.

- Use a motorized vehicle on fields, trails, and posted roads.

- Hunt any posted safety zone or enter "No Public Access" area.

- Camp without landowner permission.

- Build or use open fires without landowner permission.

- Use rifles, handguns, or shotguns with slugs on any hunt area unless specific authorization has been given by the landowner.

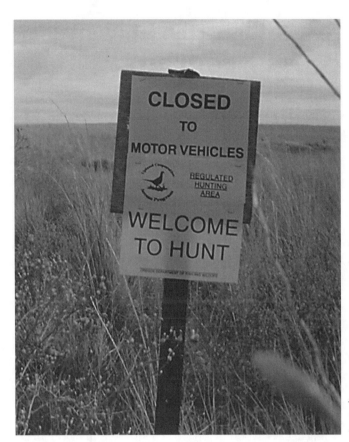

Upland Cooperative Access Program (UCAP) land near Heppner, Oregon.

While county acreage figures are available for the UCAP, most landowners—understandably—have been hesitant to approve of a map showing these lands or of a listing of participating landowners. Hunters should consult ODFW and also be willing to spend time driving around the region with a county map in hand.

Oregon's Regulated Hunt Areas

Regulated Hunt Areas (RHAs) in the Columbia Basin are similar in nature to the aforementioned UCAP lands; however, on some portions of the RHAs, hunters must possess a daily permit and abide by additional regulations. The Oregon Gamebirds Regulations pamphlet provides all details and regulations pertinent to the RHAs, which are as follows:

- Boeing Regulated Hunt Area is located adjacent to the Willow Creek Wildlife Area and is accessible via Exit 151 (Threemile Canyon) or Exit 159 (Tower Road) from I-84 west of Boardman and east of Arlington. Check stations are located at both places. Opportunities include ducks, geese, pheasant, and valley quail.

- Port of Morrow Regulated Hunt Area is located east of Boardman, with check stations off I-84 Exits 165 (US 730) and 168 (located on Bombing Range Road). Species include pheasant, valley quail, and waterfowl.

- Potlatch Regulated Hunt Area—map of this area is available at the Port of Morrow RHA South Unit check-in station at the junction of Bombing Range Road and Wilson Road. The open portion is open for waterfowl only, seven days per week, and no entry permit is required.

Oregon's State Wildlife Areas

Totaling some 170,000 acres, Oregon's state wildlife areas offer a diverse array of public wingshooting opportunities. Summer Lake and Sauvie Island—well-known and heavily hunted waterfowling areas—rank as the state's most popular destinations for goose and duck hunters, while wildlife areas such as Riverside and Lower Deschutes cater more to the upland wingshooter. Scattered throughout the state, these wildlife areas offer a glimpse of many different habitat types. Irrigon and Ladd Marsh Wildlife Areas, where pheasant rank as one of the most significant species, are heavily hunted. Soon after opening weekend, young roosters will be largely thinned out by hunters, and the remaining birds are quick to take refuge in the cattails where only a veteran, skilled dog has much chance of affording his master consistent shooting. In addition to the areas described here, there exist several smaller areas that are worth exploring. These include Elkhorn, Enterprise, Power City, Sumpter, and Jewell Meadows.

Pheasant tracks in the sand at Irrigon Wildlife Area.

Murderer's Creek Wildlife Area

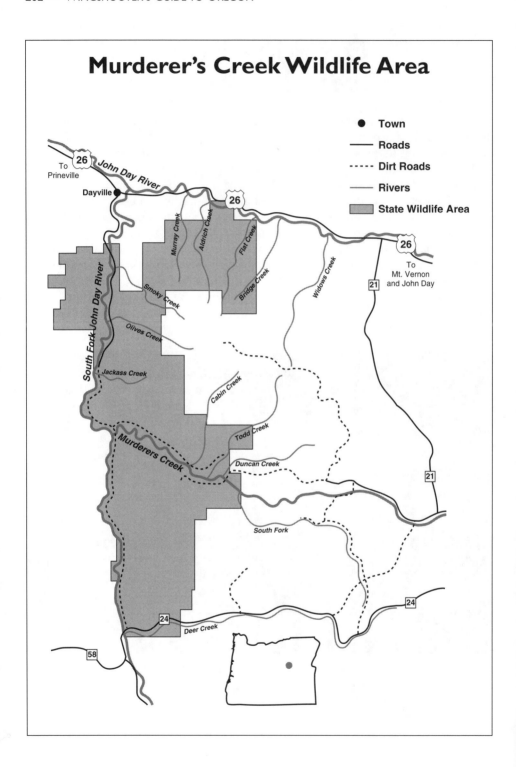

Murderer's Creek Wildlife Area

Size 42,000 acres

Species Valley quail, chukar and Hungarian partridge, ruffed and blue grouse, wild turkey, waterfowl

Location Northeastern Oregon, west of John Day

Directions From the east, follow US 395 or US 26 to John Day, then continue west on US 26 some 30 miles to the area entrance about a quarter mile east of Dayville. From the west, follow US 26 east from Prineville or follow SR 19 southeast from Condon and Kimberly. Continue east a quarter mile past Dayville to the area headquarters.

Description Murderer's Creek Wildlife Area covers scattered tracts of land along Murderer's Creek and along the South Fork John Day River south of US 26. A paved road leads south from Dayville into the area, and gravel roads continue up the river and the creek. Valley quail abound in the riparian zones near agricultural areas. Chukar inhabit the canyons of the South Fork John Day and the John Day River, while a few Huns occupy the Murderer's Creek basin. Blue grouse, though not numerous, occupy the area's highest forested ridges and saddles, and ruffed grouse are closely tied to water. Wild turkeys have been introduced here.

Notes Beware of rattlesnakes, especially early in the season. The town of John Day (see entry) lies 30 miles to the east and offers the area's only extensive array of services.

Information Murderer's Creek Wildlife Area
HCR 01, Box 911
Dayville, OR 97825
541-987-2843

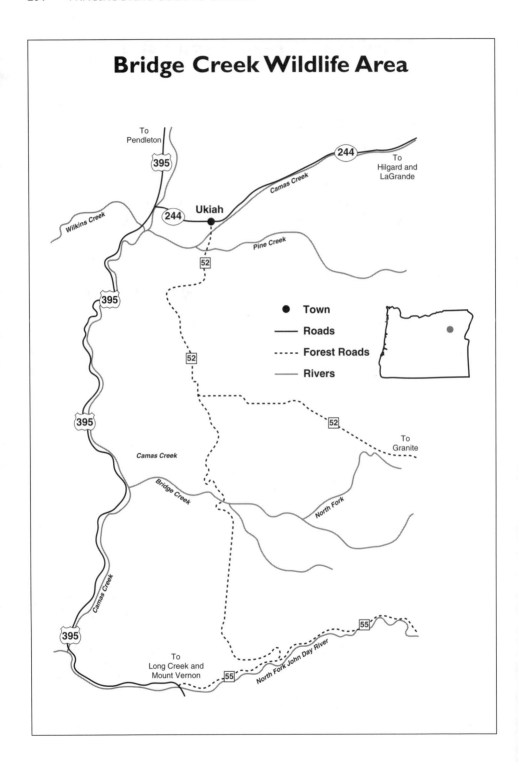

Bridge Creek Wildlife Area

To Pendleton

395

244

To Hilgard and LaGrande

Camas Creek

Wilkins Creek

244 Ukiah

Pine Creek

52

395

52

● Town

── Roads

---- Forest Roads

── Rivers

395

52

To Granite

Camas Creek

Bridge Creek

North Fork

395

Camas Creek

55

395

To Long Creek and Mount Vernon

55

North Fork John Day River

Bridge Creek Wildlife Area

Size 13,500 acres

Species Ruffed grouse, blue grouse

Location Located on the North Fork John Day drainage about 50 miles south of Pendleton

Directions Follow I-84 to Exit 209 (US 395) at Pendleton and continue south about 50 miles to SR 244. Turn left and drive about one mile to Ukiah, then turn right on Forest Road 52 heading toward Granite. Follow FR 52 about 4 miles to the signed entrance.

Description Typical of the John Day River drainage, Bridge Creek features steep, rimrock-lined canyons topped by fairly flat grasslands. Ruffed grouse occupy the riparian areas, while blue grouse live along the timbered breaks.

Information Oregon Department of Fish and Wildlife
Rt. 1, Box 18
Pendleton, OR 97801
541-276-2344

Sage, a German wirehaired pointer, find birds in heavy sagebrush country.

Ladd Marsh Wildlife Area

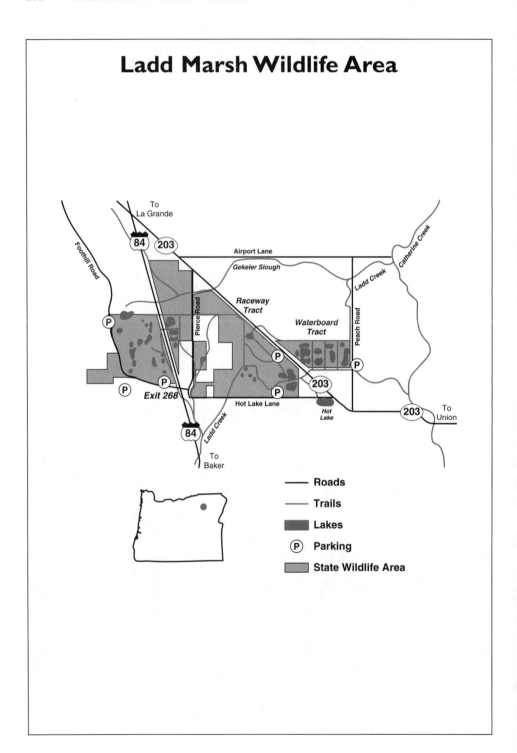

Ladd Marsh Wildlife Area

Size   3,208 acres

Species   Ring-necked pheasant, valley quail, Hungarian partridge, ducks, and Canada geese

Location   Located in Union County, south and southeast of La Grande, adjacent to Interstate 84.

Directions   Follow I-84 south from La Grande or north from Baker City. Take Exit 268 or 265. Parking areas are located along Foothill Road, Hot Lake Lane, and Union Highway (SR 203). The area headquarters is located off Pierce Road.

Description   A mixture of wetlands, grasslands, and agricultural areas, the Ladd Marsh Wildlife Area offers lots of upland habitat for pheasants and quail along with a few Hungarian partridge. After opening weekend, most of the pheasants will be found in heavy cover, especially cattail stands best hunted with a veteran dog. Valley quail abound early but soon wander to nearby private lands. Autumn precipitation determines the amount of standing water available for waterfowl. The best duck and goose hunting occurs on the Waterboard and Raceway Tracts early in the season.

Information   Ladd Marsh Wildlife Area
107 20th Street
La Grande, OR 97850
541-963-4954

Wenaha Wildlife Area

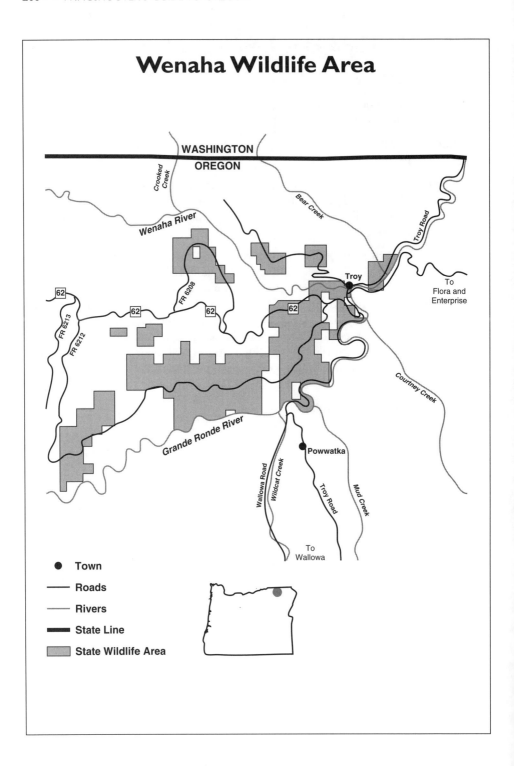

WASHINGTON

OREGON

Crooked Creek

Bear Creek

Troy Road

Wenaha River

62

62

FR 6208

62

62

Troy

To
Flora and
Enterprise

FR 6213

FR 6212

Courtney Creek

Grande Ronde River

Powwatka

Wallowa Road

Wildcat Creek

Troy Road

Mud Creek

To
Wallowa

● Town

— Roads

— Rivers

▬ State Line

▨ State Wildlife Area

Wenaha Wildlife Area

Size   13,000 acres

Species   Blue and ruffed grouse, chukar, wild turkey, waterfowl

Location   Located in the northern portion of Wallowa County near Troy

Directions Wenaha Wildlife Area includes a number of different tracts adjacent to the Grande Ronde River upstream from Troy and to the Wenaha River west of Troy. Hunting for blue grouse can be quite good along the timbered ridges and benches, especially above the river breaks. Ruffed grouse occupy riparian areas and brushy springs. Chukar inhabit the canyons where appropriate habitat is found, and wild turkey exist in scattered flocks. Turkey hunters should scout the area ahead of the season, searching for roosting areas.

Description Wenaha Wildlife Area features a mix of timbered slopes and steep grass steppe along the breaks of the Wenaha and Grande Ronde Rivers. North-facing slopes include more timber cover, and blue grouse reside along the forested ridges and in the wooded draws, often feeding at timber edges. The south slopes are drier and grassier, providing better habitat for chukar. With a little luck and legwork, hunters can harvest chukar and blue grouse not only in the same day but sometimes from the same slope. Ruffed grouse are fairly common where springs, seeps, and creeks provide water and heavy cover.

Notes   Be prepared for winter weather, which can strike at any time, especially from October on.

Information Wenaha Wildlife Area
85060 Grande Ronde Road
Enterprise, OR 97828
541-828-7721

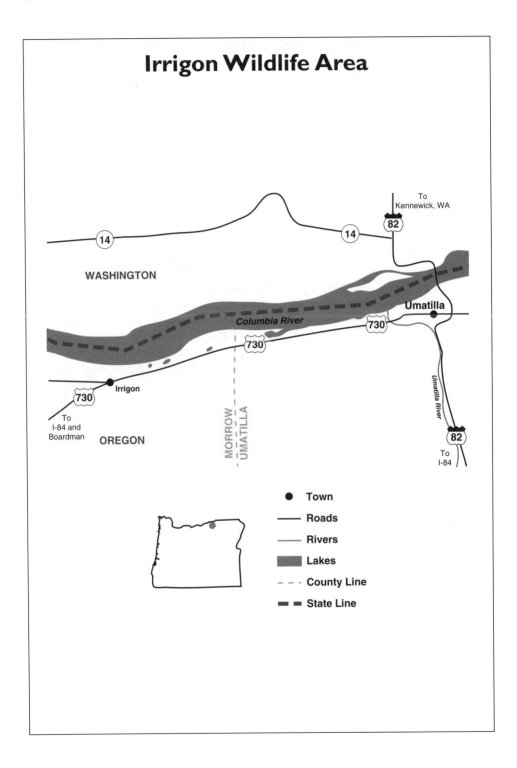

Irrigon Wildlife Area

WASHINGTON

Columbia River

Umatilla

OREGON

Irrigon

MORROW
UMATILLA

Umatilla River

To
Kennewick, WA

To
I-84 and
Boardman

To
I-84

- Town
— Roads
— Rivers
◼ Lakes
- - - County Line
▬ ▬ State Line

Irrigon Wildlife Area

Size   940 acres

Species   Ducks, Canada geese, ring-necked pheasant, valley quail, mourning dove

Location   Located a few miles northwest of Hermiston on the Columbia River between Irrigon and Umatilla

Directions Follow I-84 to Exit 168 (US 730 / Irrigon) and continue into the town of Irrigon. The wildlife area stretches along the north side of US 730 from Irrigon to the Umatilla River. Seven different access points are located off the highway between Irrigon and Umatilla.

Description Characterized by a mix of grasslands, old fencerows, brushlands, cottonwood stands, and Russian olive groves, Irrigon Wildlife Area includes several small duck ponds along with 6 miles of Columbia River frontage. Decoy hunting along the Columbia River shoreline and on the area ponds usually provides the best duck shooting opportunity in the area, especially from mid-November through December. Early morning is best. A good retriever is mandatory. Pheasant hunting is best within the first week; later, hunters with experienced dogs can hunt the cattail stands. Valley quail generally stick to the heavier cover throughout the area.

Notes   Hunters should be aware of and heed the established and marked safety zones, most of which are near residential areas.

Information Oregon Department of Fish and Wildlife
Rt. 1, Box 18
Pendleton, OR 97801
541-276-2344

Willow Creek Wildlife Area

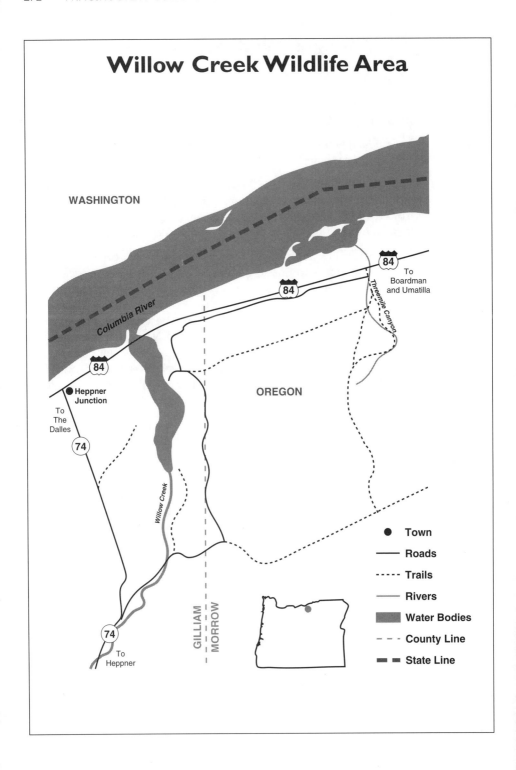

Willow Creek Wildlife Area

Size   649 acres

Species   Ring-necked pheasant, valley quail, ducks, Canada geese

Location   Located on the Willow Creek Arm of the John Day Pool on the Columbia River

Directions   Follow Interstate 84 to Exit 151 (151 miles east of Portland) and turn south, following the signs into the area.

Description   Willow Creek features a mix of upland and waterfowl habitat centered mostly around the Willow Creek Arm of the John Day Pool on the Columbia River west of Boardman. Pheasant and valley quail occur on the benches and in brushy riparian areas dominated by willow, reed stands, and other cover. Ducks become increasingly numerous as the season progresses, with the best hunting coinciding with the mid- to late autumn arrival of migrating flights.

Notes   Be sure to consult the current regulations pamphlet for specific area restrictions. Small watercraft can be launched near the parking area and from Threemile Canyon access on the Columbia River. Private property surrounds the area and is so posted. Camping is allowed in the area.

Information   Oregon Department of Fish and Wildlife
Route 1, Box 18
Pendleton, OR 97801
541-276-2344

Riverside Fish and Wildlife Area

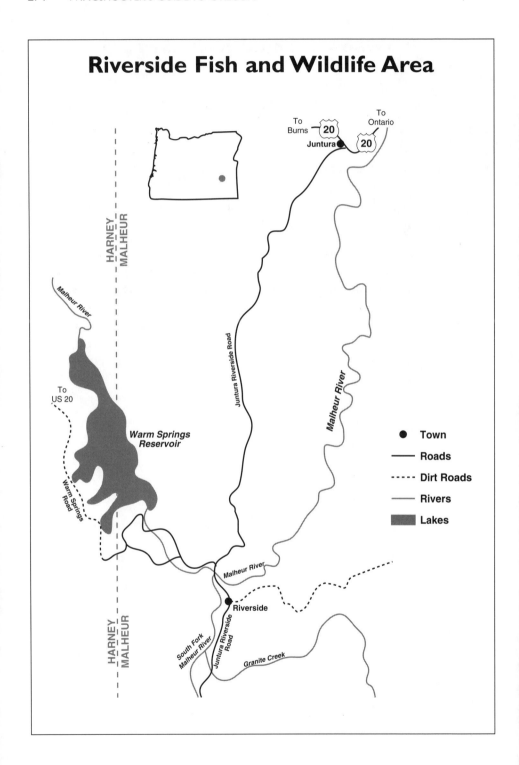

To Burns
To Ontario

20
20

Juntura

HARNEY
MALHEUR

Malheur River

To
US 20

Warm Springs
Reservoir

Juntura Riverside Road

Malheur River

Warm Springs
Road

Malheur River

Riverside

HARNEY
MALHEUR

South Fork
Malheur River

Juntura Riverside
Road

Granite Creek

● Town

— Roads

---- Dirt Roads

— Rivers

▮ Lakes

Riverside Fish and Wildlife Area

Size   4,067 acres

Species   Chukar partridge, valley quail, ducks

Location   Southeastern Oregon on the Malheur River at the west edge of Malheur County

Directions   Follow US 20 east from Burns or west from Ontario to the little town of Juntura. At Juntura, turn south on the Juntura-Riverside Road (gravel), which leads 17 miles to the Malheur River and a rough camping area. The headquarters is located down a left turn about one mile past the bridge.

Description   Primarily confined to the Malheur River corridor, Riverside is nonetheless surrounded by BLM land and therefore offers an extensive area open for chukar hunting. The habitat is typical of eastern Oregon's arid river canyons, with steep slopes covered in rabbitbrush, sage, and cheatgrass, and in many places, studded with rimrock. Valley quail are largely confined to the riparian zone along the river but abound in strong numbers during years of good nesting and rearing conditions. A few ducks—mostly mallards and teal—are taken by jump shooters each season.

Notes   The camping area is located just below the bridge. No drinking water is available. Nontoxic shot is required only for waterfowl.

Information   Oregon Department of Fish and Wildlife
P.O. Box 8
Hines, OR 97738
541-573-6582

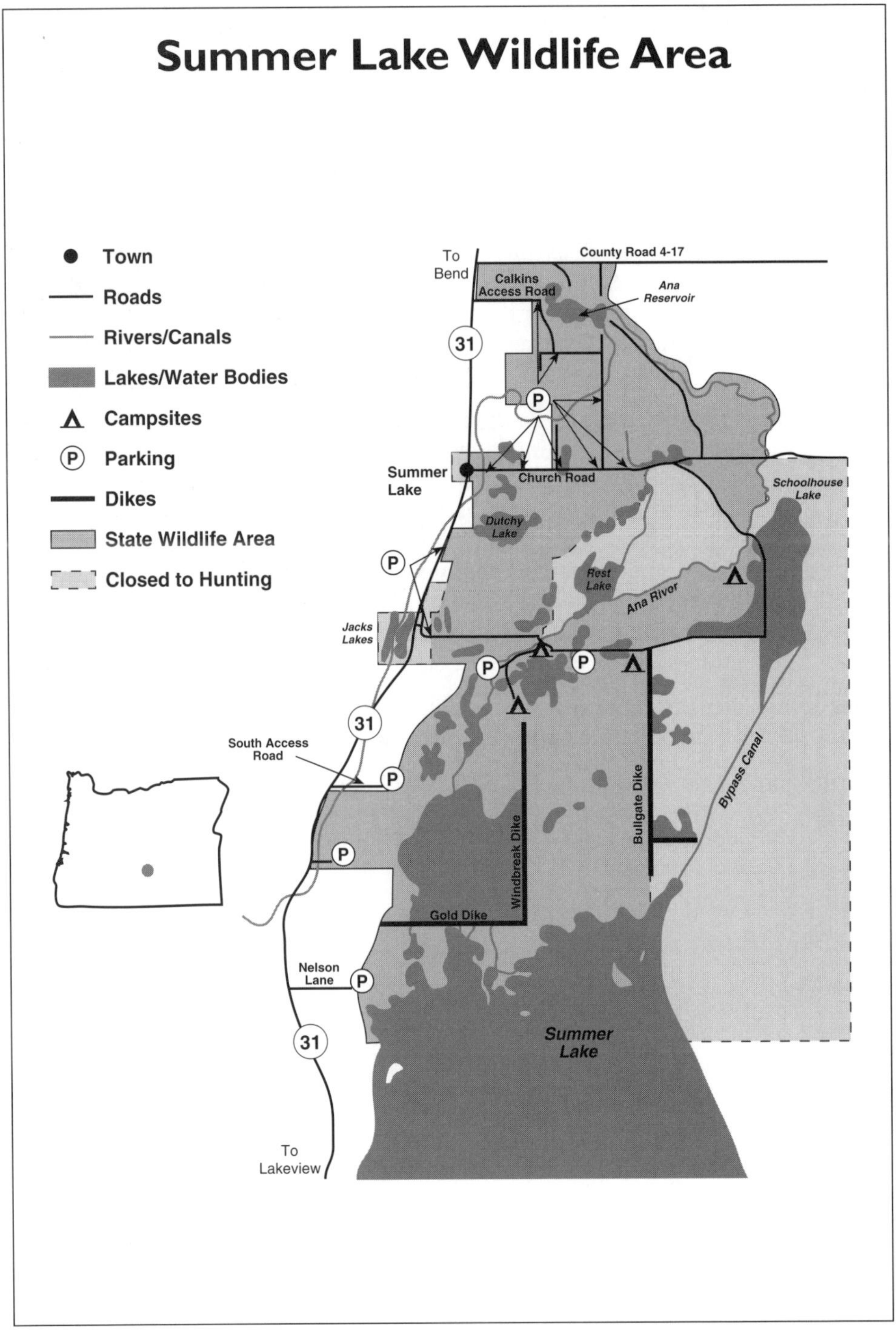

Summer Lake Wildlife Area

Town

Roads

Rivers/Canals

Lakes/Water Bodies

Campsites

Parking

Dikes

State Wildlife Area

Closed to Hunting

To Bend

County Road 4-17

Calkins Access Road

Ana Reservoir

31

Summer Lake

Church Road

Schoolhouse Lake

Dutchy Lake

Rest Lake

Ana River

Jacks Lakes

South Access Road

31

Windbreak Dike

Bullgate Dike

Bypass Canal

Gold Dike

Nelson Lane

31

Summer Lake

To Lakeview

Summer Lake Wildlife Area

Size	18,677 acres
Species	Ducks, Canada geese, snow geese, white-fronted geese, common snipe, ring-necked pheasant, valley quail
Location	Summer Lake occupies a large basin in west-central Lake County, about two hours south of Bend.
Directions	Follow US 97 south from Bend to the SR 31 junction south of LaPine. Follow SR 31 south through the town of Silver Lake, over Picture Rock Pass, and down to Summer Lake. The headquarters is located just off SR 31 at the main entrance to the area, about 1 mile south of the town of Summer Lake. From the south, follow US 395 north through Lakeview to Valley Falls, then veer right on SR 31 and continue north through Paisley and on to Summer Lake.
Description	One of Oregon's most popular waterfowling destinations, Summer Lake Wildlife Area (along with the adjacent refuge) occupies an extensive marsh that provides significant nesting, migrating, and staging habitat for a variety of birds. An intricate series of canals and dikes regulates the water table, which has no outside drainage. Summer Lake, which is a huge shallow sump with a water level determined entirely by inflow and evaporation, borders the wildlife area and refuge on its north shore. Although very popular and productive during the early part of the season, pass shooting from the dikes generally proves less effective than hunting over decoy spreads. Mallards, gadwall, and wigeon abound; pintails and teal are common, and just about every other species of freshwater duck is available.

Goose hunters can choose to target any of three species. Canada geese can be taken throughout the season. Decoy spreads along the margins of the marsh provide the best opportunity. Snow geese stage on the refuge in impressive numbers and are targeted by hunters along the north end of Summer Lake and near the River Ranch area. Large decoy spreads produce the best results, but some snow geese are taken by pass shooting from the dikes and levees. Snow goose numbers peak from late October through mid-November. White-fronted geese use the area as well, and while harvest is low, hunters can target the "specklebellies" during October.

Common snipe abound in the area, especially during the early part of the season prior to the first hard freeze. Look for snipe in the meadows, especially those with bulrush growth, and in wet fields.

Walk these areas during the midday duck-hunting lull. Pheasant and valley quail live on the area but are not particularly numerous.

Nearly throughout, the marsh is shallow enough for chest waders, but a good retriever can help locate downed birds in heavy cattail stands. By mid- to late November, expect the arrival of cold weather.

Notes   Hunters must check in and out daily, and upon leaving, must turn in a survey card at headquarters. Nontoxic shot is required for all hunting. Hunters can use bicycles to haul decoys out onto the dikes. Call the area headquarters for up-to-date hunting conditions and reports. Four camping areas are available.

Information Summer Lake Wildlife Area
36981 Highway 31
Summer Lake, OR 97640
541-943-3152

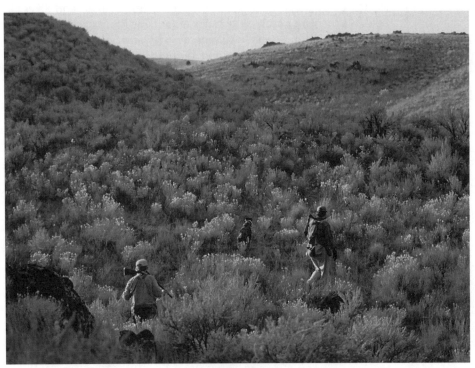

Chukar country.

White-washed at Summer Lake

The morning dawned too bright—bluebird weather. My last Summer Lake day carried all the markings of a fine bird-watching day but a poor duck-shooting day, for a bright rosy dawn intimated clear skies. Toting two dozen decoys, I walked out the dike while the preshooting-hours flights whistled overhead in abundance. By the time legal hunt hours arrived, most of the ducks would be settled into the marsh for the day.

Nonetheless, I set about arranging my spread as whispers of pink sky reached westward across the broad valley. Finally, the first tendrils of gold escaped the icy grasp of the desert rims and a brief five minutes of duck activity accompanied the arrival of shooting hours. A pair of wigeon circled low over the decoys, and I caught the drake as he turned into the wind. After that, a cozy December sun worked its soothing magic on the marsh, encouraging all manner of fowl to nestle down for a lazy day of feeding and loafing.

Indeed, the dreaded bluebird weather, killer of fine shooting days, arrived with a vengeance, and I knew from previous days afield on Summer Lake that I might just as well sit back and enjoy the ambiance. Very thin were the chances of luring ducks into the decoys, for those few that took to the wing would fly at great altitude. I spent the morning watching the drama of the marsh: muskrats and coots and buffleheads swimming amid the decoys, the latter—the so-called butterballs—often swam right up and talked to the imposters. Eagles and ravens circled high overhead. Majestic swans, gleaming white in the morning sun, flew noisily overhead. After a time, when I had determined the locations of other duck hunters, I went in search of snipe and bagged two of the little long-bills, sending several more fleeing away unscathed.

I settled back into my makeshift blind in a dense cattail stand and poured a third cup of coffee, then sat there basking in the sunlight. Not a duck in sight. I finally stood to stretch my legs and shake the icy chill out of my toes and saw to the north, at the head of the valley, a big gray curtain whose immensity obscured Squaw Butte and its attendant desert rims. Sneaking slowly down the valley a storm front was approaching. "If that thing keeps coming," I mused, "I'm in for some shooting after all."

And it kept coming. In its wake I heard faint shots from waterfowlers working the far end of the wildlife area. Lots of faint shots. The barrage continued as the edge of the storm marched southward. Within 10 minutes, the entire north side of the basin was obscured in a dense shroud of gray and black clouds. Finally, the first blast of bitter cold wind lashed across my decoy spread and sent

Winter Rim rises above the west side of Summer Lake Wildlife Area

me huddling into the protective cover of the reeds. Then the gray curtain over-whelmed me in a dizzying horizontal onslaught of snow, sleet, and wind. Within minutes the decoys were completely whitewashed on their windward side and draped in clear ice on their leeward sides. And their appearance mattered not a lick because suddenly the air was alive with ducks just begging for a place to sit down. Visibility was limited to 30 yards, so I simply stood out in the open and picked out drakes—mallards, wigeon, and gadwall—until I'd filled a bag limit, which took about five minutes.

The storm continued unabated, obliterating the sun. The air temperature plummeted. I still had decoys to collect and immediately discovered that the mesh decoy bag was frozen stiff and solid. Each decoy was coated with a half inch of ice, and each line froze immediately upon removal from the water. I did the best I could as quickly as possible. Ice-coated decoys—24 of them—make for an exceptionally heavy load, a fact I soon discovered. Add six dead ducks to the bag, along with shotgun and various other sundries, and you've got a load more fit for a mule than a 170-pound man. And I had walked a mile out onto the dike.

Frostbite and hypothermia seemed the only possible outcome for the first quarter mile, but after that, hauling my brutal burden for another few hundred yards warmed me considerably. Still, I was never so happy to see the truck, though its black finish was now awash in icy white.

In subsequent years, I remember that day with fond memories, for such glorious duck shooting occurs but infrequently. Nonetheless, despite the fond recollections of a fine shoot, in recounting that episode I cannot escape the brief shiver that remains from the memory of the coldest day I ever spent on Summer Lake.

Klamath Wildlife Area

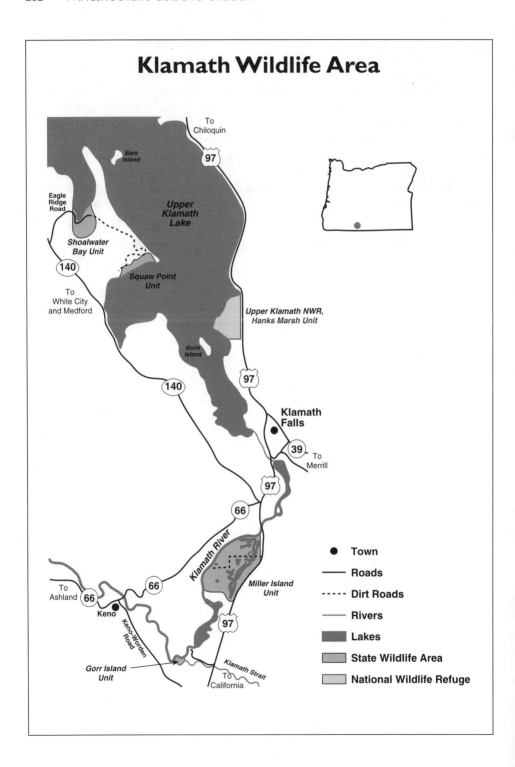

Klamath Wildlife Area

Size 3,400 acres

Species Ducks, Canada geese, snow geese, white-fronted geese, ring-necked pheasants, valley quail, mourning dove, common snipe

Location Divided into four separate units, two on Upper Klamath Lake and two on the Klamath River south of Klamath Falls

Directions Follow US 97 south to Klamath Falls. To reach Squaw Point Unit and Shoalwater Bay Unit, follow SR 140 north along the west side of Klamath Lake. To reach the Miller Island Unit and Gorr Island Unit, follow US 97 south from Klamath Falls.

Description The Miller Island Unit, which is divided into three subunits, covers a total of 2,400 acres, approximately half upland habitat and half wetland habitat. Miller Island lies 6 miles south of Klamath Falls. The Gorr Island Unit, located 12 miles south of Klamath Falls, covers 210 acres and is accessible only by boat. Shoalwater Bay Unit and Squaw Point Unit are located on the west side of Upper Klamath Lake. Totaling some 800 acres, these units are dominated by wetlands and are primarily accessible by boat. Pheasant and quail are limited to the Miller Island Unit. Pheasants are released prior to each hunt day during the season. The remainder of Klamath Wildlife Area is largely the domain of waterfowl hunters. Puddle ducks comprise a large share of the harvest, but diving ducks, including scaup, canvasback, redheads, and goldeneyes, are taken on the Shoalwater Bay and Squaw Point Units. Goose hunters find the best success on the Miller Island Unit and Gorr Island Unit. Western Canada geese prevail along with some cackling Canada geese. A few snow geese and white-fronted geese are harvested each season.

Notes Nontoxic shot is required for all hunting. Early season hunting pressure on the Miller Island Unit is regulated by a controlled hunt drawing, with hunt days usually every other day. Consult current synopsis. The remaining units are open daily during game bird seasons. Beware of marked safety zones.

Information Klamath Wildlife Area
1850 Miller Island Road West
Klamath Falls, OR 97603
541-883-5734

White River Wildlife Area

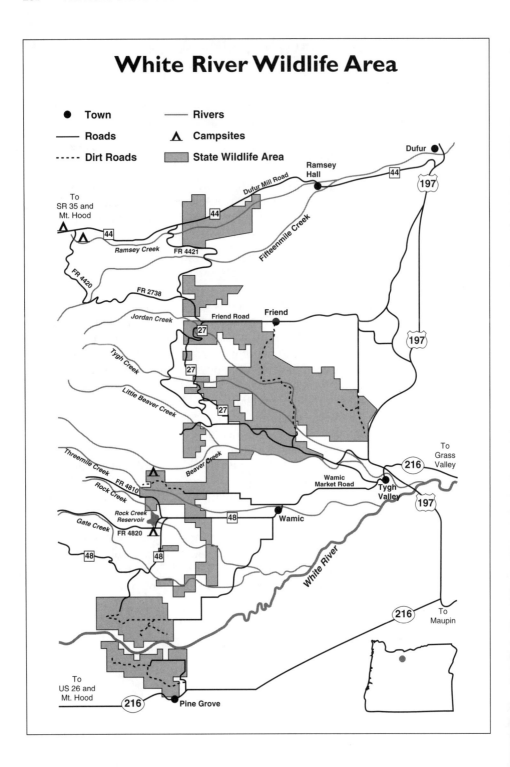

White River Wildlife Area

Size	40, 877 acres
Species	Wild turkey, ring-necked pheasant, valley quail, mountain quail, blue and ruffed grouse, mourning dove, chukar and Hungarian partridge, waterfowl
Location	North of The Dalles and west of Tygh Valley in north-central Oregon
Directions	Follow US 197 south from The Dalles for about 30 miles to reach the town of Tygh Valley. In Tygh Valley, follow the signs to Wamic on Wamic Market Road. At Wamic, continue straight ahead on Dodson Road and follow three 90-degree curves, then turn left at a gravel road that leads to the area headquarters.
Description	Turkey hunting is increasingly productive here as flocks have flourished. A diverse mix of oaks, pines, and fir offers perfect habitat for northern Oregon's highest density of Rio Grande turkeys that utilize a variety of habitats but are most commonly found in mixed stands of oak, fir, and ponderosa pine. Outside the forested tracts, this area is dominated by grass-scrub steppe, where bitterbrush and sagebrush dominate. Some 1,000 acres of pastureland is scattered about in the area. Pheasants are not plentiful but reside in and around the grain fields near Happy Ridge and Pine Grove. Valley quail exist in scattered coveys near agricultural lands, while mountain quail occur closer to Mt. Hood National Forest (they are more numerous as you climb up into the national forest). Annual harvest is low on both chukar and Hungarian partridge as well as on both species of grouse.
Notes	Check with headquarters for current road closures and travel restrictions.
Information	White River Wildlife Area 78430 Dodson Road Tygh Valley OR 97063 541-544-2126

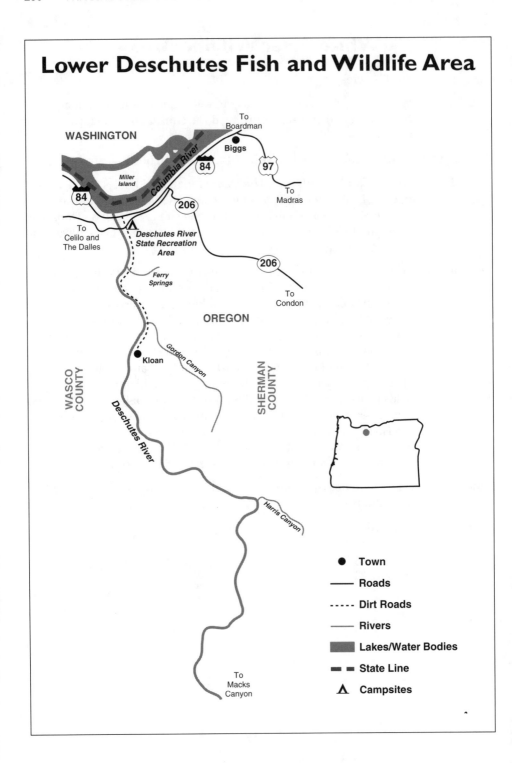

Lower Deschutes Fish and Wildlife Area

Lower Deschutes Fish and Wildlife Area

Size   8,358 acres

Species   Chukar partridge, valley quail, ring-necked pheasant, mourning dove, ducks, and Canada geese

Location   Located along the lower 17 miles of the Deschutes River

Directions   Follow Interstate 84 east from Portland to Exit 97, which leads to Deschutes State Park at the mouth of the river.

Description   The Lower Deschutes Wildlife Area extends upstream along the river for some 16 miles. Here, the Deschutes River flows through a steep, massive canyon cloaked in rock, sagebrush, cheatgrass, and other vegetation typical of Central Oregon's canyonlands. The river itself, broad and swift, is lined with alder, cottonwood, hackberry, and other shrubs and grasses. No vehicle access is available except from a steep, sometimes treacherous road leading down to Kloan, some 8 miles upriver. Otherwise, access is by hiking, biking, or jetboating up from the mouth of the river or by floating down from Macks Canyon, 25 miles above the mouth. Included in this reach are several class 3 and 4 rapids. Chukar are the predominant game bird, although a few pheasant, quail, and mourning dove are found in certain locations along the river. Waterfowlers sometimes jump shoot ducks and geese, but a strong retriever is generally required to fetch birds from the river.

Notes   Nontoxic shot required only for waterfowl. Beware of the Lower Deschutes River Refuge, which is closed to hunting. A detailed contour map is available from ODFW.

Information   Oregon Department of Fish and Wildlife
61374 Parrell Road
Bend, OR 97702
541-388-6363

Hundreds of thousands of ducks and geese migrate through Sauvie Island each year. Here, wood ducks congregate on a partially submerged tree.

Sauvie Island Wildlife Area

Size 12,000 acres

Species Ducks, geese, common snipe, ring-necked pheasant, valley quail

Location Located on Sauvie Island in the Columbia River northwest of Portland

Directions Follow US 30 northwest out of Portland heading toward St. Helens. About 10 miles north of Portland, turn right at the Sauvie Island Bridge exit and cross Sauvie Island Bridge. After the bridge, continue 1.5 miles to the junction of Reeder and Sauvie Island Roads. To reach Eastside Unit, turn right on Reeder Road to the check station. To reach the Northside Unit, continue to the end of Reeder Road, and to reach the Westside Unit, follow Sauvie Island Road.

Description This huge Columbia River island offers plentiful wetland habitat and upland habitat. This wildlife area is known primarily for its waterfowling opportunities, but pheasant and quail hunting are available as well. The area offers three different hunt units, two of which are open

Sauvie Island Wildlife Area

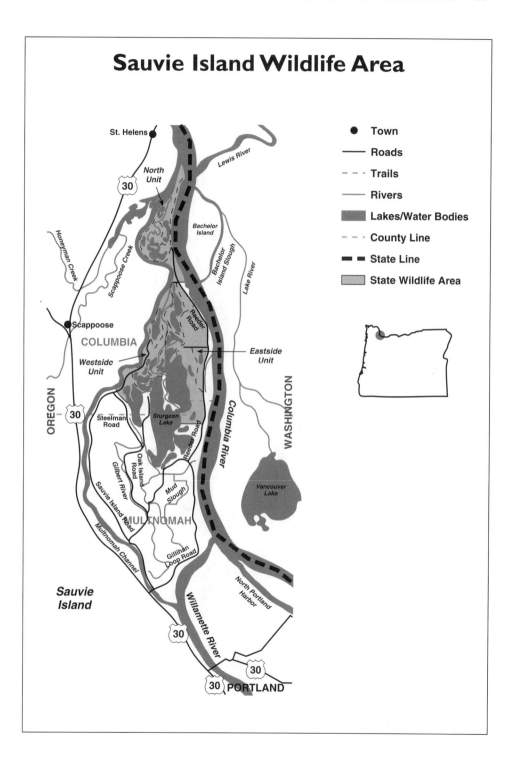

St. Helens

Lewis River

North Unit

30

Honeyman Creek

Scappoose Creek

Bachelor Island

Bachelor Island Slough

Lake River

Reeder Road

Scappoose

COLUMBIA

Westside Unit

Eastside Unit

OREGON

30

Steelman Road

Sturgeon Lake

Reeder Road

Columbia River

WASHINGTON

Oak Island Road

Gilbert River

Sauvie Island Road

Mud Slough

MULTNOMAH

Vancouver Lake

Multnomah Channel

Gillihan Loop Road

North Portland Harbor

Sauvie Island

30

Willamette River

30

30 PORTLAND

- Town
— Roads
- - - Trails
— Rivers
Lakes/Water Bodies
- - - County Line
State Line
State Wildlife Area

Sauvie Island Wildlife Area, detail

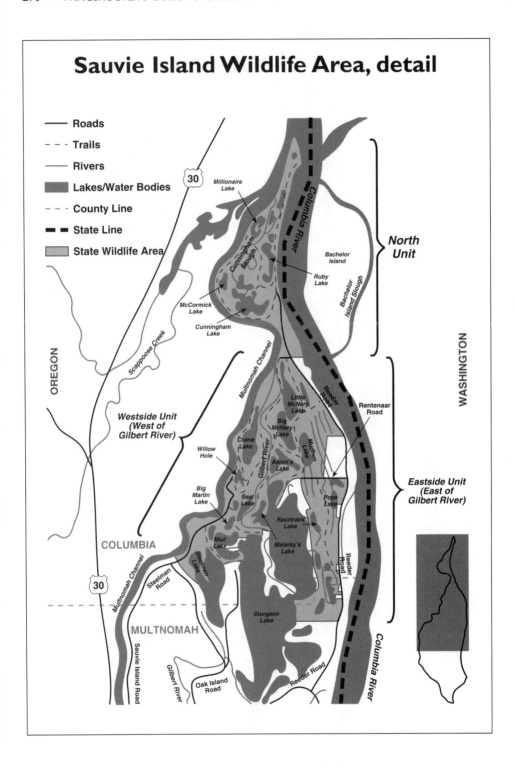

on a restricted basis: The Westside Unit is open via a drawing held an hour and a half prior to shooting hours on each specified hunt day of the season. The Eastside Unit is likewise open by permit only, but the drawing occurs by a reservation system rather than on a daily basis This is done through the controlled-hunt application procedure, details of which appear in the game bird regulations pamphlet. Northside Unit is open each day of the season and requires no check-in. On several subunits, hunters must remain at fixed locations, so if upland birds are your quarry, be sure to hunt the subunits designated as "roam areas." The entire wildlife area provides excellent goose hunting during the September Canada goose season. Upland birds, especially pheasants, are found primarily in areas of heavy cover.

Notes   The use of dogs is strongly encouraged to avoid losing downed birds. Only federally approved nontoxic shot is permitted for all game birds. All vehicles in the area are required to display a Sauvie Island Wildlife Area parking permit, which is available for purchase through many businesses on the island and through any point-of-sale license agent. Consult the current synopsis for information about youth-hunt opportunities.

Information Sauvie Island Wildlife Area
18330 NW Sauvie Island Road
Portland, OR 97231
503-621-3488

E.E. Wilson Wildlife Management Area

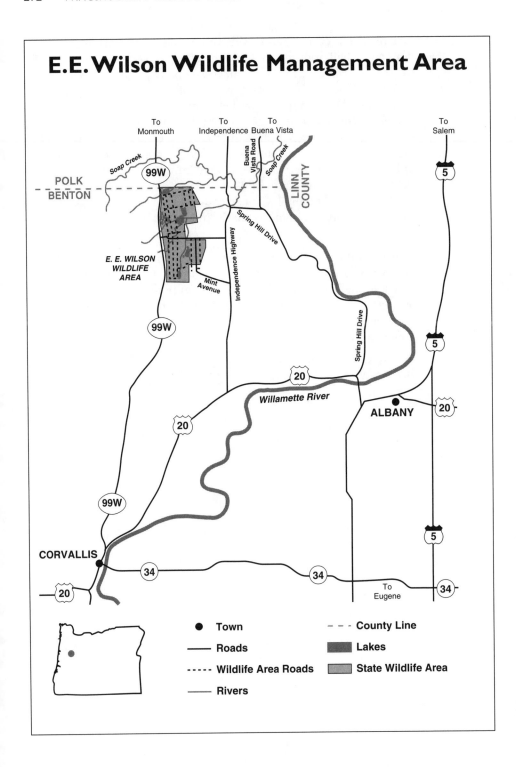

E.E. Wilson Wildlife Management Area

Size   1,683 acres

Species   Ring-necked pheasant, valley quail, mourning dove, ducks, geese, common snipe

Location   Located on the west side of the Willamette River about 10 miles north of Corvallis

Directions Follow SR 99W north from Corvallis or south from Monmouth and turn east on Camp Adair Road.

Description Once a U.S. Army base, E.E. Wilson Wildlife Area features an old grid of paved and gravel roads, many of which are still negotiable by foot, bike, and wheelchair. Most of the area is characterized by grasslands, brushlands and woodlots. Pheasant hunting is popular but is limited to stocked birds during the Western Oregon Fee Pheasant Hunt. Also popular are the youth pheasant hunts held during September. Valley quail are common in the area but prefer to stick to heavy blackberry cover where a good dog is required to find and retrieve birds. Consult the current synopsis for pheasant season dates.

Notes   Good wheelchair access. Rifles and handguns prohibited. Nontoxic shot only for all species.

Information E.E. Wilson Wildlife Area
29555 Camp Adair Road
Monmouth, OR 97361
541-745-5334

Fern Ridge Wildlife Area

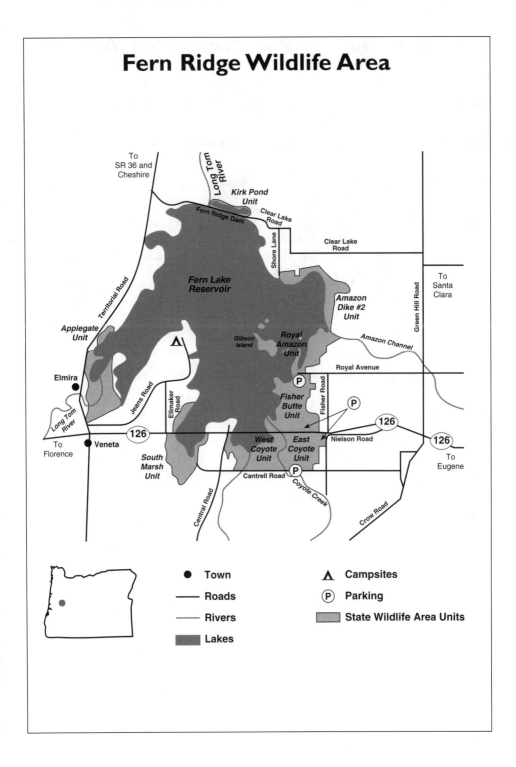

To
SR 36 and
Cheshire

Long Tom River

Kirk Pond
Unit

Fern Ridge Dam

Clear Lake
Road

Shore Lane

Clear Lake
Road

Fern Lake
Reservoir

Territorial Road

Amazon
Dike #2
Unit

To
Santa
Clara

Green Hill Road

Applegate
Unit

Gibson
Island

Royal
Amazon
Unit

Amazon Channel

Elmira

Jeans Road

Ellmaker
Road

Royal Avenue

P

Fisher
Butte
Unit

Fisher Road

P

Long Tom
River

126

To
Florence

Veneta

South
Marsh
Unit

West
Coyote
Unit

East
Coyote
Unit

Nielson Road

126

126

To
Eugene

Cantrell Road

P

Central Road

Coyote Creek

Crow Road

- ● Town
- — Roads
- — Rivers
- ▬ Lakes

- ▲ Campsites
- Ⓟ Parking
- ▬ State Wildlife Area Units

Fern Ridge Wildlife Area

Size   5, 103 acres

Species   Ducks, Canada geese, common snipe, ring-necked pheasant, valley quail, mourning dove

Location   Fern Ridge Reservoir lies several miles west of Eugene

Directions   Follow SR 126 west from town to reach the southern portion of the wildlife area. Clear Lake Road borders the north edge of the area, while Territorial Road connects Clear Lake Road with SR 126 west of the reservoir.

Description   Fern Ridge Reservoir and Wildlife Area is divided into 19 management units, most of which are open to hunting. The reservoir is drawn down during the winter, but numerous potholes, flats, and channels attract waterfowl while fringe upland habitat provides cover for stocked pheasants, a few wild pheasants, valley quail, and snipe. East Coyote, West Coyote, Fisher Butte, and Royal Amazon units offer hunting for stocked pheasants during the Western Oregon Fee Pheasant Hunt in October. Ducks attract the most hunting pressure. Controlled waterfowl hunts are available in the East and West Coyote Units. Goose hunting is limited to the September Canada Goose Season. Consult current synopsis.

Notes   Hunters using the East Coyote, West Coyote, Fisher Butte, and Royal Amazon Units must check in and out at self-service check stations prior to the controlled waterfowl hunts. During the controlled waterfowl hunts, hunters must check in and out at a staffed check station to use the East and West Coyote Units. Rifles and handguns are prohibited. Nontoxic shot is required for all game bird hunting. Check current synopsis for youth hunt days.

Information   Fern Ridge Wildlife Area
26969 Cantrell Road
Eugene, OR 97402
541-935-2591

Ken Denman Wildlife Area

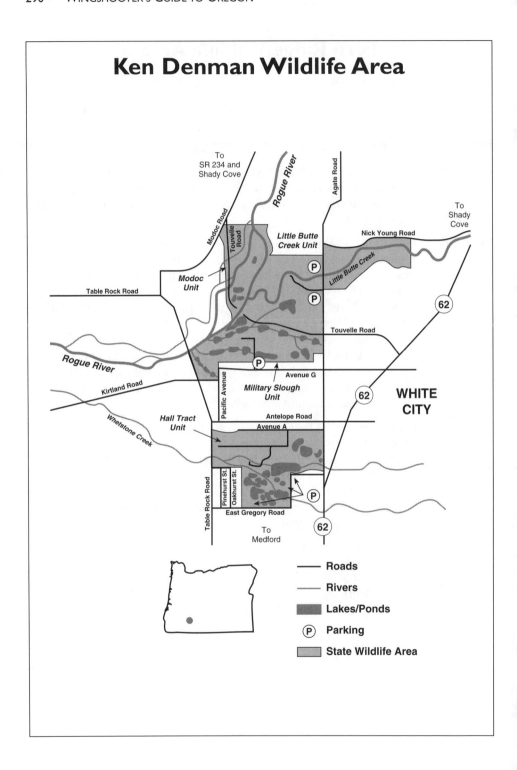

Ken Denman Wildlife Area

Size   1,799 acres

Species   Ring-necked pheasant, valley quail, mourning dove, ducks, and
Canada geese

Location   Located about 7 miles north of Medford

Directions Follow Interstate 5 to the Central Point Exit (Exit 32) and proceed
east to a left turn on Table Rock Road and then to a right turn
on East Gregory Road, which runs about 2 miles to the headquarters
on your left.

Description The so-called Agate Desert dominates this area and is characterized
by rocky grasslands. Brushy bottomlands are lined with stands of
hardwoods, including oak and cottonwood, and include some 20
small ponds. The Hall Tract and Military Slough Units feature several
miles of irrigation ditches. Most pheasants are planted on the Hall
Tract and Military Slough Units prior to the youth and fee pheasant
hunts. Valley quail prefer heavy cover in the bottomlands. Duck
hunters can jump shoot or work over decoys.

Notes   Check current synopsis for open hunting days. Nontoxic shot is
required for all game bird hunting. Rifles and handguns prohibited.
Wheelchair access at selected parking areas.

Information Ken Denman Wildlife Area
1495 East Gregory Road
Central Point, OR 97502
541-826-8774

McKay Creek National Wildlife Refuge

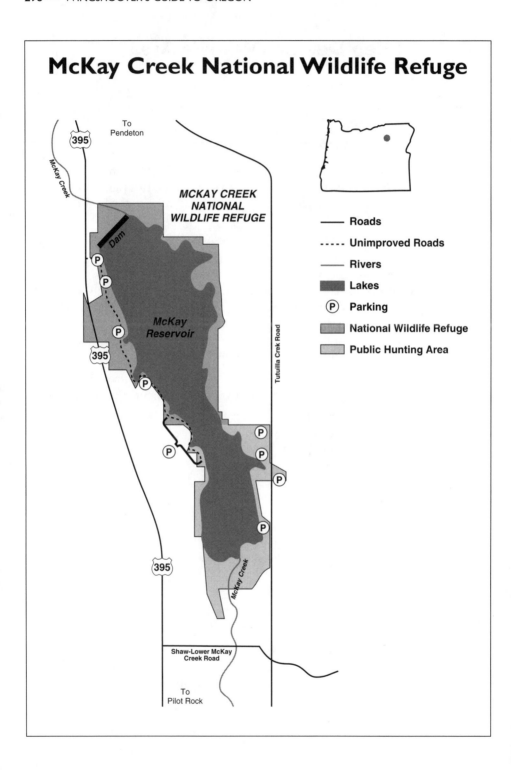

To
Pendeton

395

McKay Creek

MCKAY CREEK
NATIONAL
WILDLIFE REFUGE

Dam

P

P

McKay
Reservoir

P

395

P

Tutuilla Crek Road

P

P

P

P

P

P

395

McKay Creek

Shaw-Lower McKay
Creek Road

To
Pilot Rock

——— Roads

- - - - Unimproved Roads

——— Rivers

████ Lakes

Ⓟ Parking

░░░░ National Wildlife Refuge

░░░░ Public Hunting Area

Oregon's National Wildlife Refuges

McKay Creek National Wildlife Refuge

Size   1,836 acres (about 600 acres open to hunting)

Species   Ducks, Canada geese, ring-necked pheasant, valley quail

Location   On the east side of US 395, 8 miles south of Pendleton

Directions Follow I-84 to Pendleton, then turn south on US 395 (Exit 209 off I-84). Follow US 395 about 7 miles to a well-marked left turn into the refuge.

Description Comprised mostly of McKay (pronounced McKye) Creek Reservoir, this refuge offers about 500 acres of upland and riparian habitat and is a popular destination for pheasant hunters. By the end of opening weekend, most surviving roosters seek refuge in dense cattail stands and heavy Russian olive or willow thickets. A good dog is required to achieve consistent success here. Waterfowlers will have the best success hunting over decoy spreads along the margins of the reservoir's south half. Launches are available on both sides and on both ends of the reservoir.

Notes   Hunting is allowed only on Tuesdays, Thursdays, Saturdays, and Thanksgiving day, Christmas day, and New Year's day during the state waterfowl and pheasant seasons. Hunters are limited to 25 shells, and nontoxic shot is required.

Information Mid-Columbia River National Wildlife Refuge Complex
830 6th Street
P.O. Box 700
Umatilla, OR 97882
541-922-3232

Cold Springs National Wildlife Refuge

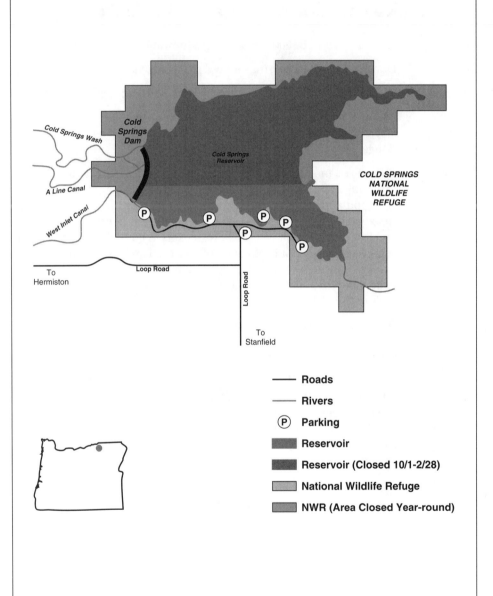

Cold Springs Wash

Cold Springs Dam

Cold Springs Reservoir

A Line Canal

West Inlet Canal

COLD SPRINGS NATIONAL WILDLIFE REFUGE

To Hermiston

Loop Road

Loop Road

To Stanfield

—— Roads

—— Rivers

Ⓟ Parking

Reservoir

Reservoir (Closed 10/1-2/28)

National Wildlife Refuge

NWR (Area Closed Year-round)

Cold Springs National Wildlife Refuge

Size   3,117 acres

Species   Ducks, Canada geese, ring-necked pheasant, valley quail

Location   Umatilla County, east of Hermiston

Directions   Follow I-84 east from western Oregon or west from Pendleton and exit at the Stanfield Exit near Hermiston (Exit 188). At Stanfield, turn east on Stanfield Loop Road and follow this road northeast and then north about 8 miles to the refuge. Several parking areas and two boat launches are located along the access road.

Description Cold Springs NWR is comprised of Cold Springs Reservoir and surrounding upland/riparian habitats. The reservoir itself offers dense cattail stands, brushy shorelines, and deepwater channels. The surrounding area features an abundance of heavy brush cover dominated by cottonwoods, willows, sagebrush, and other vegetation. Pheasant and quail inhabit the brush and are usually found in heavy cover after opening weekend. Waterfowlers find best success with decoy spreads, and the best hunting occurs from late November through early January. Mallards, gadwall, teal, and widgeon are common.

Notes   Hunting is allowed only on Tuesdays, Thursdays, Saturdays, and three holidays (Thanksgiving day, Christmas day and New Year's day). Hunters are allowed only 25 shells per day, and nontoxic shot is required. Portable blinds are allowed and temporary blinds may be constructed of natural materials, but these blinds then become available to the first arrivals on subsequent days.

Information Mid-Columbia River National Wildlife Refuge Complex
830 6th Street
P.O. Box 700
Umatilla, OR 97882
541-922-3232

Umatilla National Wildlife Refuge

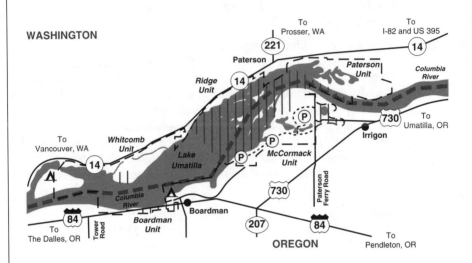

Symbol	Legend	Symbol	Legend
●	Town	Ⓟ	Parking
——	Roads	⚠	Campsites
-----	Dirt Roads	⌐ ¬	National Wildlife Refuge
▓▓	Water Bodies	工工	Areas Closed to Hunting
▬ ▬	State Line		

Umatilla National Wildlife Refuge

Size 23,555 acres (including those portions in Washington)

Species Ring-necked pheasant, valley quail, ducks, and geese

Location In northeastern Oregon, along the Columbia River from Boardman to Irrigon

Directions Follow I-84 east from Portland or west from Pendleton to the Tower Road Exit (Exit 159) near Boardman or Irrigon Exit (US 730). The McCormack Unit is located on the Columbia River from Tower Road to Boardman. To reach the McCormack Unit near Irrigon, follow US 730 east to a north turn on Paterson Ferry Road, which leads to the hunter check station at McCormack Slough.

Description The Umatilla NWR offers a diverse mix of upland bird and waterfowl habitat, all of it located on or along a wide reach of the Columbia River. Ring-necked pheasant abound throughout much of the refuge, but hunting pressure forces most of the roosters into heavy cover—especially cattail stands—where an experienced dog is required for any hope of success. On opening day and toward the very end of the season, roosters occur in more open areas, including crop circle edges. Valley quail are especially drawn to brushy draws and Russian olive stands near water. Hunting on the McCormack Unit is limited exclusively to established blind sites. These are available on McCormack Slough, on the Columbia River proper, and in the fields. Hunting is strictly controlled on this unit, so read "Notes" below and consult the refuge manager's office well before hunt day.

Notes On the McCormack Unit, upland bird and waterfowl hunting is available through a controlled system wherein the refuge is open only on specified days (Saturdays, Sundays, Wednesdays, Thanksgiving day, and New Years day). On the Boardman Unit, hunting is allowed daily through the waterfowl and pheasant seasons. Permits are required to hunt waterfowl on the McCormack Unit, and these are available either by advance reservation or on a standby basis. The drawing for reserved permits occurs during September. Interested hunters must write the refuge for details. Upland hunters must obtain a daily permit at the check-in station; 50 such permits are available each day. Advance reservations are required to hunt pheasant and quail on opening weekend. To apply for an opening weekend upland permit, send a postcard with the words "Umatilla Upland Game" and the day you wish to hunt (Saturday or Sunday). You may apply only for one day, and the card must be postmarked by

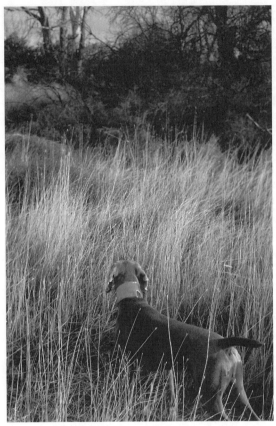

Without a dog, you could walk all day in this tall cover and not find a thing.

September 15. A lottery is used to choose 25 applicants for each day, with the permit covering the applicant and one guest. Hunters must check in and out and pay a $5 fee.

Waterfowl hunters on the McCormack Unit must use established blind sites. Slough blinds are located on McCormack Slough. Two people are allowed per blind. River blinds are staked hunting sites on the river. Three people per blind are allowed. Field blinds are located in agricultural areas, their location changing according to crop management. A daily fee of $5 per person or $10 per blind is required, and hunters must check out before leaving or moving.

The Umatilla NWR also offers two youth hunt days on the McCormack Unit. To apply, youths (age 10–17) must send a postcard with name, address, and the words "Umatilla Youth Hunt Day." Also note which day is being applied for (the first Saturday or the last Tuesday in December). These cards must be postmarked by November 1. Youths must have a hunter safety card and must be accompanied by an adult.

Temporary blinds may be constructed on the Boardman Unit, where waterfowlers are required to space themselves at least 200 yards apart. Digging or using pit blinds is prohibited. Throughout the refuge, hunters are limited to 25 shells, and nontoxic shot is required. No camping or overnight parking is allowed on the refuge.

Information Umatilla National Wildlife Refuge
P.O. Box 700
Umatilla, OR 97882
541-922-3232

Deer Flat National Wildlife Refuge

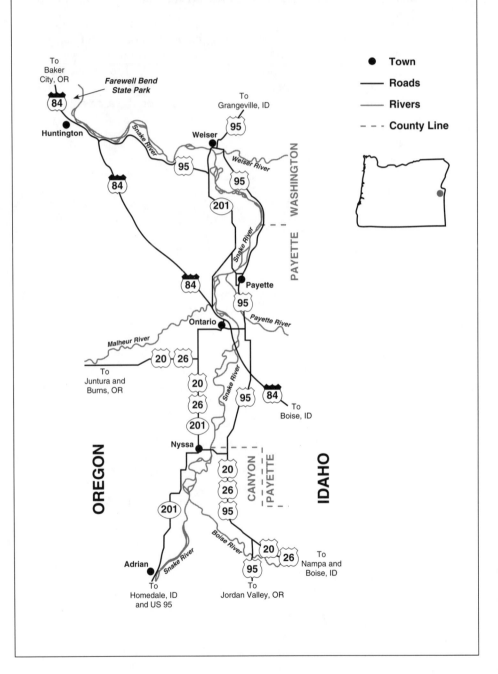

Deer Flat National Wildlife Refuge

Size 11,430 acres total, a fraction of which is in Oregon

Species Ducks, Canada geese, ring-necked pheasant, valley quail, mourning dove

Location On 16 islands of the Snake River between Adrian, Oregon, and Farewell Bend State Park

Directions Follow I-84 to Farewell Bend State Park, northeast from Ontario, or follow SR 201 to the town of Adrian, Oregon, located south of Nyssa. The islands are accessible only by boat, and in addition to the ramps at Farewell Bend and Adrian, there are launches at Ontario and on the Idaho side at Payette and Weiser.

Description The 16 islands comprising the Oregon portion of the refuge range in size from an acre to about 50 acres. Most offer grass and brush habitat with some willow and cottonwood growth in places. The islands are accessible only by boat. Pheasant and quail occupy most of the islands, especially the larger ones. Duck hunters can work over decoys along the edges of the islands or, in places, on the interior of the islands when high water floods these areas. Goose hunters should try floating decoy spreads in the lee of the islands, along with land decoys on exposed leeward shorelines.

Notes Nontoxic shot is required for all hunting. Temporary blinds may be constructed, but are subsequently available on a first-arrival basis.

Information Deer Flat National Wildlife Refuge
13751 Upper Embankment Road
Nampa, ID 83686
208-467-9278

Malheur National Wildlife Refuge

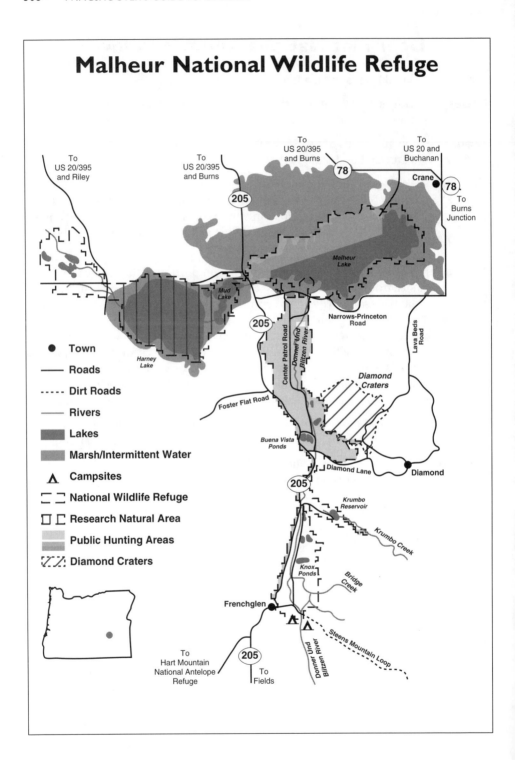

To
US 20/395
and Riley

To
US 20/395
and Burns

To
US 20/395
and Burns

To
US 20 and
Buchanan

Crane

78

78

To
Burns
Junction

205

Malheur
Lake

Mud
Lake

Narrows-Princeton
Road

Lava Beds Road

Center Patrol Road

Donner Und Blitzen River

205

Harney
Lake

Diamond
Craters

Foster Flat Road

Buena Vista
Ponds

Diamond Lane

Diamond

205

Krumbo
Reservoir

Krumbo Creek

Knox
Ponds

Bridge Creek

Frenchglen

To
Hart Mountain
National Antelope
Refuge

205

To
Fields

Donner Und Blitzen River

Steens Mountain Loop

- ● **Town**
- — **Roads**
- ---- **Dirt Roads**
- — **Rivers**
- **Lakes**
- **Marsh/Intermittent Water**
- ⋀ **Campsites**
- ⌐ ⌐ **National Wildlife Refuge**
- ⌗ ⌗ **Research Natural Area**
- **Public Hunting Areas**
- ⧄⧄ **Diamond Craters**

Malheur National Wildlife Refuge

Size   185,652 acres

Species   Ducks, Canada geese, snow geese, common snipe, ring-necked pheasant, valley quail, Hungarian partridge, chukar partridge

Location   Malheur County in southeastern Oregon

Directions   Follow State Route 78 east from Burns. After 2 miles SR 205 turns to the south, leading to the west end of Malheur Lake ("The Narrows") and eventually down to the tiny town of Frenchglen. SR 78 continues southeast and then south by the town of Crane and through the hamlets of New Princeton and Princeton, where the Princeton-Narrows Road leads west to the headquarters and on to SR 205.

Description   The focal point of this large refuge is sprawling Malheur Lake, a huge, shallow alkaline lake whose size and volume increases substantially during wet years and shrinks noticeably during dry years. During the early 1980s, unusually wet conditions caused Malheur Lake and nearby Harney Lake to reach unheard-of proportions, flooding out thousands of acres of ranch and farmlands and causing millions of dollars in damage.

Malheur NWR features diverse habitats, including shallow marshes, lakes, small ponds, flood-irrigated meadows, alkali flats, rimrocks, sage and grass steppe, and juniper stands. Average annual precipitation is only 9 inches, and long, cold winters are typical of this high-desert environment. Of the 185,652 acres comprising the refuge, some 18,000 acres are open to waterfowling and about 40,000 acres are open to upland bird hunting. The open hunting areas are divided into three different areas as follows:

Buena Vista Area is located east of SR 205, from refuge headquarters south to Diamond Lane. This 22,000-acre area is open for pheasant, quail, and partridge beginning the third Saturday in November and continuing through the end of the state seasons for each species.

Boundary Area occupies a narrow band on the west side of SR 205, from a few miles north of Buena Vista Station south to Frenchglen and also along Krumbo Creek east of Krumbo Reservoir. This area is open for all game birds during authorized state seasons.

Malheur Lake Area covers 18,000 acres along the north and west side of the lake. SR 205 crosses the area's westernmost extent at the channel that connects Malheur Lake with Mud Lake to the west. This area is open for waterfowl, common snipe, pheasant, and quail.

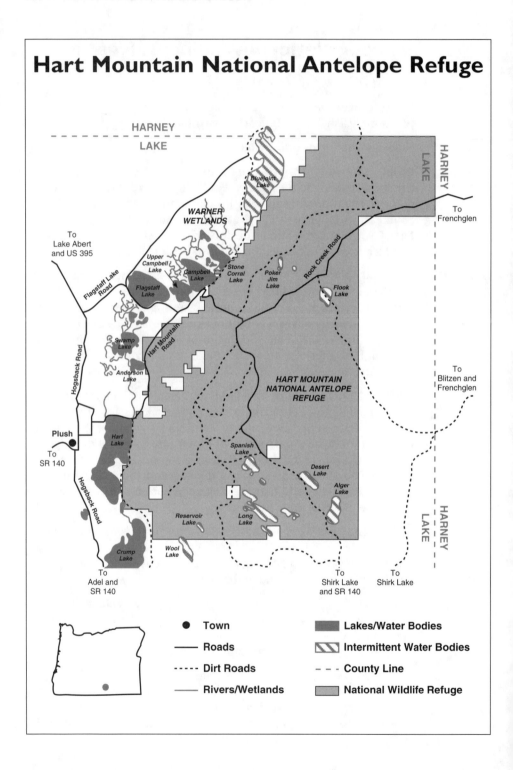

Only nonmotorized boats are allowed; temporary blinds may be constructed, which are then available on a first-come, first-served basis. Access is via an unmarked gravel road off SR 78 between mile markers 21 and 22.

Notes   Only nontoxic shot is allowed on the refuge. Camping is not allowed on the refuge, but nearby are Page Springs Campground (BLM) and Camper Corral (private), both near Frenchglen.

Information Malheur National Wildlife Refuge
HC 72, Box 245
Princeton, OR 97721
541-493-2612

Hart Mountain National Antelope Refuge

Size   275,000 acres

Species   Chukar partridge

Location   Hart Mountain is located in a remote part of southeastern Oregon, near the tiny community of Plush

Directions Follow US 395 to the SR 140 turnoff 6 miles north of Lakeview. Then follow SR 140 east

Description Located in a remote part of southeastern Oregon, Hart Mountain National Antelope Refuge was created as a haven for pronghorns. More recently, desert bighorn sheep were reintroduced and now occupy the steep slopes of the refuge. In addition to its big game, Hart Mountain is home to chukar partridge, although population density is low. Hunting for chukars is allowed on Hart Mountain's west face, south of the Hart Bar Road and north of the Grade Road. Elevations here range from 4,500 feet to nearly 7,000 feet, so hunters must be prepared for rigorous walking on these steep, rocky slopes.

Notes   Rattlesnakes are quite common in this region, so many chukar hunters prefer to wait until the weather turns cold, thereby preventing a chance encounter between snake and bird dog.

Information Hart Mountain National Antelope Refuge
18 South G Street, Room 301
P.O. Box 111
Lakeview, OR 97630
541-947-3315

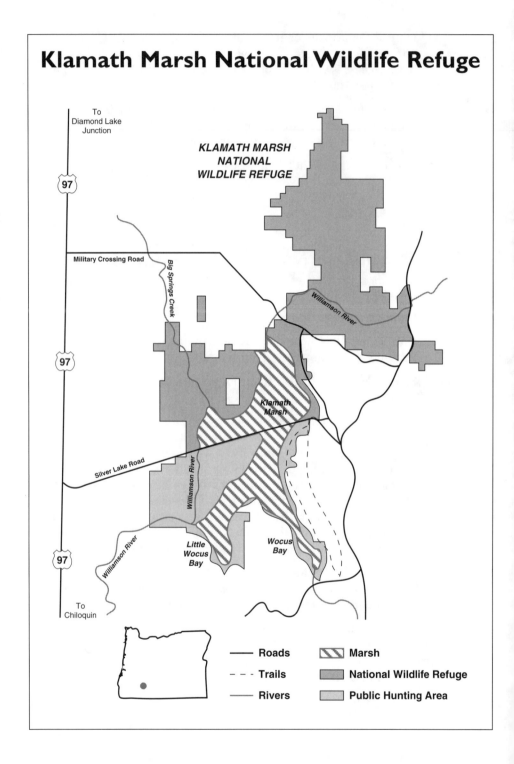

Klamath Marsh National Wildlife Refuge

Klamath Marsh National Wildlife Refuge

Size   37,600 acres

Species   Ducks, Canada geese, white-fronted geese

Location   Southern Oregon, about 50 miles north of Klamath Falls
                  and east of US 97

Directions   Follow US 97 south from Bend or north from Klamath Falls to the
                  Silver Lake Road turnoff, which leads across the marsh.

Description   Klamath Marsh is comprised of extensive cattail and reed stands
                  along with wet meadow or dry grassland habitat, depending on rela-
                  tive water levels. During excessively dry years, the marsh offers very
                  limited waterfowling because the water table drops significantly.
                  Hunting for Canada geese can be quite good along the marsh's north
                  end adjacent to Silver Lake Road, and white-fronted geese are some-
                  times available early in the season and often feed on adjacent private
                  lands just west of the marsh along Silver Lake Road. Numerous duck
                  species occur here, among the most common being mallards, pin-
                  tails, green-winged and cinnamon teal, widgeon, gadwall, ring-
                  necked ducks, and redheads. While some pass shooting is available,
                  especially during inclement weather, waterfowlers working over
                  decoys enjoy the best success. Use a pram or canoe to gain access to
                  the marsh—a launch is located at Wocus Bay off Forest Service Road
                  690, which turns south off Silver Lake Road on the east side of the
                  marsh. Refuge headquarters are located on Silver Lake Road north-
                  west of the hunting area.

Notes   Nontoxic shot is required. Only boats without motors are allowed. A
                  100-yard retrieval zone, in which no loaded weapons are allowed,
                  runs parallel to Silver Lake Road. Hunting is not allowed on refuge
                  lands north of Silver Lake Road. No camping on the refuge.

Information   Klamath Basin National Wildlife Refuge
                  Route 1, Box 74
                  Tulelake, CA 96134
                  530-667-2231

*Pintail Drake. Pintails are common on the Upper Klamath
National Wildlife Refuge.*

Upper Klamath National Wildlife Refuge

Size   14,400 acres; 6,000 acres open to hunting

Species   Ducks, Canada geese, white-fronted geese

Location   Upper Klamath Lake north of Klamath Falls

Directions The Upper Klamath NWR is divided into two units, the largest being
located on and adjacent to the northwest shoreline of Upper Klamath
Lake. To reach the area, follow SR 140 northwest from Klamath Falls
and continue along the west side of the lake until you reach Rocky
Point Junction. Turn north on West Side Road and launch at either
Rocky Point or Malone Springs Launches. The small Hank's Marsh
Unit is located just north of Klamath Falls off SR 97. Use the boat
launch at Hagelstein County Park.

Description Because hunting on the Upper Klamath NWR requires a boat to reach
fairly remote parts of the marsh, this refuge is not heavily hunted.
Nonetheless, it offers excellent prospects for a variety of ducks and
for geese. Hunting occurs along the marsh edges and in small pothole

Upper Klamath National Wildlife Refuge
Rocky Point Area

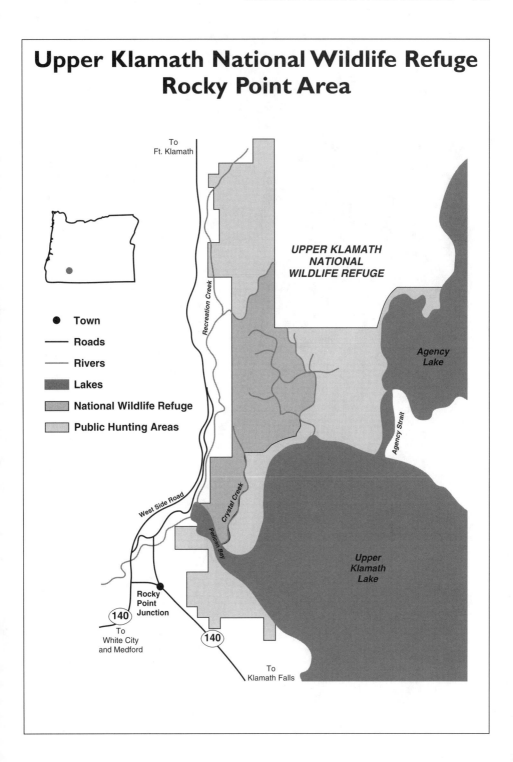

Upper Klamath National Wildlife Refuge Hanks Marsh Unit

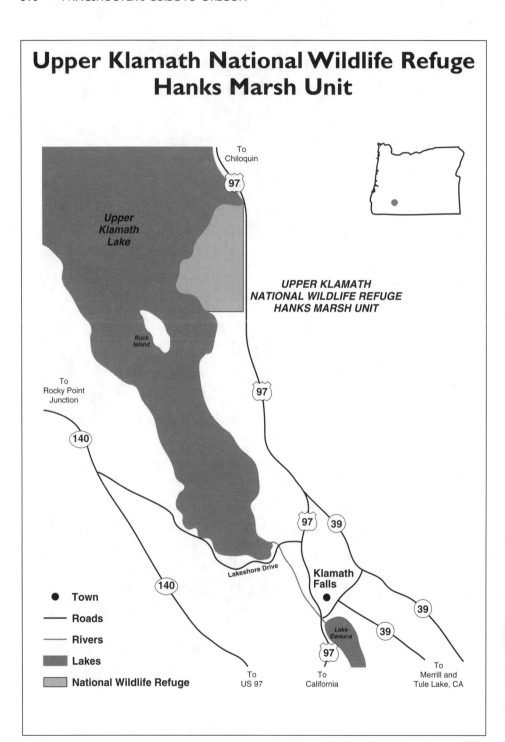

openings in the marsh, so decoy hunting is most effective. The marsh offers good prospects for both Canada and white-fronted geese ("specklebellies"), especially early in the season. Common ducks include mallard, pintail, gadwall, widgeon, green-winged teal, lesser scaup, and ring-necked ducks. Redheads, canvasback, and other species are also available. The Hank's Marsh Unit can provide good duck and goose hunting, especially late in the season if lake levels drop and birds are drawn to this area as a result.

Notes   Hunters need a boat with a reliable motor to reach the marsh because of the distances between launches and the best hunting areas. However, air-thrust and inboard water-thrust (jet) boats are not allowed. Nontoxic shot is required. No camping is allowed on the refuge. No hunting or loaded firearms are allowed on the posted "Hunter Access" routes on the marsh. No hunting from or across canoe trails (these are posted).

Information   Klamath Basin National Wildlife Refuge
Route 1, Box 74
Tulelake, CA 96134
530-667-2231

Lower Klamath National Wildlife Refuge

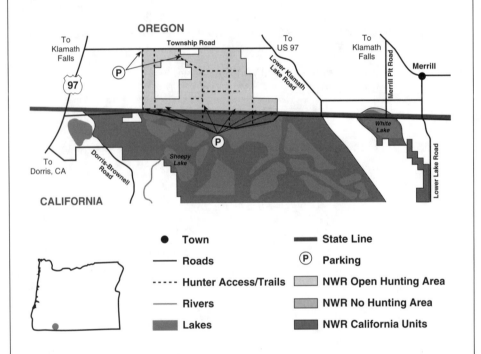

OREGON

To Klamath Falls

Township Road

To US 97

To Klamath Falls

Merrill

97

Lower Klamath Lake Road

Merrill Pit Road

White Lake

Lower Lake Road

To Dorris, CA

Dorris-Brownell Road

Sheepy Lake

CALIFORNIA

● Town

—— Roads

- - - - Hunter Access/Trails

—— Rivers

Lakes

State Line

Ⓟ Parking

NWR Open Hunting Area

NWR No Hunting Area

NWR California Units

Lower Klamath National Wildlife Refuge

Size 5,000 acres in Oregon; approximately 48,000 acres in California

Species In Oregon, primarily Canada geese and white-fronted geese along with some opportunity for ring-necked pheasant

Location South of Klamath Falls, along the California border

Directions To reach the Oregon portions of the refuge, follow US 97 south from Klamath Falls. A few miles north of the California border, turn east on Township Road, which borders the northern extent of the refuge. For directions to specific areas, check with refuge headquarters.

Description Oregon's section of the Lower Klamath National Wildlife Refuge primarily offers goose hunting in grain stubble. Canada geese are most abundant, while white-fronted geese are fairly common, especially early in the season. Cackling Canada geese are available as well as the occasional snow goose. Decoys are essential for consistent success. Some duck hunting is available when standing water covers parts of the grain stubble. Pheasant densities are fairly low, but birds are available where suitable cover exists.

Notes On the Oregon portion of Lower Klamath NWR, hunting is permitted seven days per week throughout the Oregon season, and no special permits or check-in are required. Nontoxic shot is required. No overnight parking or camping are available on the refuge.

Information Klamath Basin National Wildlife Refuge
Route 1, Box 74
Tulelake, CA 96134
530-667-2231

Lewis and Clark National Wildlife Refuge

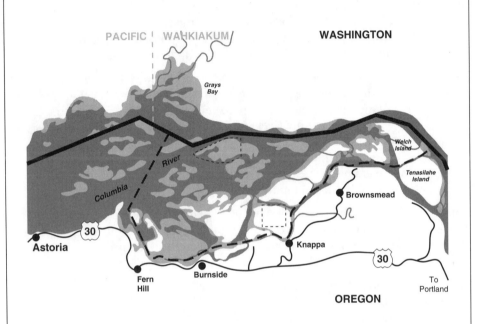

PACIFIC | WAHKIAKUM

WASHINGTON

Grays
Bay

River

Welch
Island

Columbia

Tenasilahe
Island

Brownsmead

30

Astoria

Knappa

30

Fern
Hill

Burnside

To
Portland

OREGON

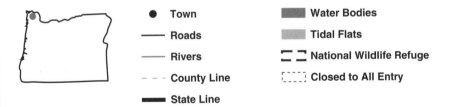

- ● Town
- — Roads
- — Rivers
- – – County Line
- ▬ State Line

- Water Bodies
- Tidal Flats
- ⊏ ⊐ National Wildlife Refuge
- Closed to All Entry

Lewis and Clark National Wildlife Refuge

Size　38,258 acres

Species　Ducks, geese, common snipe

Location　Lower Columbia River, upstream from Astoria

Description　Lewis and Clark NWR encompasses dozens of Columbia River islands upriver from Astoria. Near US 30, two different boat launches allow access to the refuge (shoreline access without a boat is quite limited). The westernmost launch is located near the mouth of the John Day River near the town of Fern Hill (don't confuse this river with the more prominent John Day River of eastern Oregon). The launch parking area is located adjacent to the highway just west of the John Day River bridge. The easternmost launch is located at Aldrich Point, northeast of Knappa and Brownsmead—turn north off US 30 onto Aldrich Point Road. A third launch is located on the Washington side of the river at Skamokawa Channel off Washington State Route 4. Remember that you are boating in tide-influenced waters, so check tide tables ahead of time and be prepared for water level changes.

Comprised entirely of estuarine wetlands habitat on and along the Columbia River, the Lewis and Clark NWR offers excellent prospects for waterfowl, especially ducks, along with good to excellent snipe hunting for those willing to walk the islands. Puddle ducks abound, especially mallard, wigeon, pintail, shoveler, and green-winged teal. Divers are also quite abundant, including ring-necked ducks, scaup, canvasback, redhead, and others. Be sure to consult current goose hunting regulations before pursuing Canada geese on the refuge.

Notes　Temporary blinds may be constructed on the refuge, and steel shot is required for all hunting. No camping is allowed on the refuge, and several areas are closed to all access (these are posted).

Information　Julia Butler Hansen Refuge for the Columbia White-tailed Deer
P.O. Box 556
Cathlamet, WA 98612
360-795-3915

Bandon Marsh National Wildlife Refuge

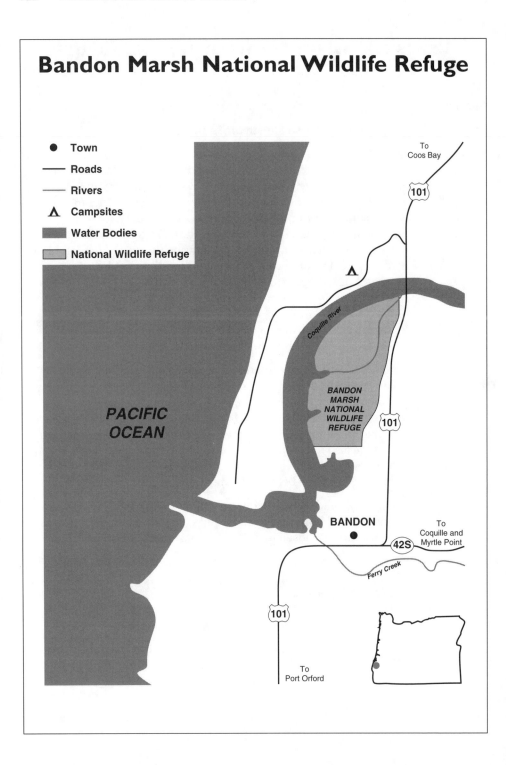

- ● Town
- — Roads
- — Rivers
- ⋏ Campsites
- Water Bodies
- National Wildlife Refuge

To Coos Bay

101

⋏

Coquille River

BANDON MARSH NATIONAL WILDLIFE REFUGE

101

PACIFIC OCEAN

BANDON
●

To Coquille and Myrtle Point

42S

Ferry Creek

101

To Port Orford

Bandon Marsh National Wildlife Refuge

Size   305 acres

Species   Ducks, geese, common snipe, band-tailed pigeon

Location   Southern Oregon coast near the community of Bandon

Directions Follow US 101 south from Coos Bay or north from Bandon. Access is by boat from Bandon (up the Coquille River), from a few parking areas along the highway, or from Bullard State Park, just north of the Coquille River Bridge.

Description Bandon Marsh is typical of Oregon's estuary environments. Here, the Coquille River surrenders its water to the Pacific but not before its delta forms a marsh drained by winding tidal creeks and characterized by extensive low-tide flats and high-tide channels. Mallard, pintail and wigeon abound; green-winged teal and shoveler are quite common. Divers use the river channel and tidal creeks. Common snipe migrate through the marsh in good numbers, with peak populations occurring late in the fall. Duck hunters using decoy spreads will achieve best results, especially when hunting the early morning and late afternoon high tides. Jump shooters can work the tidal creeks, especially at mid-stage tides, but a good retriever should be considered mandatory. Band-tailed pigeons occur in limited numbers.

Notes   The southern border of the refuge lies within the Bandon city limits and is closed to hunting. Nontoxic shot is required. Blinds may be constructed, but excessive disturbance of vegetation for this purpose is prohibited.

Information Western Oregon National Wildlife Complex
26208 Finley Refuge Road
Corvallis, OR 97333
541-757-7236

Hell's Canyon National Recreation Area

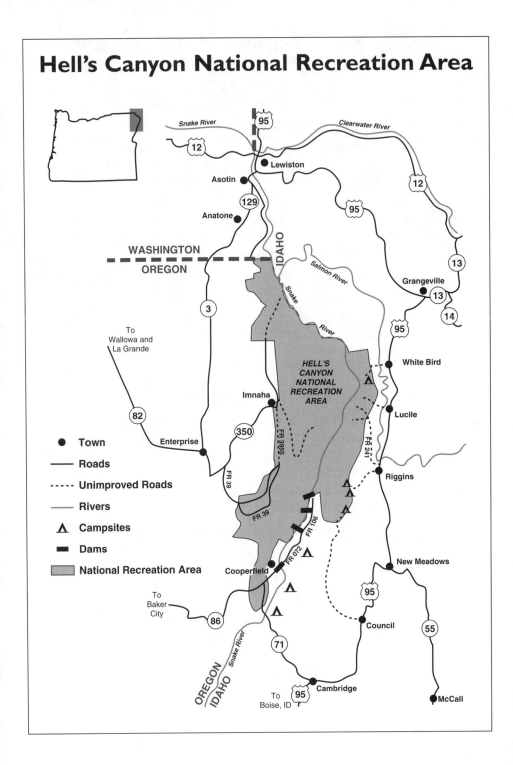

Snake River

95

12

Clearwater River

● Lewiston

Asotin ●

129

12

95

Anatone ●

13

WASHINGTON

OREGON

Salmon River

Grangeville ●

13

IDAHO

Snake

14

3

95

To
Wallowa and
La Grande

River

White Bird

HELL'S
CANYON
NATIONAL
RECREATION
AREA

Imnaha ●

Lucile ●

82

350

FR 241

FR 3955

● Enterprise

FR 39

Riggins ●

● **Town**

— **Roads**

---- **Unimproved Roads**

~~~ **Rivers**

Λ **Campsites**

▬ **Dams**

▓ **National Recreation Area**

FR 39

FR 106

FR 072

New Meadows ●

Cooperfield ●

95

To
Baker
City

86

Council ●

55

71

OREGON

IDAHO

Snake River

To
Boise, ID

95

● Cambridge

● McCall

Other Public Hunting Areas

Hell's Canyon National Recreation Area

Size   650,598 acres (Oregon and Idaho)

Species   Chukar partridge, blue grouse, ruffed grouse, ducks, and geese; some opportunity for Rio Grande turkey, ring-necked pheasant, valley quail, mourning dove

Location   In and around Hell's Canyon on the Snake River in northeastern Oregon

Directions Follow I-84 to La Grande or Baker City. From La Grande, follow SR 82 to Joseph and then follow the signs to Imnaha and the Imnaha River (Little Sheep Creek Road). When open, the Hell's Canyon Scenic Loop (Forest Route 39) continues up the Imnaha River and then over to SR 86, which then heads west to Halfway and eventually to Richland and Baker City. From Baker City, follow SR 86 east to Hell's Canyon. Be sure to obtain a copy of the Hell's Canyon NRA map (see address below).

Description The Hell's Canyon National Recreation Area encompasses not only the massive canyon itself (the deepest such gorge in North America) but also the Imnaha River Canyon and many secondary drainages. Both the Snake River (Hell's Canyon) and the Imnaha River offer strong populations of chukar, making this the top game bird in the region. However, blue grouse are equally abundant on timbered ridges throughout the area. In some places, the two game birds occupy the same slopes, with chukar living closer to the water along the grassy, rocky canyon breaks, and blue grouse thriving high up in the timber and in the forested draws that reach down the mountains. Hunting this rugged country demands that both wingshooter and dog be in top physical condition.

Notes   Check with Hell's Canyon NRA to purchase a map of the area and also to ask about road closures.

Information Hell's Canyon National Recreation Area
88401 Highway 82
Enterprise, OR 97828
541-426-5546

Wanaket Wildlife Mitigation Area

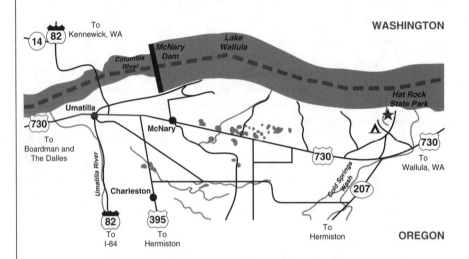

●	**Town**	▩	**Lakes/Water Bodies**
★	**State Park**	Λ	**Campsites**
—	**Roads**	▬ ▬	**State Line**
∿	**Rivers/Ditches**		

Wanaket Wildlife Mitigation Area

Size   2,800 acres

Species   Ring-necked pheasant, valley quail, ducks, Canada geese

Location   In the Columbia Basin, between the communities of McNary and Hat Rock, north of Hermiston

Directions   From the west, follow I-84 to the Irrigon/US 730 exit (Exit 168) and continue east through Irrigon and Umatilla. Continue eastward past Umatilla and past McNary Dam. The area lies adjacent to the highway past McNary and before Hat Rock. From the east, exit I-84 at Stanfield (Exit 188) or at I-82 (Exit 179). Follow either route to its respective junction with US 730 and turn east.

Description   This area was created under the Northwest Power Planning Council's Wildlife Program to replace habitat lost due to hydropower development in the Columbia Basin. Managed by the Confederated Tribes of the Umatilla Indian Reservation, Wanaket offers upland habitats characterized by brushy grasslands along with wetlands in the form of small pothole ponds surrounded in many cases by cattail stands. The area is home to good numbers of pheasant and quail; ducks are most numerous from late November through December after the arrival of northern migrants.

Notes   Nontoxic shot is required for all hunting. Hunting is limited to particular days, and hunts are allocated by daily drawing. Maps are available from the tribal office.

Information   Confederated Tribes of the Umatilla Indian Reservation
Wildlife Program
P.O. Box 638
Pendleton, OR 97801
541-278-5268

Steens Mountain
National Recreation Lands

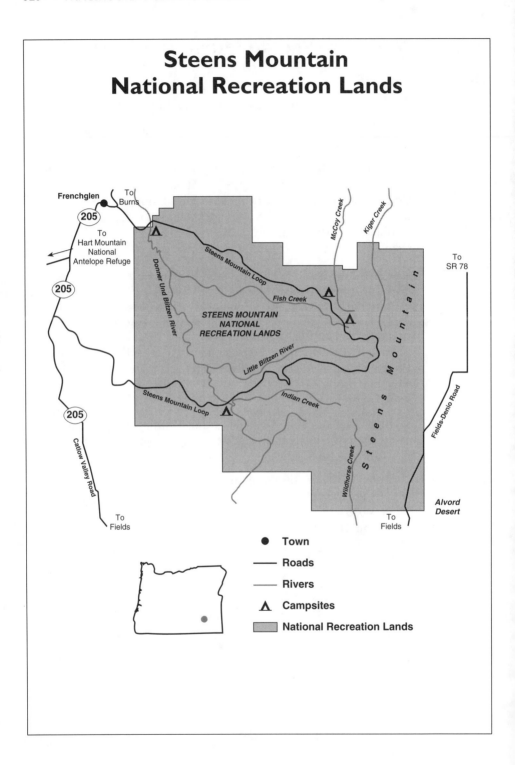

Steens Mountain National Recreation Lands

Size   193,856 acres

Species   Chukar partridge, sage grouse, valley quail, mourning dove, Hungarian partridge, ring-necked pheasant, ducks, Canada geese, snow geese (see Notes, below)

Location   Southeastern Oregon in the Steens Mountains near Frenchglen (Harney County)

Directions   From Burns, follow State Route 205 to Frenchglen, then follow Steens Mountain Loop Road to reach the summit. To reach the east side of the Steens Mountains, follow SR 78 southeast from Burns, eventually crossing over the northern extent of the range. Soon thereafter, watch for a right turn on Fields-Denio Road, which runs north-south along the base of the mountains all the way to the tiny town of Fields. At Fields, SR 205 (Catlow Valley Road), arriving from the west side of the mountains, intersects Fields-Denio Road.

Description This 193,856-acre area includes the highest points of the remarkable Steens Mountain Range, including 9,773-foot Steens Mountain itself. A huge fault-block escarpment, the Steens Mountains rise unceremoniously from the west, gaining a rather gradual 5,000 feet before peaking at over 9,000 feet and then falling suddenly and precipitously away to the east. The east face of the Steens forms a stunning and brutally steep, rugged expanse of exposed rock that causes a rain shadow in its wake on the desert floor some 5,000 feet below. The Donner and Blitzen River's headwaters form here and bisects the area with its northwesterly course, providing a canyon home for chukar partridge. Chukars also inhabit the east face of the Steens, where seeps, springs, and stream-cut gorges provide ideal habitat. Sage hens can be found throughout the range, even atop the highest ridges. Typically, the Steens Mountain Unit is granted 150 or so sage grouse tags and is one of the more productive hunt units.

Notes   Within the boundaries of the Steens Mountain NRL, chukar and sage grouse are the primary resident game bird. Hunting for most other species occurs along the margins of the area, such as on the Malheur National Wildlife Refuge, which borders the northwest corner of the area and on the wetlands below the east face of the Steens Mountains (e.g., Mann Lake). A good map of the Steens Mountain NRL is available from the area headquarters or from many of the other BLM offices in the state.

Warner Wetlands

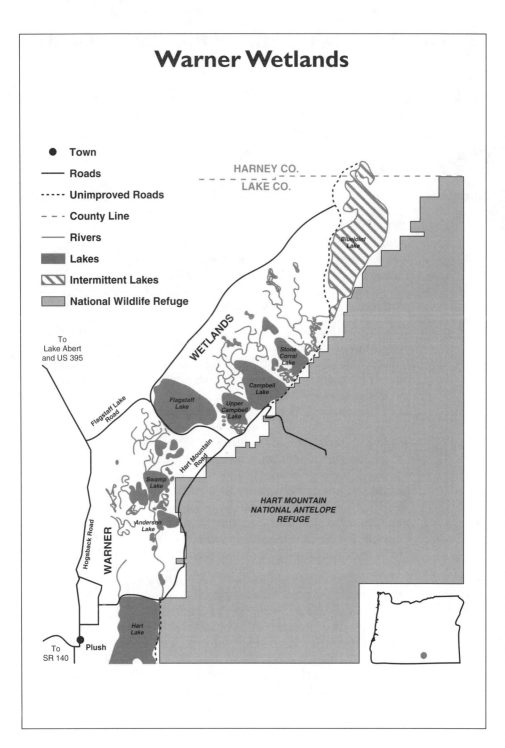

Town

Roads

Unimproved Roads

County Line

Rivers

Lakes

Intermittent Lakes

National Wildlife Refuge

HARNEY CO.
LAKE CO.

Bluejoint Lake

To
Lake Abert
and US 395

WETLANDS

Stone Corral Lake

Campbell Lake

Flagstaff Lake Road

Flagstaff Lake

Upper Campbell Lake

Hart Mountain Road

Swamp Lake

HART MOUNTAIN
NATIONAL ANTELOPE
REFUGE

Hogsback Road

WARNER

Anderson Lake

Hart Lake

To
SR 140

Plush

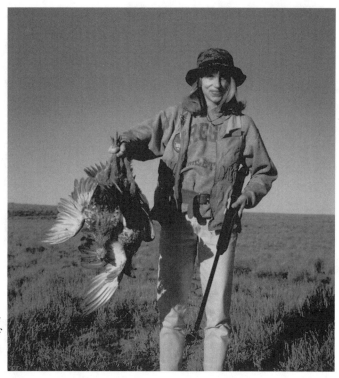

DeAnn Montgomery with a brace of sage grouse from southeastern Oregon.

Information Steens Mountain National Recreation Lands
Managed by Bureau of Land Management, Burns District Office
HC 74-12533 US 20 West
Hines, OR 97738
541-573-4400

Warner Wetlands (BLM)

Size   55,350 acres

Species   Ducks, Canada geese, white-fronted geese, common snipe

Location   Warner Valley of southeastern Oregon

Directions   Six miles north of Lakeview, turn east off US 395 onto SR 140, which
goes over Warner Summit. Turn left (north) on the Plush Cut-off Road
and continue north through the tiny town of Plush and up into the
Warner Wetlands. Several local roads provide access to the area,

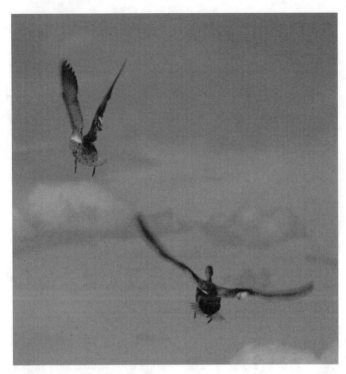

Gadwall in flight.

including Flagstaff Lake Road and the Hart Mountain Road, which leads about 10 miles up to a parking area on the northeast shore.

Description Warner Wetlands is comprised of a series of broad and shallow, desert sump lakes whose status as lakes depends upon recent climatic conditions. The area has no outside drainage. During dry years, when inflow is minimal and when evaporation takes a heavy toll on the water table, the wetlands offer limited waterfowl habitat. But during wet years, Warner Wetlands offers substantial opportunity for duck and goose hunters in an area that attracts relatively few people. During dry years, hunting opportunities are largely confined to the south third of the wetlands, which are dominated by shallow marshes. During wet years, when channels and sloughs of the north end of the wetlands run full, this area offers excellent prospects to scull-boat hunters. Marsh and pond areas are ideally suited to decoying. Mallards, gadwall, wigeon, shoveler, and pintail abound; redheads and teal are quite common as well. Canada geese are most common on the south third of the area and small flocks of white-fronted geese migrate through early in the season.

Notes Early season hunting is usually best because severe winter weather often hits the area by late November. Before making the long drive to Warner Wetlands, check with ODFW in Lakeview for current water and weather conditions. Few amenities are available, so bring your own water, shelter, firewood, etc.

Information Bureau of Land Management
Lakeview Resource Area
1000 South 9th Street
P.O. Box 151
Lakeview, OR 97630

Oregon Department of Fish and Wildlife, Lakeview
541-947-2950

Crooked River National Grassland

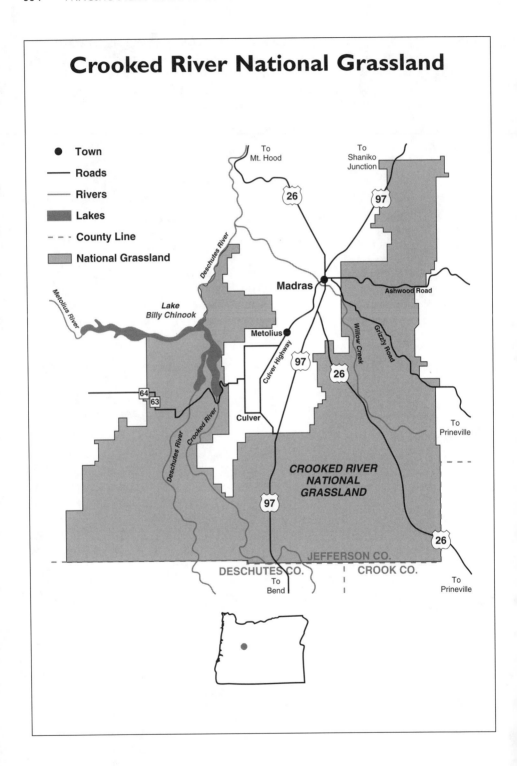

- ● Town
- — Roads
- ~~ Rivers
- ▮ Lakes
- - - - County Line
- ▮ National Grassland

To Mt. Hood

To Shaniko Junction

26

97

Deschutes River

Metolius River

Madras

Ashwood Road

Lake Billy Chinook

Metolius

Willow Creek

Grizzly Road

Culver Highway

97

26

64

63

Culver

Crooked River

Deschutes River

To Prineville

CROOKED RIVER NATIONAL GRASSLAND

97

JEFFERSON CO.

DESCHUTES CO.

CROOK CO.

26

To Bend

To Prineville

Crooked River National Grassland

Size   111,379 acres

Species   Valley quail, ring-necked pheasant, chukar partridge, Hungarian partridge, mourning dove, ducks, and geese

Location   Central Oregon in Jefferson and Crook Counties

Directions Follow any highway leading to central Oregon (e.g., US 26 from Portland or SR 22 from Salem), then follow US 97 to Madras. The grasslands encompass several areas, the most popular of which is the large tract east of US 97 and southeast of Madras.

Description The Crooked River National Grasslands encompasses rolling hills and flat brushlands with an abundance of cover for valley quail. Pheasants and Huns exist in small numbers where appropriate habitat is found. Chukar partridge inhabit the breaks of the Crooked and Deschutes Rivers (one tract of the grasslands borders the Deschutes and Crooked River Arms of Lake Billy Chinook). Chukar populations are highly variable in this part of Oregon, with birds being rather abundant during years of mild winters and ideal spring nesting conditions but scarce and scattered otherwise. Valley quail comprise the single most important species, and the surest way to locate coveys is to first find water sources and then use a good dog. Dove hunters who scout ahead of time may find good shooting, and some limited waterfowling opportunities exist on area reservoirs and canals.

Notes   Check with the headquarters (address below) for information about maps and access.

Information Crooked River National Grassland
813 Southwest Hwy 97
Madras, OR 97741
541-475-9272

Oregon Department of Fish and Wildlife
2042 Southeast Paulina Hwy
Prineville, OR 97754
541-447-5111

Willamette River greenheads.

Willamette River Greenway

Size   Stretches along various reaches of the Willamette River from Eugene to Portland

Species   Ducks, Canada geese, mourning dove

Location   Willamette River corridor in western Oregon's Willamette Valley

Description   The Willamette River Greenway, which exists in some 40 different parcels of land along the river, offers excellent access to this life-blood waterway. Most access is by boat (see listing of launches below). Waterfowl hunters generally find good to excellent prospects for mallard, pintail, wigeon, wood ducks, green-winged teal, ring-necked ducks, and other species. The river also offers good hunting during the September Canada Goose Hunt. Use land and water spreads along gravel bars and islands where the geese often roost during the day. Some advance scouting pays dividends for water-fowlers who decipher the daily movements of the geese. Mourning doves can be quite abundant some years and regularly use the river's gravel bars during morning and evening.

Notes   The Oregon State Parks and Recreation Department offers a brochure titled "Willamette River Recreation Guide," which includes good maps of Greenway lands. Send $1 to Oregon Parks and Recreation requesting a copy (address below). Much of the access to the Willamette River Greenway parcels is by boat only. The Oregon State Marine Board publishes a map detailing the locations of all the public and public access boat ramps on the river. The following ramps are of significance to waterfowlers (starting with the ramps below Eugene and going downriver, match number to map):

Willamette River Greenway

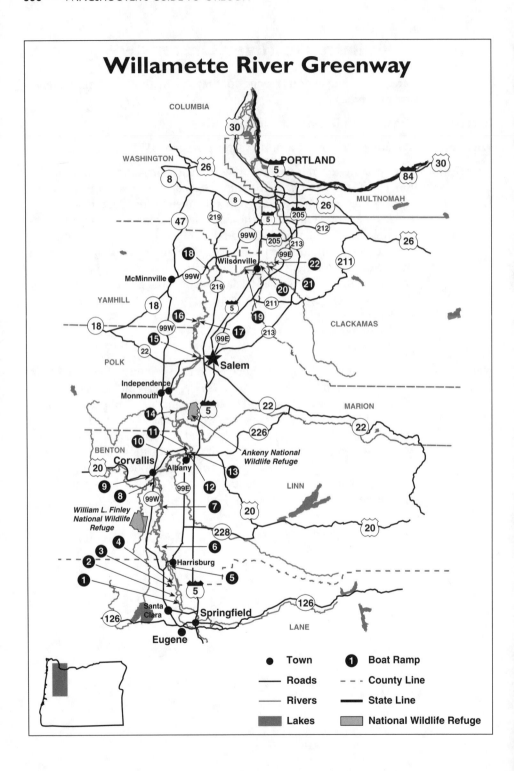

COLUMBIA

WASHINGTON

PORTLAND

MULTNOMAH

McMinnville

YAMHILL

Wilsonville

CLACKAMAS

Salem

Independence
Monmouth

POLK

MARION

Ankeny National
Wildlife Refuge

BENTON

Corvallis

Albany

LINN

William L. Finley
National Wildlife
Refuge

Harrisburg

Santa
Clara

Springfield

LANE

Eugene

● Town   ❶ Boat Ramp
— Roads   - - - County Line
— Rivers   — State Line
▓ Lakes   ▒ National Wildlife Refuge

Willamette River Greenway Boat Launches

No.	Launch Name/Location	Ramp Type	Facilities
1.	Whiteley Ramp, north of Santa Clara, west bank	Improved	Parking
2.	Hileman Landing, north of Santa Clara, west bank	Unimproved	Parking
3.	Marshall Island, between Santa Clara and Harrisburg, west bank	Improved	Parking, restrooms
4.	Christensen's, between Santa Clara and Harrisburg, east bank	Unimproved	Parking
5.	Harrisburg, at the town of Harrisburg, east bank	Improved	Parking, restrooms
6.	McCartney Park, north of Harrisburg, east bank	Improved	Parking, restrooms
7.	Peoria Park, between Harrisburg and Corvallis, east bank	Improved	Parking, camping, restrooms
8.	Willamette Park, Corvallis, west bank	Improved	Parking, restrooms
9.	Corvallis Ramp, Corvallis, west bank	Unimproved	Parking, restrooms
10.	Hyak Park, west of Albany, west bank	Improved	Parking, restrooms
11.	Takena Landing, Albany, west (north) bank	Improved	Parking
12.	Montieth Dock, Albany, east (south) bank	No ramp (dock)	Parking, restrooms
13.	Bowman Park, east of Albany, east bank	Improved	Parking, restrooms
14.	Buena Vista Park, southeast of Independence, west bank	Improved	Parking, restrooms
15.	Wallace Marine Park, Salem, west bank	Improved	Parking, restrooms, moorage
16.	Wheatland Ferry, north of Salem, west bank	Improved	Parking,
17.	Willamette Mission State Park, north of Salem, east bank	Improved	Parking, restrooms, moorage
18.	San Salvador, south of Wilsonville, east bank	Improved	Parking, restrooms
19.	Roger's Landing, west of Wilsonville, north bank	Improved	Parking, restrooms

20. Boone's Ferry Landing, near Wilsonville, south bank	Improved	Moorage, restrooms, fuel
21. Molalla River State Park, west of Wilsonville, south bank	Improved	Parking, restrooms
22. Hebb Park, west of Wilsonville, north bank	Improved	Parking, restrooms, moorage

Information Oregon Department of Parks and Recreation
1115 Commercial Street Northeast
Salem, OR 97310

Oregon State Marine Board
P.O. Box 14145
Salem, OR 97309-5065

Oregon's Estuaries

Size   Various

Species   Waterfowl, common snipe, band-tailed pigeon, ruffed grouse

Location   Along the Oregon Coast, essentially from Gold Beach to Astoria

Directions Among the most significant estuaries are: Young's Bay (Astoria), lower Columbia River (see listing for Lewis and Clark National Wildlife Refuge), Tillamook Bay, Netarts Bay, Nestucca Bay, Salmon River, Siletz Bay (Lincoln City), Yaquina Bay (Newport/Toledo), Alsea Bay (Waldport), Siuslaw River (Florence), Umpqua River (Reedsport), Coos Bay, and Bandon Marsh (see under *National Wildlife Refuges*).

Description Oregon's estuaries offer diverse, interesting, and challenging hunting for a variety of ducks and also some of the West's premier wingshooting for common snipe, which migrate along the coast in large numbers. Waterfowling can take the form of decoying, jump shooting, sculling, and even pass shooting. The saltwater environment, complete with its changing tides, dictates hunting strategies that often differ from those employed on freshwater environs. See accompanying article about estuary duck hunting. Snipe hunters and duck hunters alike should exercise extreme care in negotiating the estuaries by foot, as narrow tidal creeks are often surprisingly deep, and estuary mud can range in consistency from firm to quick-mud. Band-tailed pigeons migrate along the coast in many places and on some of the estuaries can provide fair shooting for those with good timing. Look for birds in old growth Sitka spruce and Douglas fir stands and in dead snags along the margins of the estuaries. Ruffed grouse inhabit the wooded fringes of some of the estuaries; look for them along steep drainage's above the marsh fringes.

Notes   Except where otherwise regulated (e.g., refuges, wildlife areas), hunters can use lead shot to hunt snipe on the coastal estuaries. This is because snipe are regulated as migratory game birds (like mourning doves) rather than as migratory waterfowl. However, one may not hunt ducks with lead shot in possession, so those who wish to hunt both must either use steel shot for both or divide the hunt in two, trading steel for lead at the vehicle. Other shorebirds—all of them protected—occur in abundance on Oregon's estuaries. Hunters should learn the habit and appearance differences between snipe and similar-looking birds, such as dowitchers (see entry on common snipe). Band-tailed pigeon seasons are short and restrictive—be sure to check current synopsis.

Information Contact ODFW office nearest your destination.

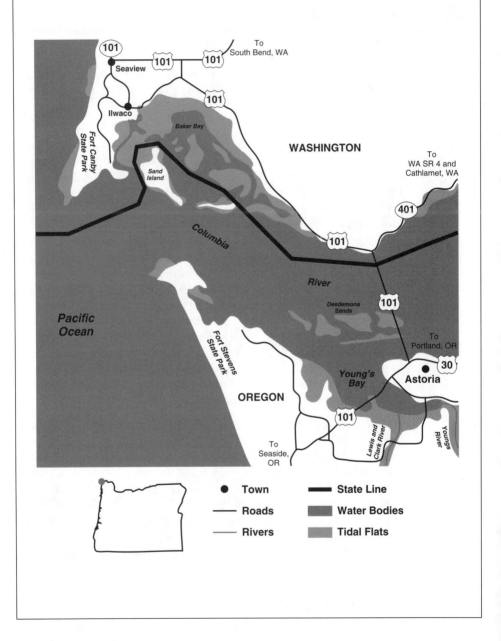

Oregon's Estuaries:
Young's Bay and Lower Columbia River

Oregon's Estuaries:
Tillamook Bay and Netarts Bay

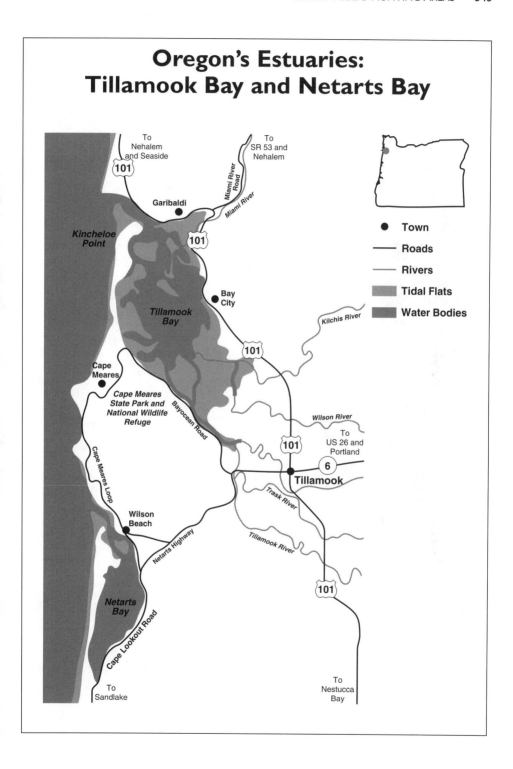

To
Nehalem
and Seaside

To
SR 53 and
Nehalem

101

Miami River Road

Miami River

Garibaldi

101

Kincheloe
Point

Bay
City

Tillamook
Bay

Kilchis River

101

Cape
Meares

Cape Meares
State Park and
National Wildlife
Refuge

Bayocean Road

Wilson River

To
US 26 and
Portland

101

Cape Meares Loop

6

Tillamook

Trask River

Wilson
Beach

Netarts Highway

Tillamook River

Netarts
Bay

Cape Lookout Road

101

To
Sandlake

To
Nestucca
Bay

● Town
— Roads
— Rivers
  Tidal Flats
  Water Bodies

Oregon's Estuaries: Nestucca Bay

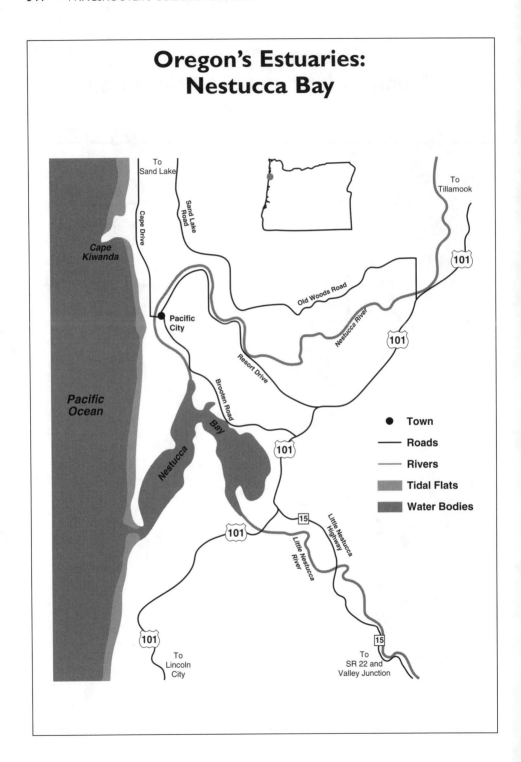

Oregon's Estuaries:
Salmon River and Siletz Bay

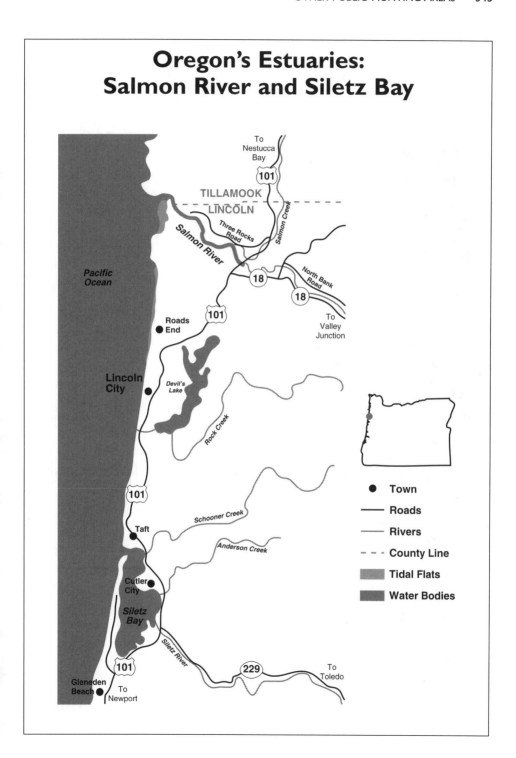

Oregon's Estuaries:
Yaquina and Alsea Bays

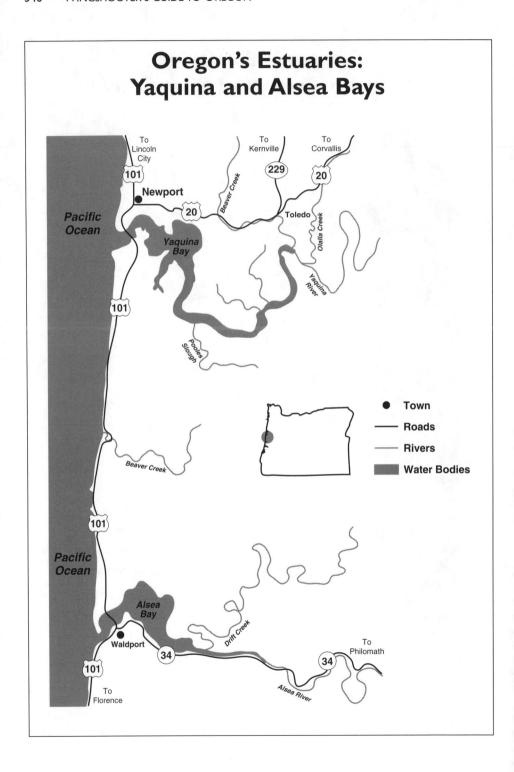

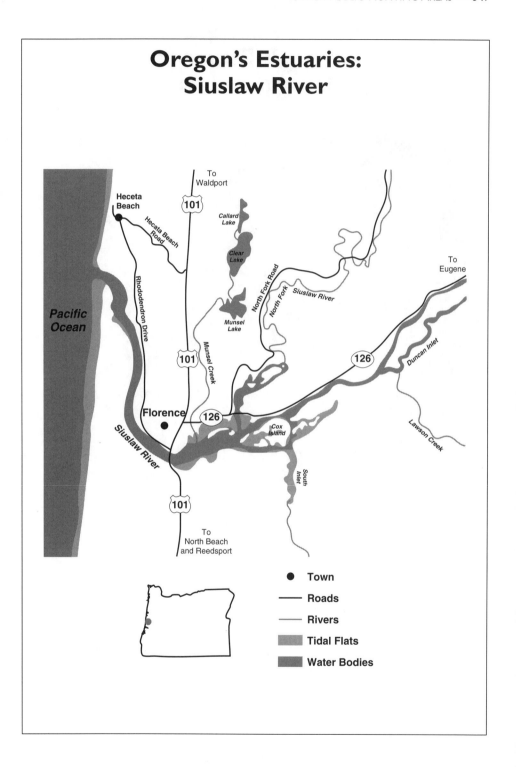

Oregon's Estuaries: Siuslaw River

To Waldport

Heceta Beach

101

Callard Lake

Clear Lake

Heceta Beach Road

Pacific Ocean

Rhododendron Drive

North Fork Road

North Fork

Siuslaw River

To Eugene

Munsel Lake

101

Munsel Creek

126

Duncan Inlet

Florence

126

Cox Island

Lawson Creek

Siuslaw River

South Inlet

101

To North Beach and Reedsport

● Town

—— Roads

— Rivers

Tidal Flats

Water Bodies

Oregon's Estuaries: Umpqua River

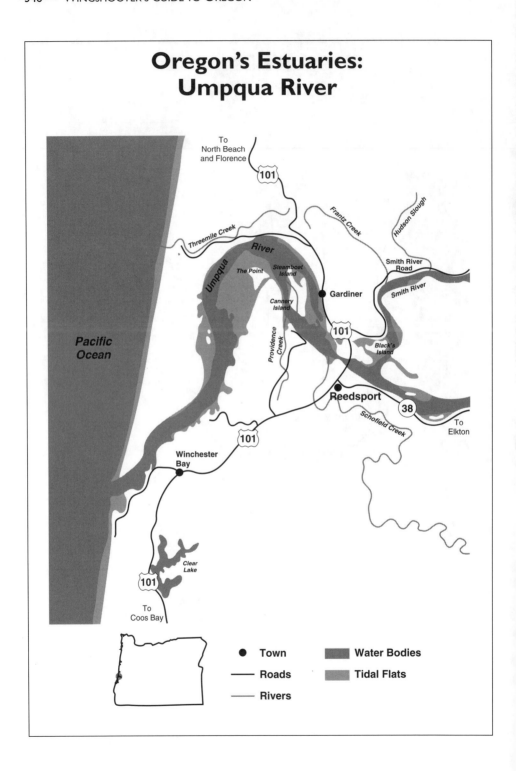

To
North Beach
and Florence

101

Frantz Creek

Hudson Slough

Threemile Creek

Umpqua River

Smith River
Road

The Point

Steamboat
Island

Gardiner

Smith River

Cannery
Island

101

Pacific
Ocean

Providence
Creek

Black's
Island

Reedsport

38

To
Elkton

Schofield Creek

101

Winchester
Bay

To
Coos Bay

Clear
Lake

101

● Town   Water Bodies

— Roads   Tidal Flats

Rivers

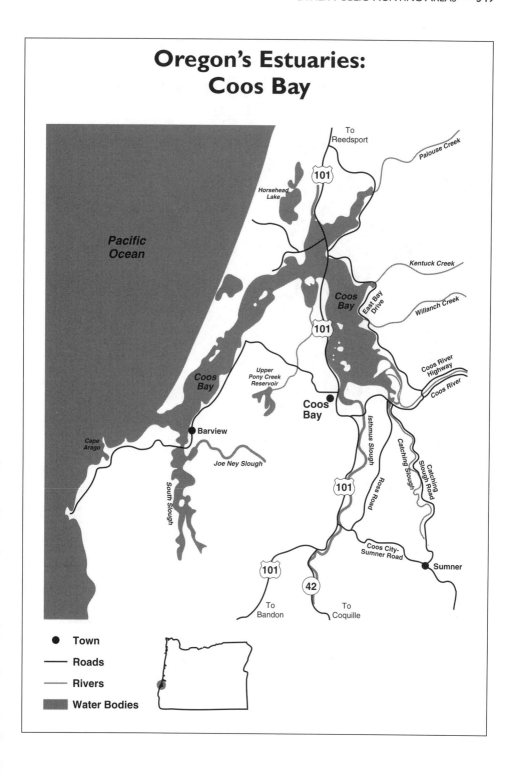

Oregon's Estuaries: Coos Bay

To Reedsport

Palouse Creek

101

Horsehead Lake

Pacific Ocean

Kentuck Creek

Coos Bay

East Bay Drive

Willanch Creek

101

Coos River Highway

Coos River

Upper Pony Creek Reservoir

Coos Bay

Coos Bay

Barview

Cape Arago

Joe Ney Slough

Isthmus Slough

Catching Slough

Catching Slough Road

South Slough

Ross Road

101

Coos City-Sumner Road

Sumner

101

42

To Bandon

To Coquille

● Town

— Roads

— Rivers

▨ Water Bodies

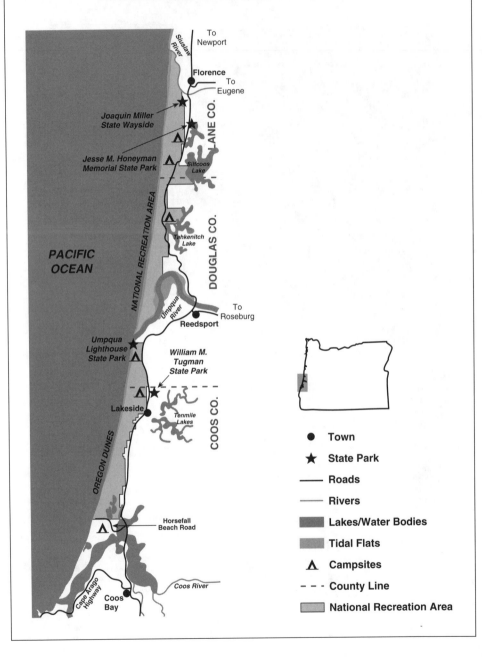

Oregon Sand Dunes National Recreation Area

Oregon Dunes National Recreation Area

Size   31,000 acres

Species   Ducks, Canada geese, common snipe, black brant, band-tailed pigeon

Location   On the Oregon coast between Florence and Coos Bay (on the west side of US 101)

Directions From the north, follow US 101 or SR 126 to Florence. The Oregon Dunes NRA begins on the south side of the Siuslaw River at Florence with access sites available in some places right along the highway and also at various state parks. From Roseburg, follow SR 38 down the Umpqua River to Reedsport. From the south, follow SR 42 up from Winston to Coos Bay. At Coos Bay, cross the US 101 bridge over the bay heading north. The first access to the dunes is from the Horsefall Beach area (depart US 101 at a signed left turn just past the bay bridge. Between Coos Bay and Florence, look for additional access points at state parks. Before venturing out, obtain a copy of the Oregon Dunes NRA map from the headquarters in Reedsport (see address below).

Description Oregon Dunes National Recreation Area comprises a 45-mile-long strip of beach featuring extensive large sand dunes, beach grass, sedge and reed marshlands, and myriad pothole lakes and ponds. These lakes and ponds provide an opportunity for waterfowl hunting, especially during windy, wet weather. A map and a willingness to walk can lead duck hunters to many underhunted areas where decoying and jump shooting bring success. A good retrieving dog should be considered mandatory. In a few places, sufficient habitat exists to allow for fair to good snipe hunting. Walk the margins of ponds and lakes; also hunt above the tide line on the edges of the estuaries and on the islands in the estuaries, especially where sedges and bulrushes grow.

Notes   All Oregon hunting regulations apply while hunting on the Oregon Dunes NRA. Be careful to avoid private lands and remember that hunting is not allowed within the boundaries of the state parks in the area. Contact the Oregon Dunes NRA headquarters to obtain maps.

Information Oregon Dunes National Recreation Area
855 Highway 101
Reedsport, OR 97467
541-271-3611

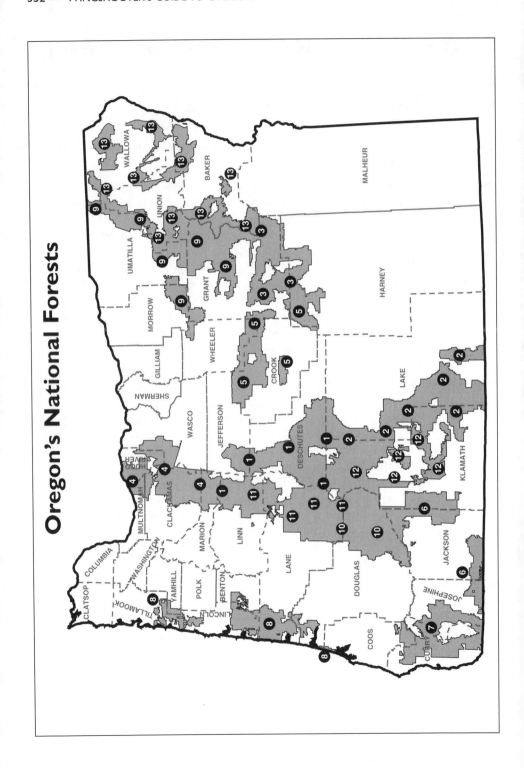

Oregon's National Forests

National Forests in Oregon

Oregon includes some 15.6 million acres of national forest lands administered by the USDA Forest Service. These forest service lands extend across all but the southeastern portion of Oregon and envelop virtually all of the state's major mountain ranges, offering excellent public access to countless tracts of prime game bird habitat. National forest lands are especially important to hunters who pursue grouse, mountain quail, and wild turkey. Each of the national forests in Oregon (there are 13 of them) has its own headquarters from which wingshooters can purchase good maps. In addition to the national forest maps themselves, which provide good overviews of the area, hunters should purchase the ranger district maps. These maps are topographical and of a larger scale than the forest maps, detailing individual ranger districts within the national forests. They are a great aid not only in determining access routes but also in locating likely habitat.

1. **Deschutes National Forest**
   1645 US 20 East
   Bend, OR 97701
   541-388-2715

2. **Fremont National Forest**
   524 North G Street
   Lakeview, OR 97630
   541-947-2151

3. **Malheur National Forest**
   139 Northeast Dayton Street
   John Day, OR 97845
   541-575-3000

4. **Mt. Hood National Forest**
   16400 Champion Way
   Sandy, OR 97055
   503-668-1700

5. **Ochoco National Forest**
   3160 Northeast Third Street
   Prineville, OR 97754
   541-416-6500

6. **Rogue River National Forest**
   333 West 8th Street / P.O. Box 520
   Medford, OR 97501
   541-858-2200

7. **Siskiyou National Forest**
   P.O. Box 440
   Grants Pass, OR 97526

8. **Siuslaw National Forest**
   4077 Southwest Research Way
   Corvallis, OR 97339
   541-750-7000

9. **Umatilla National Forest**
   2517 Southwest Hailey Avenue
   Pendleton, OR 97801
   541-278-3716

10. **Umpqua National Forest**
    P.O. Box 1008
    2900 Northwest Stewart Parkway
    Roseburg, OR 97470
    541-672-6601

11. **Willamette National Forest**
    Federal Building
    211 East 7th Avenue
    Eugene, OR 97401
    541-465-6521

12. **Winema National Forest**
    2819 Dahlia Street
    Klamath Falls, OR 97601

13. **Wallowa-Whitman National Forest**
    P.O. Box 907
    Baker City, OR 97814

Bureau of Land Management (BLM)

The Bureau of Land Management (U.S. Department of Interior) manages 15.7 million acres in Oregon, the bulk of which is found in the arid country of southeastern Oregon. Malheur, Harney, and Lake Counties all abound in BLM-administered lands, but the BLM also manages the 2.2 million acres of timber-rich Oregon and California Railroad lands in western Oregon. For bird hunting enthusiasts, BLM holdings in southeastern Oregon are especially significant and important because many thousands of acres of prime chukar partridge habitat is available on pubic grounds, making Oregon one of the best states for those interested in pursuing this remarkable game bird. The BLM offers some detailed maps that show land ownership. These can be a great help to chukar hunters trying to determine where public lands end and private lands begin. These maps are available for purchase through the district offices, whose addresses and phone numbers are listed below.

BLM Oregon State Office
1515 Southwest 5th Avenue
P.O. Box 2965
Portland, OR 97208
503-952-6002

BLM Coos Bay District
1300 Airport Lane
North Bend, OR 97459-2000
541-756-0100

BLM Eugene District
2890 Chad Drive / P.O. Box 10226
Eugene, OR 97440
541-683-6600

BLM Lakeview District
1000 Ninth Street
Lakeview, OR 97630
541-947-2177

BLM Medford District
3040 Biddle Road
Medford, OR 97504
541-770-2200

BLM Prineville District
3050 Northeast 3rd Street
P.O. Box 550
Prineville, OR 97754
541-416-6700

BLM Roseburg District
777 Northwest Garden Valley Boulevard
Roseburg, OR 97470
541-440-4930

BLM Salem District
1717 Fabry Road Southeast
Salem, OR 97306
503-375-5646

BLM Burns District
HC-74, 12533 Hwy 20 West
Hines, OR 97738
541-573-4400

BLM Spokane District
1103 North Fancher
Spokane, WA 99202-1275
(509) 536-1275

BLM Vale District
100 Oregon Street
Vale, OR 97918
541-473-3144

Appendix I
Traveling with Dog and Gun

My first experience flying with my hunting dog proved an educational experience for both of us. I discovered in short order that the airline had precious little information available in an organized format yet had ample rules and regulations that seemed to change with each new person to whom I spoke. The bottom line, as it turned out, was as follows:

1. The dog must have a health certificate prepared by a veterinarian (this took all of 5 minutes and cost around $25). This must include proof of rabies vaccination.
2. You must request passage for your dog and then await approval of your request from the airline. Do this well ahead of your flight date and then get a confirmation number.
3. The dog must be checked as baggage and is charged an extra fee of around $50 each direction.
4. The dog must have a travel kennel, and airlines are quite specific about kennel requirements as follows:
   - The kennel must be large enough so that the dog can stand up with head room, turn around, and lie down in a comfortable position.
   - The kennel must include empty water and food containers attached in such a way that they can be filled from the outside.
   - The kennel must include at least one label with your name, address, phone number, destination, and dog's call name.
   - A second certificate, issued by the airline agent, must state the last time the dog was fed and watered (must be within four hours of departure) and must include instructions for feeding in the event of a delay or change in the schedule.
   - The kennel should be labeled with stickers reading "Live Animal" and "This Side Up."
   - Place absorbent material in the bottom of the kennel.
5. Tranquilizers for dogs are available, but these are not recommended because of potential dangerous problems resulting from high altitude.
6. Federal regulations exist regarding safe temperatures for transport of dogs:
   - Animals will not be accepted if the temperature is below 10°F at any point in transit.
   - If the temperature at your destination is below 45°F, a certificate of acclimation stating that your dog is used to low temperatures will be necessary. This is available from your vet.
   - Temperatures above 85°F can be dangerous for animals in transit. Many airlines will not accept dogs if the temperature at any transit point is more than 85°.

Shannon Alexander with his German wirehaired pointer, Bailey.

Oregon's autumn temperatures vary widely. September can be brutally hot statewide or pleasantly cool. Often, one part of the state is cool while another is hot. October generally brings mild temperatures throughout the state. By late November, many parts of eastern and central Oregon are bitter cold, while western Oregon is cool and wet. Most flights into Oregon arrive at Portland International Airport (PDX). At PDX you can expect hot weather at least through mid-September most years. Conversely, Portland rarely experiences bitter cold or snow. Eugene (Eugene Airport) offers a similar, though wetter, fall and winter climate.

For airline travel, shotguns must be packed in a locked gun case separate from ammunition, which itself must remain in a case designated as such in the original manufacturer's containers. Ammunition must be checked through as well. In addition, you will be required to sign a waiver stating that the gun is unloaded at the time of check-in.

Appendix II
Hunter Conditioning
and Equipment

Some of Oregon's myriad wingshooting opportunities require serious physical effort on the part of the hunter. No doubt the most strenuous on a daily basis, chukar hunting often requires substantial climbs up steep desert canyons and then miles of hiking once altitude is gained. Most if not all of the legwork occurs on rocky, uneven ground that chews up boots, feet, ankles, and knees. An early morning chukar hunt might begin in 20-degree weather and end in 85-degree heat; or you might get a dose of snow, rain, or sleet accompanied by a bitter cold desert wind.

Likewise, hunters who pursue blue grouse and mountain quail typically walk substantial distances at moderate to high elevations in Oregon's major mountain ranges. Seasons for both birds begin on September 1, when 90-degree afternoons are common. Hunting for mountain quail often resembles chukar hunting: both birds are partial to steep, rocky slopes. In the quail's case, these mountain slopes are covered in brush and young timber. The pursuit of mountain quail can sometimes leave hunters more sweaty, scraped, and exhausted than chukar hunting.

Hunting these upland game birds—Hungarian partridge, pheasant, and valley quail included—becomes a much more enjoyable proposition for hunters who take time to get in good physical shape prior to the season. Walking and running comprise the two most significant fitness activities that upland hunters can undertake several months prior to the season. As your fitness program progresses, begin carrying a weighted pack and start hiking and jogging on inclines. The addition of a weight-training program can only further benefit your conditioning in the field during the upcoming season. If you are new to such activity, consult both a physician and a trainer.

My personal preparations include year-around attention to physical fitness with increased cardiovascular work during spring and summer. Each summer I plan several major hikes and backpacking excursions, including climbing various peaks. The combination of a heavy pack, long hike, and high elevation pays dividends when the bird season begins. My weight training program continues unabated throughout the year.

Clothing

Your choice of clothing is dictated mostly by the environment in which you hunt and the kind of weather you expect. When hunting chukars, consider wearing a pair of gaiters or pants that cuff down around the uppers of your boots, thus preventing your socks from collecting cheatgrass seeds. Brush pants and/or gators also help a great deal in grouse and quail hunting, where all sorts of burrs and seeds compete for the right to stick to your clothing.

Hunting boots must be broken in prior to the season. I prefer high-topped models with good ankle support. Waterproof boots are a good idea for Oregon upland hunters, especially if ruffed grouse and valley quail are your quarry. Oregon's chukar season extends into January, as does the grouse and mountain quail season in western Oregon. By that time, snow blankets the mountains and dusts many chukar ranges. Waterproof boots and warm socks keep your feet dry and comfortable.

Layer your clothing so you can remove outer clothing as the day warms or as you heat up from exertion. A 25-degree eastern Oregon morning seems a lot less chilly once you climb about halfway up a desert rim in pursuit of chukars. Other important items include shooting glasses, a brimmed hat, shell vest with game pouch, and one or two extra pairs of socks if you intend to cover a lot of ground.

Equipment

Always carry more water than you think you will need. My dog comes first when it comes to my water supply. I always note the locations of water sources in the different places I hunt, thus knowing where and when I can lead my dog to a drink. I also carry high-energy snacks for both the dogs and me. Permanent items in my hunting pack include matches in a waterproof container, compass, knife, first-aid supplies for dog and man, sunscreen, extra dog whistle, and a tissue paper. In unfamiliar areas, I carry a topo map.

Vehicle Equipment

The equipment you carry in the vehicle depends on where you hunt and for how long. Some things should be considered essential, such as emergency auto supplies (flares, shovel, jumper cables, tow chain, tire chains, jack and tire iron, gloves, duct tape, etc.). If you venture to the far reaches of chukar country in southeastern Oregon, carry two extra tires along as well as at least 10 gallons of gas. Be wary of the frozen road trap: Early in the morning you creep up a desert rim following a nice, hard frozen road; you hunt all day and then return to the vehicle late in the afternoon and head back down the road only to bury the truck in axle-deep mud rendered nice and gooey by the daytime sun.

Along with the typical vehicle equipment, I carry an ice chest, plastic ziplock bags, extra food and lots of water, a sleeping bag even if I'm not planning to camp, extra shells and gun cleaning supplies, binoculars, extra cloths, flashlight, shovel and axe, and dog supplies. If you have a cellular phone, lock it in the lock-box or glove compartment.

Appendix III
Gun Dog Conditioning

Gun dog conditioning is critical for both the enjoyment of your hunt and for the well-being of your biggest asset in the field—a good bird dog. Upland dogs probably cover three to five times the miles you walk in a day afield. An unconditioned dog will be spent in a matter of hours, especially when hunting tough country, such as that you'll encounter in pursuit of chukar, blue grouse and mountain quail.

Off-season conditioning will keep your dogs in peak shape and make all-day hunters out of them. Take them running with you as often as possible. Get them out in the field often and let them run. Prior to the season, both hunter and dog will benefit from long runs and hikes.

Because of the terrain I hunt in Oregon, which always seems to include rocky ground to one extent or another, I take great pains to toughen the dog's feet. The easiest way to accomplish this is to cover in gravel the dog's run or kennel. Also get the

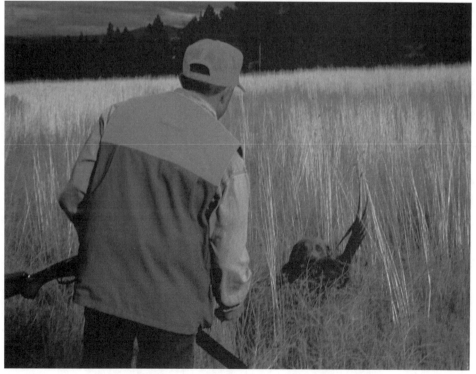

A dog sure helps bring the birds home in this kind of cover.

dog outdoors often, so his or her feet quite simply spend a lot of time pounding on different surfaces. I might add that I train my dogs from a very early age to submit fully to my efforts to examine their pads, not to mention their eyes, ears and mouths.

I usually feed my dog early on the day of the hunt, but only with half a ration, the other half being reserved for an evening feeding. During the hunt, I offer the dog an occasional small snack. Packets of honey make a great energy-boosting snack for dogs.

During the early season, hot weather can lead to heat prostration in dogs. Carry lots of water with you in the field and allow the dog frequent drinks throughout the day; in hot weather, allow the dog to drink his fill during the mid-day break. I also train my dogs to drink from a plastic squirt bottle. They pick this up readily with just a little practice, but teach them at home, not in the field. Also carry some form of collapsible water dish (my Filson hat has on many occasions served perfectly as a water dish).

In *Wingshooter's Guide To North Dakota*, author Chuck Johnson says: "At times dogs can run so hard that they lose their electrolytes. Keeping a bottle of Pedialyte with you can alleviate this problem. Mix some in with the drinking water when you suspect a problem is occurring. This product can be found in most drugstores and is most often used to restore electrolytes in infants."

In your vehicle, carry at least five gallons of water and a complete dog first-aid kit. After the day's hunt, allow the animal to lounge around prior to feeding. Then let him sleep as long as he wants. A well conditioned bird dog will wake up the next morning ready and eager to start the drill all over again.

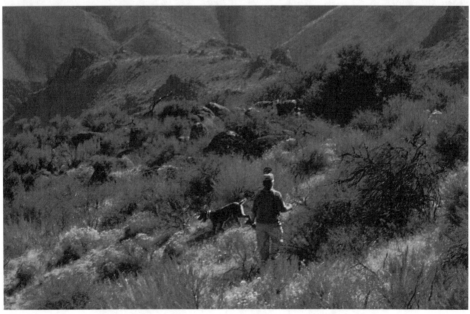

Jeff Funke and his German wirehair hunting chukar.

Appendix IV
Equipment Checklist

CLOTHING

_____ Polypropylene underwear

_____ Inner socks

_____ Wool socks

_____ Long sleeve canvas/chamois shirts

_____ Pants, double-faced

_____ Hunting boots

_____ Billed hat

_____ Bandana

_____ Shooting gloves

_____ Shooting glasses

_____ Ear protectors

_____ Hunting vest/coat

_____ Down vest/coat

_____ Rain gear

_____ Hip boots/waders for waterfowl hunting

_____ Chaps

DOG SUPPLIES

_____ Food, bowls

_____ Beeper collar

_____ Lead

_____ Dog boots, pad toughener

_____ Hemostat

_____ Whistle

_____ Water bottles

_____ _Field Guide to Dog First Aid_

_____ Dog first aid kit

_____ Record of dog vaccinations

_____ Scissors

_____ Toenail clippers

HUNTING SUPPLIES

_____ _Wingshooter's Guide to Oregon_

_____ Shotgun/shells

_____ Cleaning kit

_____ Maps

_____ Knife

_____ Fanny pack

_____ Water bottle

_____ Camera, film

_____ Binoculars

_____ Game shears

_____ Ice chest

_____ Notebook, pen

_____ License

_____ Matches

_____ Axe, shovel

_____ Sunscreen

_____ Twine

_____ Decoys, decoy anchor

_____ Compass

_____ Flashlight

_____ Bird calls

_____ Spare choke tubes

_____ Magnifying glass for maps

Appendix V
Preserving Game Birds for Mounting

by John and Laurel Berger, Berger's Taxidermy

Exploding into the sky with a cackle and brilliant color, the rooster pheasant flushed and I momentarily lost my mind. Regaining my composure, I pulled the trigger and with the crack of my shotgun, the bird fell. That pheasant was a memory well worth preserving, and it now glides across our living room wall in a graceful, open-winged mount.

When deciding if you should mount a game bird, there are a few things to consider. The bird should be mature and have good plumage—we recommend saving birds that have been shot late in the season, ideally after the first of November. However, this doesn't apply to all game birds. Look for pinfeathers on the head and neck, and check the beak, feet, tail, and wings for shot damage. Since most taxidermists use the bird's skull, a bird that has been head-shot may be too damaged or disfigured to be mountable. All of these factors will affect the quality of a finished mount.

If a downed bird is wounded and in good enough condition to mount, do not ring the neck because it will cause skin damage and hemorrhaging. We feel the best method is to grasp the bird from the back just behind wings and then, with your thumb on one side of the rib cage and your fingers on the other, squeeze firmly. This will kill the bird in a humane and timely manner without causing damage to the feathers.

Keep the birds that you plan to have mounted separate from the others in your bag. Carrying them from the field by the feet saves them from damage and allows some cooling. We do not recommend carrying the bird in your game vest because feathers may become damaged, broken, or bloodstained.

After you've chosen the best bird or birds to mount, stop any bleeding by placing tissue or a cotton ball in the wounds. Wipe off any blood that may have run onto the feathers with a dabbing motion. Try not to push the blood down into the feathers. Also, place a cotton ball in the mouth to catch any body fluids that may potentially leak out onto the feathers.

Although some washing may be necessary before mounting, a taxidermist prefers that the bird be blood and dirt free upon delivery. Gently smooth the feathers into place, tuck the head to the chest, and wrap in clean paper towels. Place the bird head first into a plastic bag and store in a cool, protected place until the bird can be frozen.

Another popular method for preserving a bird is using a nylon stocking or cheesecloth. After caring for the bird, place the bird, with its head tucked, chest first into the nylon or cheesecloth. If you choose this method, remember that the only way to get the bird back out is to cut a hole in front of the chest and head and then push it through. If you pull it out by the feet, there will be feather damage.

Once the bird is securely in the nylon or cheesecloth, put the bird in a plastic bag to prevent dehydration or freezer burn. It is best to freeze the bird as soon as possible, and it can be stored in the freezer until you are able to get it to a taxidermist. Make sure that the bag is labeled with the type of bird, date harvested, as well as your name and license number. Taxidermists are required to have this information while the bird is in their possession.

When possible, take two birds to the taxidermist for determining which bird has the best plumage and is in the best shape for mounting.

With just a little care, you can preserve the memory of your hunt through the art of taxidermy. Bird mounts are easy to care for and will provide you with years of enjoyment.

Tip: To clean a mounted bird, use a cottonball dampened with rubbing alcohol. Start from the head using a sweeping motion in the direction of the feathers and work down the bird. Dust is lifted onto the cottonball, and the alcohol will evaporate. Make sure to change the cottonball regularly because they become soiled quickly.

Appendix VI
Field Preparation of Game Birds for the Table

by Chuck Johnson

The two most important tools for preparing birds in the field for the table are game sheers and a knife with a gut hook.

During early season, when temperatures are in the 70° to 90° range, I draw my birds immediately or shortly after I leave the field. You can draw your birds by several methods.

I make a cut with my sheers at the end of the breast, making a small entry hole into the body cavity. I then take my gut hook, insert it into the cavity and pull out the intestines and other body parts.

The other method I use is to take my sheers and cut up the center of the bird's back, splitting the bird in two. Then you can use your gut hook and knife to clean out the intestines and other body parts.

I like to place my birds in a cooler during the hot early season. When the temperatures are cooler (below 55°), I store my birds in either a burlap or net bag. This type of bag allows air to circulate around the birds.

I like to hang my birds before cleaning and freezing. I hang my birds in a room where the temperature is less than 60° F. I have found that two to three days hanging time is best for the smaller birds (i.e., huns, grouse, woodcock). I hang my larger birds (pheasants, ducks) from four to five days. Hanging birds is a matter of individual preference. My friend, Datus Proper, hangs his birds for a much longer period of time than I do. I suggest that you experiment and then pick a hanging time that suits your tastes.

When the temperature is over 60°F, I clean my birds and freeze them immediately. We wrap our birds in cling wrap, place them in a ziplock bag, and then mark the bag with the type of bird and the date.

Appendix VII
Information Sources

Oregon Department of Fish & Wildlife, Headquarters
2501 Southwest First Avenue
Portland, OR 9727
503-872-5268

ODFW, Columbia Regional Headquarters
17330 Southeast Evelyn Street
Clackamas, OR 97015
503-657-2000

ODFW, Northwest Regional Headquarters
7118 Northeast Vandenberg Avenue
Corvallis, OR 97330
(541) 757-4186

ODFW, Southwest Regional Headquarters
4192 North Umpqua Hwy
Roseburg, OR 97470
(541) 440-3353

ODFW, High Desert Regional Headquarters
61374 Parrell Road
Bend, OR 97702
(541) 388-6363

ODFW, Northeast Regional Headquarters
107 20th Street
La Grande, OR 97850
(541) 963-2138

Oregon Department of Forestry
2600 State Street
Salem, OR 97310
503-945-7211

Oregon State Marine Board
435 Commercial Street Northeast, #400
Salem, OR 97310
503-378-8587

Oregon Parks and Recreation Department
1115 Commercial Street Northeast
Salem, OR 97310
503-378-6305

Division of State Lands
775 Summer Street Northeast
Salem, OR 97310
503-378-3805

U.S. Fish and Wildlife Service
Pacific Region
911 Northeast 11th Avenue
Portland, OR 97232
503-231-6118

United States Geological Survey (topographic maps)
Federal Center
Box 25286
Denver, CO 80225
303-236-7477

Index